FRIENDS
of the
Davenport Public Library

"Celebrate The Printed Word"
Endowment Fund
provided funds for the
purchase of this item

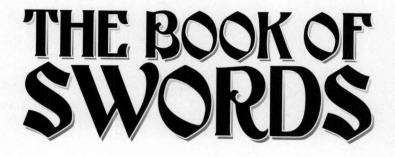

THE BOOK OF SWORDS

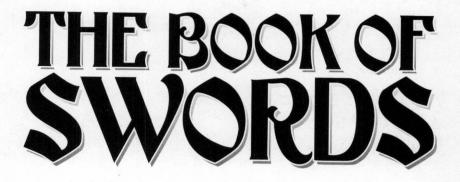

THE BOOK OF SWORDS

HANK REINHARDT

BAEN

A Baen Books Original

Baen Publishing Enterprises
P.O. Box 1403
Riverdale, NY 10471
www.baen.com

ISBN 10: 1-4391-3281-X
ISBN-13: 978-1-4391-3281-4

First printing, August 2009

Distributed by Simon & Schuster
1230 Avenue of the Americas
New York, NY 10020

Library of Congress Cataloging-in-Publication Data

Reinhardt, Hank, 1934–2007.
  The book of swords / Hank Reinhardt.
      p. cm.
  ISBN-13: 978-1-4391-3281-4 (hc)
  ISBN-13: 978-1-4391-3282-1 (trade pb)
  ISBN-10: 1-4391-3281-X
  1. Swords—History. 2. Weapons—History. I. Title.
  U852.R45 2009
  623.4'41—dc22

                                               2009018226

10 9 8 7 6 5 4 3 2 1

Pages by Joy Freeman (www.pagesbyjoy.com)
Printed in the United States of America

▶ Contents ◀

▶ Editor's Preface ◀

The following book by Hank Reinhardt represents ten years of writing, on and off, and a lifetime's experience with bladed weapons. When Hank died unexpectedly in October 2007 after complications from heart surgery, he left a first draft of the complete manuscript that he'd printed out to send to readers. He also left multiple versions of each of the files—word processing and backup were not Hank's fortes. He often joked that if it didn't involve the principles of wedge or lever it was too complicated for him. (This was not true, by the way, but an example of his modesty; he was a great synthesizer of knowledge across many fields, from metallurgy to biomechanics, from history to economics—as this book amply attests.) Still, as I learned from Hank, swords are all about the wedge and lever; and he loved talking to people about them.

My task as wife and editor—as it would have been had Hank lived to supervise my work—was to collate all the different versions and create a master file with the best of each iteration. I also duly sent out the manuscript to Hank's first readers and incorporated their comments. It was no easy task for any of us; Hank's loss was too fresh.

But the manuscript reads like Hank spoke, so in some way Hank lives on through this book. He was a great teller of tales. And he was a great explainer of things; this book reflects that. He was known for his ability to cut through to the heart of a matter—and he eschewed any of the obfuscatory b.s. that goes along with so much scholarship and teaching of martial arts. Unlike those writers of historical manuals or current purveyors of seminars, Hank wasn't out to make money by keeping secrets, drawing out a living from reluctant students. And since this book is being published after his death, you, the reader, know that's true.

This book by no means encapsulates all of Hank's knowledge of weaponry. For one thing, he never stopped experimenting and was constantly expanding his knowledge base. He never called himself an "expert" on arms and armor, but a "serious student." He thought anyone who was a self-styled expert was probably both pretentious and ignorant. For instance, he never would have been able to write this brief overview of his credentials; he would have preferred the work just to stand on its own. And to fully appreciate Hank's deep understanding of weapons you had to see him fight.

From the time he was old enough to hold a broomstick, he sparred with almost every kind of weapon there was. For his seventieth birthday, we had cake and champagne at his house in Georgia and then he went out back to spar with several young men using the new sparring weapons he had invented (and for which a patent has been granted). The incredible speed and reaction time of his prime was slightly diminished, and forty-plus years of smoking severely cut into his wind, but he was still game, and won more bouts than not.

Hank expanded his knowledge of weapons in three ways: practical usage, including sparring, cutting experiments and actual design of modern swords; extensive research of previously published material on weapons, from the Greek epics and Norse sagas to photographic representations of the arms and armor collections of the world's museums; and visual and physical inspection of antique weapons in those collections and museums. He was able in his work as sword designer for Museum Replicas, Ltd., the mail order company he co-founded with Atlanta Cutlery's Bill Adams, to cross the world studying weapons in the world's finest museums, from Nepal to Sweden, England to Spain. He was also a modest collector of antique weapons himself, starting from the time he was stationed in Germany as a G.I. in the 1950s picking up his first polearm, to the time he died, scanning eBay for interesting South Sea maces.

So this work is not written as a traditional work of scholarship with footnotes and bibliographies and formal summaries of rival theories. Hank wrote down the things he thought were important about swords, garnered from a lifetime of study, and he wrote them down as he would have had he been talking to you at a dojo, or seminar, or party or convention, or a visit to his weapon-filled house, complete with digressions, tales from the Norse sagas, snippets of poetry and references to historical occurrences he just assumed everybody was familiar with. I've even left in his awful puns.

But just because Hank wrote in a conversational tone, don't underestimate the content. You will find several instances of original scholarship, including his discussion of the effectiveness of the rounded tip of the Viking sword and its similarity to the geometry of the Japanese katana, and his thoughts about the form of the Viking halberd.

Hank spent a large part of his life sharing his knowledge of and enthusiasm for fighting, the things men fight with, and the things men fight for. This book covers the first two subjects. His first readers were, for the most part, those he sparred with: Greg Phillips, Jerry Proctor, Whit Williams, Nils Onsager, and Mike Stamm. Other readers were also his longtime friends Charlotte Proctor, Patrick Gibbs, Hili Gastfriend and Gerald W. Page, who could be counted on to point out places where Hank's intention was not as clear to the layman as could be wished. I also thank Jimmy Fikes, another longtime Hank friend and a man whom Hank considered a blacksmith and knifemaker of mystical talents; Bruce Brookhart, his colleague at Museum Replicas, Ltd.; and Steve Shackleford, editor of *Blade* magazine, for their help on this book.

Peter Fuller, one of the finest armorers of our time, was invaluable not only for his help with technical matters, but also for providing all of the line drawings used here, and coordination of all of the illustrations. Suzanne Hughes, with the help of her husband Steve Hughes, provided all of the photographs of items from Hank's own collection. There are not enough thanks in the world to give them for donating their time and expertise. Thanks also go to Jennie Faries and Joy Freeman who made it possible for the drawings and photographs to be so elegantly displayed in the typeset book.

Because Hank had only finished a first draft, some questions that arose from his manuscript had to be answered by his readers or by my own research. He also did not provide full reading lists for each chapter; where the recommendations are directly his, as in the first chapter, they are indicated. Where not, we have looked to his other writings and in his extensive personal library of arms and armor for works we feel he would have endorsed. A lot of nonsense has been written about weapons; reader beware. Hank never took anything on faith, but always tested against common sense and his own experience.

If there are any errors of fact or infelicities of phrasing in the book, the fault is almost undoubtedly mine, done in the editorial process in Hank's absence. I would appreciate hearing feedback from readers. Comments can be sent to me via the publisher at toni@baen.com. Hank's website is being maintained as a source of his work, and will, at some point in the future, also list all of the works in his library, available on written request to those who are also researching issues that so interested Hank all his life. That website, maintained by volunteer and longtime friend-of-Hank Julie Wall, is: www.hankreinhardt.com.

—Toni Weisskopf Reinhardt
2009

▶ Introduction ◀

The sword is the most revered of all of man's weapons. Although the club is older, the knife more universal, and the firearm much more efficient, it is to the sword that the most decoration, myth, mysticism and reverence has been given.

The sword has been the symbol of Justice, of Vengeance, and of Mercy. The katana has been called "The Soul of the Samurai." The Vikings lavished love, care, and attached wonderful names to their weapons. No one artifact has so captured the imagination as has the sword. It captured my imagination when I was seven years old, and it still fascinates me some sixty years later.

When I was twelve years old, my brother-in-law returned from the WWII in the South Pacific and gave me two Japanese bayonets. With a neighborhood kid I promptly went out and started fighting with them. The result was that I had two bayonets with blades that looked like hacksaws from the nicks. This clearly was not the way it happened in books and movies! This was the beginning of a lifelong quest to find out how swords were actually used in combat.

About the same time I started fighting with broomsticks and garbage can tops. This was a lot of fun until the mothers started screaming about knots on little darlings' heads. They paid no attention when it was explained that the recipient failed to parry. Regretfully, irate parents put an end to the blossoming experiments on the use of the sword. Alas, thus is serious scientific study forestalled. . . .

I continued my solo study of the subject matter and managed to buy various small edged weapons while still a teenager. My first was a kukri, a knife used by the Gurkhas of Nepal. Serious collecting didn't start until I was twenty-three, in the U.S. Army and stationed in Germany. There I ran across a Swiss short sword

1

circa 1840 and a rapier (in very poor condition), circa 1650. I bought both, and the craze was on.

While in Germany I traveled extensively, visiting many museums, and frequently talking with armor curators (who rarely found anyone who shared their passion). After my separation from the army, and back in the States, I continued my studying and collecting. [Editor's Note: Hank's collection of antique and reproduction weapons at the time of his death included over 600 items; his collection of books on arms and armor included over 700 volumes.]

In 1984 Bill Adams and I started up Museum Replicas, Ltd., and issued a catalog devoted to the sale of replica arms and armor. This allowed me greater latitude in my studies, and I began to travel much more, visiting even more museums in Europe and Asia. Now, my interest in arms and armor wasn't limited to European items, but embraced Asian, African and Polynesian as well.

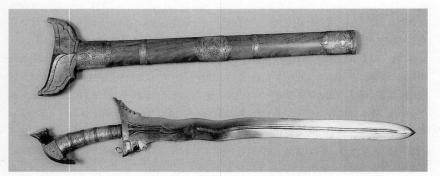

Indonesian kris, circa 1900, 30 inches overall length. HRC550.

My research into the actual use of the weapons has been helped a great deal by the study of original sources, such as Icelandic sagas, Froissart's *Chronicles* and many medieval manuscripts. In addition to this I have engaged in many experiments, such as cutting into mail, cutting armor, and testing weapons to see just how effective they are. Along with several friends, I have engaged in a great deal of sparring combat. However, this time we used padded weapons. (Wives can put an end to scientific inquiry as well as parents.)

There have been many excellent books on the sword, particularly its development and history. The European sword has been well studied, so too the Eastern weapons, particularly the Japanese katana. Other authors have approached the study of the sword from a historical viewpoint, from Ewart Oakeshott, who wrote with an eye to classifying different types of medieval swords, to Richard Burton, describing swords around the world.

So it may be presumptuous of me to feel that I can add to the work. But I do feel that my own experimentation and its results are well worth recording. What I intend to show in this volume is the result of a lifetime's practical research into swords, how they were made and how they were employed, and to correct some of the incredible amount of misinformation given about swords, all types of swords.

As our society has grown more and more advanced, and more reliant on technology, there has been an increased interest in the weapons of the past. The romance of the sword is very much alive, both in the East and the West.

But as our technology has improved our living conditions it has also obscured our vision of the past. Not only is our vision obscured by distance, but movies, books and fiction of all types have romanticized the past, and particularly the sword, beyond all recognition of the real thing.

In order to understand the sword it is necessary for us to understand the material from which it is made. This appears to be so basic an idea that it isn't worth the effort to write down or even read it. But the truth is that very few people understand iron and its physical properties, and in order to understand the sword, and its use, it is necessary to understand iron and how the weapons were made then, and now.

Let me explain. In my time, I have been asked if the Vikings used stainless steel in their swords, as it wouldn't rust on their long voyages. I had one person write and tell me that he had left his sword outside in the rain, and it had developed a "fungus," funny red splotches on the blade! Since stainless steel was not developed until the 20th century, and ferric oxide (known as "rust") has been around since the beginning of time, you can understand my feelings that this ignorance should be dealt with.

Curiously enough, it wasn't until 1786 that de Morveau proved that it was carbon that turned iron into steel. (Carbon was only discovered about ten to twelve years previous to that.) Before then it was thought that steel was the *pure* form of iron, and that by using coke, coal, etc. and heating the iron white hot, that impurities were being burnt out, instead of vice versa.

In order to understand swords, how they are used, what they can and can't do, it is necessary to know something about iron and steel. Years ago, when swords were in actual use, this would not be necessary. People were familiar with iron implements and knew what to expect. However, this is not true today. Movies, television and books have all contributed to this lack of knowledge. The most outrageous comments are made and believed, and these comments are made by people who have no knowledge of the subject! Sometimes these "experts" will deliberately lie in order to dramatize something. For an example, in the movie of Shakespeare's *Henry V*, director Sir Lawrence Olivier has a scene with a knight being hoisted up by a crane and lowered onto his horse. When it was pointed out that this was not only incorrect, but actually ridiculous, Olivier replied that he didn't care, it made a good scene!

But this is just one of many such errors that have been perpetuated in modern times. Swords are shown slammed edge on against each other with no damage, smashed into concrete pillars, and cutting steel and stone with ease. I think my favorite myth is that of the Japanese katana that cut a machine gun barrel in half.

These have all led to a belief that swords can actually do these things! This book will be about how swords were actually used, with concrete, demonstrable evidence as well as historical anecdotal evidence presented. Drawing on information from grave excavations, illustrations of battle scenes, and many classical and medieval literary sources, I will discuss how contemporaries showed swords being used.

Further, I will draw on my own personal experience with devoted friends also interested in the use of the swords. I will show readers the things you do not do because they get you killed and things you do not do because it tears up the sword. And I will illustrate the best way to use many different types of swords.

Building on Oakeshott and others, this volume will add to the body of knowledge of the history of swords by illustrating not only the beauty of the form of the sword, but also their beauty of function.

—Hank Reinhardt

Copper and Bronze

It wasn't until the invention of bronze that the sword became possible. Before that time, knives, axes, spears, and even clubs were multi-purpose, used as both tool and weapon. But with bronze, an alloy of tin and copper, an item that was purely a weapon became possible. It is easy to postulate, but not prove, that with the invention of the sword a pure warrior class became possible. Bronze was expensive, and only a few individuals could afford swords, but this gave them an unquestioned advantage over opponents armed with flint knives and axes.

It is probable that the invention of bronze was first achieved by copper-using people, and in many cases fully developed bronze weapons were introduced into Stone-Age cultures. In Northern Europe there are flint daggers and flint "swords" that appear to be copies of bronze weapons. In Denmark there is a polished stone axe head that is an excellent copy of a bronze axe. The flint knapping is excellent and appears to be a brave but futile attempt

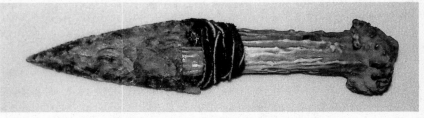

A flint knife made by Greg Phillips.
From the collection of Laura Brayman. Photo by Charlotte Proctor.

to stay up with the new metal. It's rather like developing a truly superb carriage about the time the automobile came along.

The estimated time frame for the development and use of metals is constantly undergoing revisions backward. Until recently, the discovery and use of copper was thought to have occurred about four thousand years ago. However, several fascinating new discoveries have pushed the time frame back at least a thousand years, and raised even more interesting questions. One of these discoveries was the body of a man preserved in ice. I will digress a bit to tell his story, to show a little of the cultural context in which these early weapons were used, before I get to more technical matters.

OTZI

The Otzal Alps lie between Austria and Italy. They are partially covered with glacial ice so that only small sections ever melt. In 1991, two hikers discovered a man's body. At first the authorities were uncertain as to how old the body was, but when scientists were able to examine the corpse, it was found to be about 5,300 years old! The body was in a remarkable state of preservation. But what was even more remarkable, and thrilling, was that his tools and clothing were found with him.

The individual, who has been nicknamed Otzi, had bearskin-soled shoes that were stuffed with grass, fur leggings, a fur jacket, a grass overcape and a fur hat with ear flaps. All of the clothing was well made and highly serviceable. In addition, he also carried some fire-making tools, some fungi that were probably used as medicine, and some berries to eat. His equipment consisted of a double-edged stone knife that was hafted with wood, a bow that was only partially finished, twelve blank arrow shafts, two arrows that were broken, and, most amazing of all, a copper axe.

The copper axe was quite well made, with an edge width of about two inches. It was attached to a shaft two feet long. The length of the shaft suggests to me that the axe was primarily a weapon, as tools usually have a shorter shaft. Chemical tests on the body also indicate that Otzi himself was the likely candidate for having cast the axe, as his body contained chemicals that are produced during the casting process.

But let me digress here to tell a bit more of Otzi's story, because it's fascinating. He not only deserves a book about him, but should get a novel as well.

Otzi was between 25 and 45 years old, about 5 feet 4 inches in height, and weighed about 150 pounds. Speculation was that he had been caught in a sudden storm and had frozen to death. The body and equipment were studied a great deal, but it was close to ten years before someone thought to put the body through an imaging scanner. When they did, the scientists received quite a shock. Otzi had not died of natural causes or under accidental circumstances. Otzi had been murdered.

Under his left shoulder blade was a stone arrowhead. The arrow had passed through the left arm, cutting through the triceps, probably some nerves, and had penetrated the body, probably the lung, although I am not certain of this. Medical opinion is that he would have died from the wound in about two to four hours. Once the arrowhead was located, an even more thorough search of his body was made and turned up some more wounds. These wounds were on the hands, and are what are generally referred to as "defensive wounds." When someone is attacked with an edged weapon they will usually attempt to fend off the attack with their hands. This results in many deep gashes in the hands and rarely results in stopping the attack.

We have an individual with a valuable axe, a half-finished bow, and a quiver with twelve unfinished arrows and two broken arrows, and an unsolved murder. It's impossible for me not to speculate on the tale of Otzi.

A hostile encounter leaves Otzi with his bow broken. He would retrieve the two arrows, broken in the fight, as the heads would be useful later. He finds some wood suitable for a bow and begins to prepare it. He does make some arrows, but does not have time to finish them. He is again attacked. This time the fight is probably hand-to-hand, and Otzi again makes his escape. But as he's fleeing uphill, an arrow finds him. Although mortally wounded, he keeps on, probably losing his pursuers, maybe in the dark, or because a storm came up, or just because of the cold of the mountain. He falls, only to be found 5,300 years later.

Interesting. One of oldest mummies found in Europe, and he was murdered, or, if you like, killed in battle. For Otzi didn't die quietly without a struggle. Subsequent tests revealed blood samples from at least three individuals on Otzi, his clothes and his weapons. We don't know if he was the good guy or the bad guy, what we do know is that it is a fascinating development.

While everything about Otzi is fascinating to us for what it can tell about a time that is mostly unknown to modern civilization, from the parasites in his intestines, to his wounds, clothing and tattoos, I am most concerned with that copper axe. This indicates that copper was much more in use than had been previously known, and that the earliest use dates back much further than had been stipulated before his discovery.

To further substantiate this, there was a recent discovery in Jordan of a copper weapon and tool producing factory. The factory is about five thousand years old, and in many respects this is a more important find than Otzi, though less viscerally exciting.

THE MANUFACTURE OF COPPER

At the end of the 20th century, an amazing discovery was made at an excavation in the desert of southern Jordan. Located not far from the Dead Sea, Khibat Hamri Ifdan was a massive metal working complex. Although the site was found in the 1970s it was not fully excavated until 1999. The findings have been most impressive.

Archeologists uncovered a factory that was dedicated to producing copper tools: axes, hammers, knives and other items, including copper ingots. This operation was not a small four- or five-man job shop, but was quite large, obviously a factory. The factory contained about seventy rooms and, at the last counting I have heard about, the team had uncovered hundreds of ceramic molds, broken and discarded items, and approximately 5,000 tons of slag. This much slag indicates that the plant must have produced hundreds of tons over its lifetime.

It also appears, and is reported, that although the plant produced many tools and items, the primary operation was the making of copper ingots. This indicates a rather large trading network, as locals could not use as much copper as was produced. The plant was destroyed about 2700 BC by an earthquake. This time frame is right at the beginning of the Bronze Age. Frankly, I don't think anyone expected to find such a large operation at this period in time. Prior to this, the largest operation known was in Hissarlik, Turkey (believed to be the Troy of legend), and Hissarlik produced only about 70–80 items. An operation of this size indicates that the production of copper had been known long before had previously been believed. You simply do not organize a large operation such as this unless you have the artisans, the knowledge, and the market for the items that you will produce.

It is doubtful that swords were ever produced in copper. A few may have been tried, but abandoned once they were found unserviceable. Copper is simply too soft to make a good sword. Knives and axes and hammers, yes. Still, it is easy to see the antecedents of sword-making factories here.

In order to produce so much copper, it is necessary to have several different occupations come together: mining, mold making, wooden pattern making, charcoal manufacturing, heating and smelting—not to mention the trade routes that must be established and serviced. What an exciting time that must have been for the adventurers who took up trading! The world was a huge place back then. I am sure that many traders never ventured too far afield, but I am also sure that the more enterprising and adventurous sort spent years in travel, even unto the Cold Northern Seas. Which brings us back to bronze, and the true beginning of the age of swords.

We know the process for producing an item of copper or bronze. First a master is made. This can be of wood or clay. Once this is made, a mold is made that will separate and allow the master to be removed. The mold can be of clay, stone or even ceramics. It is possible, and it was done, to make a master of wax, and then burn it out, but this was later once the casting was well established. It is doubtful that this was done for simple tools, though, as it would be too expensive. The mold is filled with molten copper or bronze, and once it has

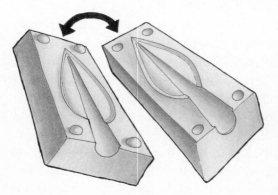

A *mold for a copper spear head.*

cooled, the mold is separated. Another method, almost as common, was simply to carve the mold out of stone. This was practical for flat type axes and other items that were one sided. Of course you can make a left and right side of stone, and have a more durable mold, but this would seem to be more expensive than merely using a ceramic material.

Very early copper working may have been done by just one or two people. But it quickly becomes evident that superior items can be produced at a faster rate by several people working in sequence. You need someone to dig the ore, someone to smelt it, a master maker to carve or mold the master, someone to make the molds, someone to cast and pour the metal. You will also need someone to gather the wood for the fire. The culture was much different then. You couldn't call up and order coal, or turn on the electric furnace. In short, this was a cooperative venture involving a large number of people, and remained that way even until modern times. The casual solo blacksmith who took iron ore and forged a blade, ground it to shape, filed, sharpened and polished, then made a hilt, balanced it, and also made a scabbard, is so much romantic nonsense. Oh, I wouldn't say that it never happened; it is quite possible that a few tried it that way. Certainly legends tell of this happening, and always a very special sword is produced. But there were romantics back then, too, and since the sword was venerated in most societies, special blades were even more desired and sought after. But it really didn't work. Today you have some superb sword and knife makers who do each part of the whole process, but today's swords are art items, and not utility pieces. But I digress; we are still talking about copper and bronze.

Knives, axes, spears and clubs can all be made from copper. And all can be capable weapons, just not *good* ones. But the same is not true of swords. Copper simply does not have the strength to support a long blade. However, with the addition of about ten percent tin to the mixture, it becomes a very tough material, of surprising strength and durability.

Bronze weapons soon began to dominate the battlefields of the world. The spread of bronze is the cause of much speculation, and is likely to remain more speculation than fact. Was it because of trade, war, or simply spontaneous development in many different places? We simply do not know how the knowledge of bronze working was spread. What we do know is that there was a surprising amount of trade between the Mediterranean and England and Ireland and even China at that time.

THE BRONZE AGE

The invention of bronze was a significant event in the history of man. With bronze, man was at last able to develop a tool that was pure weapon: the sword! Compared to flint, obsidian and copper, bronze was really a magical material. Bronze is hard enough to take a sharp edge, and yet not become brittle, and it was quickly made into that familiar shape we call a sword.

It would be interesting to create a neat chart of the development of the sword, but while a great deal is known, not enough is known to be able to state that bronze was developed in a specific area, and spread in such a way. It appears to be an invention that occurred within a few hundred years around 2000 BC in the Middle East as well as China.

Reproduction bronze dagger. HRC175.

As far as I have been able to determine, there does not seem to be a "national" or "ethnic" grouping to these swords. One is as likely to show up in Turkey as in Ireland. Let me also add that I have handled many more steel weapons than bronze ones, and I am aware that my knowledge of bronze weapons is limited.

Bronze spread throughout the Middle East, and then into Europe. Mercantile trading must have been quite an adventure back then, taking bronze tools and weapons into Europe to trade for amber and raw materials. The traders who followed the rivers into Northern Europe were probably a tough, hardy lot, and well able to defend their wares. The dangers of sea and forest were not undertaken lightly four thousand years ago.

The merchants traveled the Mediterranean to Iberia, maybe into the vast Atlantic and the frozen seas to the north, England, or the Scandinavian countries. All with storm and shipwreck and pirates a constant threat, and not even knowing how they would be received when they got there. Or maybe they took the land route through what we call the Balkans into what is now Germany, trading ingots of bronze or even weapons for tin and amber and furs. They faced unknown tribes, and could never be sure if they were saying the right thing or insulting the chief beyond all recall.

Could you trade with this new tribe, or would they attack and try to take your goods? You would never know until the transaction was finished. Wild lands, wild animals, and even wilder men: facing these required toughness, cunning and determination. One thing is for certain. It could not have been a dull life.

Not only were items made of bronze spread throughout Europe, but the knowledge of how these items were made was also disseminated. Soon there were bronze manufacturing centers all through Europe. This spread of information and goods was not done overnight. Indeed, it took several hundred years at least. For many years stone and bronze existed side by side. As mentioned earlier, there are several examples of stone daggers that are copies of bronze daggers, and flint swords as well. This is both pathetic and heroic.

MANUFACTURING IN BRONZE

Just like manufacturing in copper, manufacturing in bronze is not a simple procedure and requires more than one or two men. It also requires the extra step of alloying the tin and the copper. A bronze sword must be cast. It cannot be forged like iron. In order to make a sword, one must have the required amount of bronze, a good furnace in which to melt it, and molds in which to pour it. First a pattern must be made. This was probably done in wood, although I do not know of extant archeological remnants that would verify this. After the pattern was completed, a mold was made. This was done in clay, with a coarse clay on the bottom, and a much finer clay on the top. The pattern was then impressed into the clay and another mold for the top was made. After the molds were completed, they were then baked until it was dry and hard. (Dry was very important: molten bronze poured on water could have an interesting effect on those standing around.*) Gates were provided so that gasses could escape, and the sword was cast.

After the sword cooled, the mold was broken and the sword taken out and finished. The blade edges were hammered thoroughly. The hammering was very necessary, as this work added about twenty percent to the hardness of the edge. The sword was then polished and decorated.

Without a doubt the manufacturing process was quickly streamlined. We can see this from the recent excavations in Jordan. This was not a small operation, as it had sections devoted to certain tasks. This is practical and economical. There is a tendency today to think that our ancestors were not nearly as bright as we are. This is nonsense. They did not have the amount of knowledge available that we do, but for sheer IQ and ingenuity they were easily our equals.

In the manufacture of items with a specific usage, you are limited by the material being used. All swords can be broken down into swords used for cutting, for thrusting, and for both cutting and thrusting. You can't make a practical sword out of rock, bone, wood or glass. Rock and bone are too brittle, wood too dull and glass too fragile. Bronze, on the other hand, can make a pretty decent sword. It is easily seen that a sword designed for a single purpose will do that one thing better than one that attempts to do both. Bronze Age weapons are no exception to this rule.

Weight can be a problem, and bronze is almost one-third heavier than iron. While bronze is heavy, it is also attractive. Many Bronze Age swords are as elegantly beautiful in shape and design as anything ever produced in steel. They have the additional advantage that the metal itself, when properly polished, is strikingly beautiful.

In today's world we are used to brass, a copper-zinc alloy, and encounter bronze only rarely, and never in swords. This can easily lead to a misunderstanding of the bronze swords in their design and use. Because bronze is heavier than iron, and because it is also softer, it requires more metal to give it strength, and this makes it even heavier. This leads to a certain similarity in the

---

*If there was moisture of any kind in the mold, the molten bronze would make the mold explode—right in your face. Such a drastic change in temperature between the molten metal and the water always ends with a violent result. It's like having your engine overheat, and then pouring cold water into your radiator; you'll crack your engine block.   —Peter Fuller

A shotel is usually sharpened on the inside, but many are sharpened on both edges.

forms of all bronze swords, even from widely separated areas. It seems likely that this was due to several things: dispersion of both knowledge of manufacture and the weapons themselves, plus the fact that the designs are quite effective.

There is one exception to this statement: early Egyptian and Assyrian swords are quite different, but both show a mutual influence. There are many illustrations of Egyptian swords, and one or two originals, that show swords that are a long triangle in shape, and are cut and thrust weapons. These are, in both form and function, almost identical to many swords shown on Assyrian bas-reliefs. But one Egyptian sword, the kopesh, is believed to be the ancestor of the Greek kopis, and subsequently the falcata and then the kukri. Now, the kopesh is sickle-shaped, but in the few that I have seen, the edge is on the outside of the curve in some of the swords, and on the inside in others. (On the kukri and falcata, the edge is always on the inside, and the lineage attributing the kopesh as their ancestor may simply be apocryphal.) When the edge is on the outside of the curve, it bears a great deal of resemblance to some Assyrian and Sumerian swords that have been excavated. In Abyssinia a sword that was in use until quite recently is the shotel. This is a highly curved sword that is usually sharpened on the inside, but many, including one in my possession, are sharpened on both edges. Although we cannot know for sure, it seems reasonable to assume that it is a descendent of the kopesh.

There has not been an in-depth study of Chinese bronze weapons. I feel that this has been due to political climates and proximity rather than a lack of interest. The few Chinese weapons that I have been able to see, both in photographs and in person, are quite attractive, well made, yet with a definite touch of the exotic about them. I would dearly love to see a good study made of all of them, and not just the sword.

THE SHAPE OF THE BRONZE SWORD

Bronze Age swords did show some variation because they varied in their use. There were cut-and-thrust swords, short cut-and-thrust weapons, rapiers, and long slashing weapons. But due to the limitations of the material the weapons were heavier, thicker, and slower than comparable ones made of iron. Nevertheless, they were still effective enough to kill people.

The classic Bronze Age rapier is found from Ireland to Greece and from Denmark to Italy. We do know that there were extensive trading networks linking Europe with the Middle East, so it is impossible to tell from whence the sword originated. However, we also know that many were made in separate locations such as Ireland and Crete, as we have archeological evidence of this. There is a sword found in Lissane, Ireland, dated between 1500–1000 BC, that is almost completely identical to a Cretan rapier of a slightly earlier date. It is not only the rapiers that are similar, but the cutting swords as well. From the accompanying drawings you can see the great similarities of these swords, although they come from different parts of the world.

Most of these weapons were rather long, with blades of more than thirty

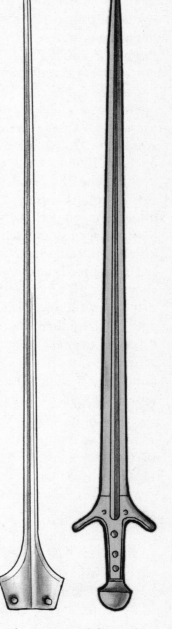

The Lissane (left) and Cretan (right) blades are surprisingly similar.

inches. All of the thrusting swords have thick and rigid blades. The thickness gives them great power in a thrust. It is doubtful that they were used in what we would consider "fencing"; the sword is simply too heavy. Although a blow from one of these might be as severe as a blow from a mace or club, undoubtedly the blade would bend. But I do believe that a style of fighting did evolve around this type of sword. I have no proof of this, just a strong hunch. Possibly they were used with the right hand on the grip, and the left hand on the blade, such as you might use a short spear. Certainly the thickness and the weight of the sword would give them enough power to penetrate most armor of the period.

It is generally believed that these weapons were the first true swords, and that they developed from the knife. There is a lot of evidence in support of this. There are many bronze knives that have been sharpened to such an extent that they no longer resemble knives, but rather stilettos. It does not take much imagination to see a bronze knife maker looking at one of these, and thinking about making a longer knife. Since these are weapons, it is obvious that a much longer blade would be better in combat than a short one. To strengthen the case even more, grips are attached in such a way as to make it impossible to use the sword in any cutting actions. Some of the early rapiers have the handles fixed by a rather odd method. The grip is a separate piece, and is fastened to the sword blades by rivets. The butt of the sword blade is curved, and the handle riveted over it. This grip is weak, and this is why I began to wonder if they may not have been used with two hands. The grip attachment is so weak that if a thrust was made and hit slightly off center, it could cause the grip to break. Again, pure speculation on my part, with no evidence except my own playing around to support it.

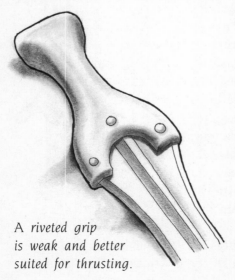

A *riveted grip is weak and better suited for thrusting.*

While this kind of riveted handle is not very strong, as long as the user's force is directed forward in a thrust, it is sufficient. The moment you tried to cut with it, though, or should the blade be struck hard from the side, the rivets would start popping and the blade come loose and fall off. This leaves one with only the grip. Not only is this disconcerting and dangerous, it also plays holy hell with the Heroic Image that we warriors like to cultivate.

The majority of the extant swords with this construction show damage, and are oft times missing their grips. As a result, this particular method of attaching the hilt was discarded, and two other methods were used, both of which worked very well. One was to draw the blade out into a tang, and attach the grip to this. This method was a forerunner of the way sword grips were attached in the Middle Ages, and how most modern functional reproductions are produced. Although superior to the first method, it was still not as optimal as it could be. While this method works very well in steel, bronze is not strong enough and it often broke. Again, I'm sure this was rather disconcerting to the warrior in the middle of a vicious fight. I can imagine what it would be like to land a blow, swing your sword aloft for a killing strike, only to have the blade fly away from you like someone who owes you money!

Cutting swords appear to have arrived slightly later than the rapier, but again, this is something that we can only speculate about. Certainly the cutting swords have a much stronger grip. With the development of the improved grip, we now encounter what we can call the typical Bronze Age sword. This is a leaf shaped blade with a narrow waist, swelling to a very effective cutting section, and then tapering to a deadly point. This is one of the most beautiful of shapes, and is also quite effective. This blade shape shows up in many places, even as far

Bronze sword with leaf-shaped blade, 950 BC.

Bronze sword, 400 BC, 23 inches long.

Reproduction steel leaf-shaped blade. HRC198.

away as Africa, and two thousand years later. Most of the cutting and cut-and-thrust swords have grips that are cast integral with the blade. This is much stronger, as the grip is part of the sword. Of course this also adds weight, and the weight may be the reason that two other methods were tried. One method was the tang construction that was later so successful with steel swords.

The other method was much more successful in bronze weapons. In this the grip is made with two extended flanges. Then a piece of material is inserted between them, and the flanges folded over. The material could be plain wood or ivory or any decorative material. These grips follow a timeline. Once the grip was cast integral with the blade, they never went back. But flanged and solid bronze grips coexisted until the bronze sword was replaced by the steel ones.

The cross sections of bronze swords do not vary as much as those later ones made of steel. Indeed, on many of these bronze swords it is difficult to tell what the original shape actually was. A sword could have been quite broad, and yet over years of use be transformed into a much more narrow sword, with much thicker cutting edges. There are swords whose edges are so thick as make you wonder if they were really maces. However, a closer inspection leads one to think that they are swords that saw a great deal of use, and whose edges have simply been worn away. Some blades were made with a well defined central ridge that strengthened the blade. Others had thick diamond cross sections, and still others had thick center sections, and wide flat blades.

A mid-rib cross-section provided the strength needed for cutting blows.

The most common form of cross

section is that of a raised center section, almost a mid rib, with the blade sloping down to the edges. This provided the strength needed for cutting blows. It appears that some swords were made with blades that are thick on the edge, while some have much thinner blades and thin, very sharp edges. It is difficult to tell how much of this is intentional, and how much is due to use, corrosion, and sharpening. Certainly many of them do show file marks. I believe that some swords were made with a thicker edge simply to enable them to cut through some of the armor worn, and I also believe that there are others that were made with thin, flat edges. It should always be remembered that the swords, even mass-produced, were still individual items. A Bronze Age warrior might easily grind and file his sword into a shape that he preferred. (Steel swords would always show a greater variety in shape, since they were individually forged, and bronze weapons were cast). There are a few bronze swords that are flat and would be capable of delivering a terrific cut. How well they would hold up is the question. I do not know of any research along these lines for Bronze Age swords. A larger number of these swords have the flattened diamond cross section of many medieval swords.

I know of two bronze swords that are pure choppers with no capability of thrusting. They are both located in Sweden. Both are large and heavy, and each has a small bronze pellet that appears to be there for weight. One of the swords has two of these pellets and also has a curved section that appears to be for carrying the sword. They are thick and heavy, and it would take a strong man to use them in battle, but they would deliver a blow that would likely not be forgotten.

There has been some confusion regarding some bronze daggers. Early attachments of the handle to the blade with rivets made a very poor juncture. While this is known to have been done, there are many bronze blades that are not properly daggers, but rather what are termed halberds. These weapons had the blade attached at right angles to the line of the hilt. Usually the blades were attached to the shaft by being inserted into a slot in the shaft, and then rivets inserted. This is also not as strong as a socket, but was more substantial than being tied on. The Chinese liked this weapon, but quickly learned to make the halberd with a socket.

FIGHTING WITH THE BRONZE SWORD

Bronze swords were used in conjunction with a shield. The shield is the earliest bit of defensive armor known. Just about everyone used the shield at one time or another. (The Japanese appear to be the only civilized society in which the shield was not in general use at one time or another.) Bronze swords were not designed to be both offensive and defensive weapons, so what happened when someone was caught without a shield is anyone's guess. But the guy without the shield was in deep trouble. With the shield, the fighting techniques were pretty much the same as they were a thousand years later, though probably a little less refined. This would be due to the type of armor more than lack of knowledge or skill.

Although this will be dealt with more fully in a later chapter, suffice it to say that steel armor was more protective than bronze. A steel sword striking a steel helmet was more likely to skip off or fail to bite, so more effort would be made to hit the enemy in the unprotected area, shoulders for instance, than on the head.

Reproduction bronze helmet.
HRC342.

However, with bronze it's different. Bronze helmets are not as thick and protective. A hard blow with a bronze sword could crack or crush the helmet. The sword would be only slightly damaged, especially if it was one with a thicker edge. Armor and helmets were designed for protection against glancing blows, and not for well aimed full force hits. I imagine in the heat of battle there would be a lot of glancing blows. Blows would be coming from all directions, even from those on your own side. Swords would be knocked aside, bounce off of shields, rebound right and left, and be thrown up in spasms as someone was hit and killed. We know that such combat took place from the *Illiad* and the *Odyssey*, not to mention pictorial representation on vases, and from other written sources. In short, armor was needed not only as protection from your enemies, but your friends as well. It could not give you complete protection, but it was a lot better to have some protection than none at all.

Although weapons were cast, most of the armor was cold worked. Bronze is easily worked once you realize that it quickly work hardens. Then it has to be annealed. The easiest way to anneal bronze is to heat it up quite hot, and then quench it in water (note that this is the reverse of annealing iron). Helmets and breastplates were forged. The very early armor, like the Dendra panoply, is really rather ugly. It took a good while for them to come up with the muscle breastplate that we all love.

Here weight enters into the subject once again. Bronze is heavy, and the result is that the armor cannot be made too strong, or the weight will be prohibitive. People who get to see a real helmet or breastplate for the first time are usually shocked at how thin the metal is. Thin—but a good armorer would work harden the metal, so that it would be thin, but strong. Not perfect, but a lot better than nothing.

Bronze is a comparatively simple material to work and cast. If you have all the ingredients—the right amount of tin, the right amount of copper, proper molds with gates, and a sufficiency of heat—then your casting is generally going to come out pretty well. During the Late Bronze Age (1550 BC–1200 BC) castings were very good, and it is obvious that the metal workers knew their craft. The one real advantage here is that the swords were consistent in their hardness and their quality.

But even as bronze workers improved their craft, another discovery was waiting in the wings. One that would be the most important ingredient in war even until today. As Kipling phrased it, "Iron—Cold Iron—was the master of them all!"

Suggestions for further reading from Hank:

Bottini, Angelo et al., *Antike Helme*. Verlag de Roemisch-Germanischen Zentralmuseums, Mainz, 1988.

Byock, Jesse L., "Egil's Bones," *Scientific American*, Jan. 1995, Vol. 272 #1, pages 82–87.

Peake, Harold and Herbert John Fleure, *Merchant Venturers in Bronze.* Yale University Press, New Haven, 1931.

Eogan, George, *Catalog of Irish Bronze Swords*, Stationary Office—Government Publicans, Dublin, 1965.

Eogan, George, *Hoards of the Irish Later Bronze Age.* University College, Dublin, 1883.

Gamber, Ortwin, *Waffe und Rustung Eurasiens.* Klinkhardt & Bierman, 1978.

Ottenjann, Helmut, *Die Nordischen Vollgriffschwerter der Alteren und Mittleren Bronzeit*, Verlag Walter De Gruyter & Co., 1969.

Seitz, Heribert, *Blankwaffen.* Klinkhardt & Biermann GMBH, Munchen, 1981.

Snodgrass, Anthony, *Early Greek Armour and Weapons from the End of the Bronze Age to 600 B.C.*, Edinburgh University Press, Edinburgh, 1964.

Suggestions for further reading from the editors:

Buehr, Walter, *Warrior's Weapons.* Thomas Y. Crowell Company, New York, 1963.

Connolly, Peter, *Greece and Rome at War.* Greenhill Books, London, 1998.

Macqueen, J.G., *The Hittites and Their Contemporaries in Asia Minor.* Westview Press, Boulder, 1975.

▶ 2 ◀

Iron and Steel

Metallic sword and knife-making doubtless began when ancient man discovered little green stones on the ground which, when heated sufficiently, yielded copper. This liquid metal then was poured into molds to form axes and knives. These tools were soft, but could be work hardened by hammering.

Later, these early smiths learned how to alloy tin with copper to make bronze and with zinc to make brass. Both these alloys produced weapons of superior strength and hardness. But there was a far better metal on the horizon.

Iron is one of the most useful metals known to man. It is also one of the most common elements on the planet. In its pure state iron is only slightly harder than copper. But iron is a reactive metal and will combine with many other elements. With the addition of other elements, the properties of iron change drastically. Rarely is iron found that does not have some impurities mixed in with it. Of all the impurities, none is quite so important as carbon. But I get ahead of myself.

No one knows who first discovered iron, or where. In the past it was believed that the Hittites were the first, but that is being challenged as more and more information becomes available. At the time of this writing, the first makers and users of iron are not known.

More than likely the discovery was an offshoot of the bronze industry. It is quite likely that iron was discovered while mining for tin and copper. Probably this new metal was initially discarded

23

and considered to be just trash. It was possible that it took quite a while for anyone to pay any attention to the material. However, once its abilities were realized, it quickly supplanted bronze as the ideal metal for swords and other weapons.

When you compare the different properties of bronze and iron you can see that it took a great leap to make iron into something useful. Bronze can be cast easily; it can be annealed by heating it up and plunging it into cold water, and thin sheets can be easily worked with a hammer. Iron behaves differently. While it will work harden and thus crack under the stress of cold forging, it has to be heated to be annealed, and then must be cooled very slowly. If it were quench-hardened, as they would do with bronze, it would not soften. If by some chance there were some carbon present, it might get very hard. In short, its behavior was quite different than bronze or copper.

But don't think that once iron was discovered bronze was dropped immediately. Far from it. Just as bronze weapons coexisted with Stone Age ones, so too did iron weapons coexist with bronze ones. Bronze continued to be important in the accoutrements, fittings, guards, pommels, etc., not to mention that maces could still be made from bronze. Even today, brass is still used for modern gun cartridge cases.

Although it took a great deal of time, someone finally figured out that iron could be quite useful, and then iron weapons began to appear. The Iron Age is generally considered to date from about 1400 BC. But this is a date used more for convenience than for anything else. We are already aware that copper was discovered a lot sooner than was thought, and that might be true for iron as well.

The Hittites are frequently given the credit for the discovery of iron, and many believe that the brief Hittite Empire was created by their mighty iron weapons. This is highly doubtful. First, there is no direct evidence that the Hittites used iron in abundance. Second, early iron swords were not much better than their bronze counterparts. Although lighter than bronze swords, they would bend just as easily. It probably took some time for methods to be discovered that yielded a steely iron. In the clash of armies it is quite doubtful that this small advantage would have been sufficient to insure victory and conquest. But it is undeniable that at about this time iron weapons and artifacts begin to appear.

You also have the very likely scenario that the discoverers did not run out and share the information with their neighbors. Undoubtedly the first iron weapons were more curiosities than decidedly better weapons. But in the forging of the blades under heat, some of them absorbed some carbon, and thus came out much tougher than bronze.

Man's nature has not changed in a few thousand years, and when the ancients learned their smiths could make a better blade, they tried to keep it a secret and sell their iron weapons at a premium. After all, the swords were stronger, tougher, lighter, and could be made longer, and, it was felt, be more effective.

It is human nature to keep your foe at a distance if possible. It is widely believed that a longer sword can give you an advantage. (This is only partially true. History shows us that a shorter weapon, used properly, is better than a long one. Consider the Greek phalanx and its twelve-foot-long spears versus the Roman short sword, the short Zulu assegai battling the traditional long African throwing spear, the Spanish sword-and-buckler men against the Swiss pikemen, and even the long rapier against the small sword.) Since the iron sword was a better product, why not get top dollar for it? Although this is just supposition on my part, I have a strong feeling this is what happened.

Restricting the flow of knowledge can only last so long, and in the end the knowledge of iron working spread over most of the world. Although the knowledge of how to smelt the iron and forge blades was pretty common, the ability to make fine swords was not.

There were many "secrets": secret formulas for smelting the iron, secret formulas for forging, and above all, the secret of properly tempering the blade. Smiths all over the world were pretty successful at restricting *this* knowledge. There was also a lot of mystery to this art, real and imagined. This "mystery" coupled with "the grass is always greener" concept, led to the legends of Toledo, Damascus, Japanese, and Persian swords, and the fabled Indian wootz steel (of which more below).

In a pre-industrial society, the ability to work iron and produce weapons and tools was considered almost magical, and its practitioners were linked to the gods themselves. Although the degree of reverence varied from culture to culture, the blacksmith was a powerful figure, and the blacksmith who produced weapons was even more important. This was true in many societies. Even the practical Romans had Vulcan, the crippled smith of the gods. Indeed, this crippling of the smith may have had some basis in fact. Both the Norse god Weyland and the Roman Vulcan were lame. Obviously this could be simply borrowing from one religion to another, and I am certainly not an expert on mythology. Certainly it is a good way to keep a good smith from running away. But we can read, and see, the importance of the smith in early societies. In Japan, Persia, China, Europe, and even in tribal Africa, the smith was of great importance and highly valued.

It is easy to see how this can happen. Consider taking a lump of metal and changing it into a shining sword blade that is capable of cutting through flesh and bone, and even mail. The whole process can appear magical! Since nothing was known of chemistry or metallurgy, even the practitioners themselves could think of it as magic!

Let me add something here on a personal level. I do not believe in magic. I am a hard core realist, and might best be described as a pragmatic empiricist. Having said that I am also forced to admit to having witnessed things I simply do not understand.

I have seen Jim Fikes, a blacksmith living in Jasper, Alabama, at this time, forge and temper a knife; while others, using the same steel and methods, do the same thing, at the same time. Then testing time comes around. Jim's knife holds an edge much longer, and can be made sharper, than any of the others. This is not hearsay, but it is true, as I was doing the cutting. I made the effort and cut the material as identically as I could, and the results were amazing. I still don't believe in magical swords, but I can be persuaded that there could have been knives and swords that were amazing.

There was one important reason that allowed this "mystery" of making a sword or knife to continue and flourish. The reason was very simple. The makers themselves did not know why the swords they produced were good, mediocre and a few really bad. These last they threw back into the pot to be re-melted and re-forged. What they did know was that if they used ore from a specific place, and did certain things by rote, taking a specified time to do it, and in a certain manner, they frequently came up with a good sword blade. And rarely, a truly superb sword blade appeared. But they did not know why.

The real secret to this was simply carbon content in the iron. But since the science of chemistry and metallurgy had not yet been developed, no one knew it. The average person is quite surprised to learn how late it actually was before the impurity, carbon, was proved to be what turned iron into steel. Some recent discoveries in England have shown that very high quality steel was produced in England in the "Dark Ages" (circa 476–1000 AD). Hamwic was a Saxon port that is under modern Southampton. Much of it has now been excavated, and a very interesting discovery was made. Several blooms of very high quality steel were found, plus several knives with high quality steel edges. These blooms are homogenous steel, with about two percent carbon. Properly forged, this could produce exceptional quality blades.

Shortly before this discovery, another one equally fascinating was announced. It seems that a monastery, abandoned when Henry VIII split from the Catholic Church, was also a metal producing factory. This is not unusual in itself. But what is unusual, is that the process they used was identical to the Bessemer process that was invented by Sir Henry Bessemer in the 19th century, and was in use in manufacturing until quite recently.

In 1740, Benjamin Huntsman, a maker of watch springs, found that he could produce much superior steel by melting the steel, allowing the slag to rise to the surface, and then skimming it off. This is much the same technique as was used in producing Wootz steel of India. But carbon wasn't discovered until 1774 by Swedish metallurgist Sven Rinman. In 1786 French chemist Guyton de Morveau showed that the substance isolated by Rinman was carbon, introduced into the iron, that turned the iron into steel.

As early as 1540 AD an Italian had suggested that steel was the "pure" form of iron, and to achieve this purity the iron was heated up and charcoal, leather, and other such substances added to help burn out the impurities. Since charcoal and leather both contain carbon, he was on the right track, but going in the wrong direction. It was the impurities—sulfur, phosphorus, nitrogen, hydrogen, total oxygen, and sometimes carbon—that frustrated steel production. Modern steelmakers grapple with these impurities today, but with a clear understanding of what they are fighting. The ancient blacksmith could only fall back on empirical knowledge gained from trial and error.

FROM IRON TO STEEL

Let us take a look at iron and what it can and cannot do. Hollywood, popular fiction, and our own wishful thinking have given to swords properties and abilities that simply do not exist in the real world. Martial arts movies have the hero jumping straight up for twelve feet, and sword films depict blades cutting down large trees, shearing through metal and stone with ease, hitting other blades edge to edge, and never showing a scratch.

Iron is malleable and not too heavy. It can be worked cold, and in thin sheets can be made to take on all sorts of shapes (witness plate armor). Iron is chemically quite active, and will combine readily with many substances. When heated to a cherry red it becomes plastic and can be shaped easily. Work hardening will add a small amount of toughness to iron. But if it is hammered cold too much, it will begin to crack, and even when work hardened it will not have a great deal of toughness. If you add

Samples of Peter Fuller's modern reproduction plate armor (left) and helmets (below).
Photos by Peter Fuller.

carbon to the iron, the crystalline structure changes. And so do the properties of the metal.

Now this certainly isn't a book on metallurgy, but understanding the basic material that is used to make a sword, and its properties, is important to understanding the weapon, and how it was, and was not, used.

Carbon is the principal alloying element in the manufacture of knives and swords. Although other elements can be added, and will produce some minor changes, it is carbon that makes the most difference. Today we can add chromium and produce stainless steel, add various other trace elements like molybdenum and vanadium, and produce tougher, stronger and better blades. Some of these trace elements were in the various legendary ores, and they produced swords that were better (forging and tempering being equal) than other blades made from bog iron ore or ore with none of the valuable trace elements.

Iron that contains .05 percent to .20 percent carbon is considered low carbon steel, and is little better than iron. At best it can be called a "steely iron." Although better than bronze, it does not make a good sword. Medium carbon steels, containing up to .70 percent, make a good blade. It can be tempered and, although it will not harden to the same degree as high carbon steel, it will harden and take an edge. The best swords are made from high carbon steel, with a carbon range of up to 1.00 percent. Any higher than this and the carbon shows a strong tendency to make the blade entirely too hard, and subject to easy breakage. (Understand that these figures apply to swords made prior to the 20th century. Modern alloys can make very good sword blades without the same amount of carbon.)

But carbon content alone does not make a good sword. Heat treating, or tempering, is the most important factor. You can have a sword with a medium carbon blade, and one with a high carbon blade, but if the one with the high carbon blade is not tempered properly, it will be inferior to the other. The tempering process was another area that allowed for "secrets." Water is an excellent cooling medium, but it has one problem. Unless the water is highly agitated, it will immediately steam and create a barrier that will delay the cooling process, thus you get uneven cooling. This is particularly true for a large object like a sword. This is why running water was used, and why a fall of water was preferred.

But fresh water isn't the only medium; brine is very good, as well as oil. All of these make good tempering mediums.

One quenching medium that was not used was a slave, into whom the red hot sword was supposedly thrust to gain some occult property. This is one of the more popular and ridiculous myths that permeate this field. Aside from the moral considerations that our ancestors did, and did not, have, it simply wouldn't work anyway. The human body simply could not remove heat quickly enough to make an effective tempering medium. Nor could it be done in a uniform manner. It sounds good and romantic and magical, but it simply isn't true.

THE FORGING PROCESS

The forging process was usually started with a "cake" of steel. This was a piece of steel about two pounds in weight and was usually obtained through trade. A swordmaker was lucky if he lived close enough to a good source of metal. But this usually wasn't the case.

The steel was heated to a cherry red and then pounded into a bar. This process was repeated several times, and eventually it was shaped into the sword blade. The Japanese had a process whereby they would take the carbon containing iron and fold it over many times. This allowed the carbon to disperse throughout the sword, making a blade that was generally homogeneous. This folding ensured that any welding flaw did not go fully through the blade, thus helping to keep the blade from breaking under stress.

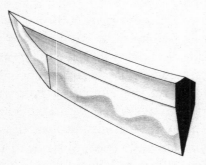

The Japanese also used several other techniques designed to produce a superior blade. They would enclose a high carbon center with a mild steel skin, allowing the edge to protrude. This kept a very sharp, hard edge, but with a soft back that could absorb shock. They also tried the reverse, with a soft core encased in high carbon steel. This served the same purpose.

*Cross-section view of
a Japanese sword.*

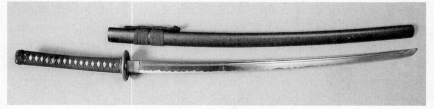

Reproduction katana. HRC106.

The Europeans used a different technique. They would twist bars of high carbon steel with bars of low carbon, rough shape the sword, and then weld on a high carbon edge. The purpose was the same, to give a hard edge with a core that could take the shock of a blow and not break.

The two processes do not appear to have occurred at the same time. This method of manufacturing the katana is believed to have appeared about 1000 AD in Japan, and continues even today by some of the Living Treasures of Japan, those smiths who still forge superior swords. However, in Europe around 900 AD, smelting techniques had improved so that it was possible to get a cake of steel large enough to make a full steel sword. Not long after the debut of these swords, pattern welding as a method of making swords vanished, and all-steel swords began to appear.

There is an interesting historical novelty here. The first all-steel swords have a distinct shape. The blade is wider at the hilt, and tapers somewhat to the point. This puts the weight of the sword closer to the hand, and thus makes it quicker. Also, all of these early blades are marked with the name "Ulfberht" in nice large letters. Shortly thereafter copies marked "Inglerii" appear. We don't know anything concrete about the significance of these names.

It is rather hard for me to write without digressing. There are so many aspects that need to be brought out, and so many tales about swords, that it's really hard to stay on course. But here I go, back to making the sword.

Reproduction Ulfberht blade. HRC210.

After the sword was forged to shape it was filed, partially polished, and then hardened. This last was done by heating the sword to a bright red, and then immersing it in a tempering medium, in order of preference: water, brine, or oil, this last being more forgiving and easier on the steel. As soon as possible after the blade had been quench hardened, it was tempered.

The sword at the end of the hardening process was extremely hard and brittle, and most blades tended to warp under the stress. However, since the crystalline structure of the metal was still unsettled, there was a 15-minute window of opportunity when the smith could straighten the blade without breaking it. Then came the tempering.

The sword was heated to the desired temperature, usually around 400 to 500 degrees, and kept at that temperature for an appropriate time, so that the temperature is consistent throughout the blade. It was cooled quickly in the medium of choice.

This produces a blade that is hard, yet also tough. By varying the amount of heat applied to the blade you can get varying degrees of hardness and flexibility. This frequently depended on how the sword was to be used as well as the length of the sword. A shorter weapon could be harder, as it would not be subjected to the same amount of torque as would a longer weapon. (Note that too much hardness could cause the edge to chip easily.) A longer weapon would have to have a greater degree of flexibility as simple leverage would add a great deal of force that would be applied to the blade in combat. The individual struck with a sword is highly unlikely to remain still, and his inconsiderate movements would place great stress on the blade.

One of the favorite themes in fiction is a rapier so superbly tempered that the blade can be bent so that the point touches the hilt, and when released, springs back to true. I have such a sword at home, that I picked up in Toledo, Spain. It is pretty, in a rather garish fashion, and is completely worthless as a weapon. I sharpened the blade, and could not penetrate a cardboard box! The blade flops all over the place, and you can't cut with it or thrust. But it is flexible!

Regardless of movies and fiction, the rapier was required to have a rather stiff blade. The rigidity was necessary, as it was a thrusting weapon, and had to at least penetrate a breastbone, and may have had to deal with mail as well. As the rapier progressed and eventually changed into the small sword, its form changed to reflect the stresses it would be subject to. The blade was generally tempered to a strong spring. This allowed it to absorb the shock it would encounter, but still be rigid enough to penetrate. The stiffness was aided by cross sections. Many cross sections had a diamond shape, some with hollowed faces for less weight. One beautiful sword in my collection, which I came to own by way of Ewart Oakeshott, has a cross section that is literally a cross. Some cup hilts have blades that are thin rigid needles. The most effective small sword has a cross section that is triangular, with deeply hollowed faces. This is an extremely light and quick weapon.

But I digress. Let us return to the heat treating of the sword.

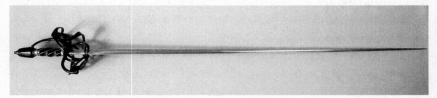

Reproduction of an original rapier from the
collection of Ewart Oakeshott. HRC24.

There is another form of tempering called "slack tempering." In this procedure the sword is heated up red hot, and then inserted into the cooling medium. It is kept there for a predetermined period, usually just a few minutes, and then withdrawn. This is done while the blade is very hot. The cooling medium has not sucked all the heat out of the blade. The residual heat then builds back up in the blade and then the sword is again quenched. This time it is left until cool, taken out and quickly straightened. This method is quick and requires less work, and was generally done on the cheaper swords. It does not give a good even temper, and results in a blade that has soft and hard spots.

Another form of heat treating was also used. This is called "case hardening." This was used a great deal in more primitive areas where the metal working skill did not approach that of Japan, Europe or the Near East.

The weapon was forged and pretty much completely polished. Then it was covered with some form of carbon-bearing substance, such as leather, charcoal or plant matter, generally placed in a sealed container and heated up to a red heat. It was then taken out, left to cool, and lightly polished. It was heated up one more time and quenched again. This operation left a thin skin of very hard steel, sometimes as hard as 64–65 on the Rockwell scale. The problem was that the surface hardening is only about ¹⁄₁₆ of an inch deep or less. The result was a very soft blade with a very hard skin. It was excellent for slicing, but rarely would it stand up to any real abuse. Javanese and Filipino knives and swords are generally made this way. Although they are highly regarded, and attributed with almost magical qualities in their areas, they really can't stand up to rigorous use.

The problems facing the early swordsmiths, regardless of their location, was how to get enough carbon into the iron. Remember, they didn't really know what the substance was. Early furnaces lacked the ability to reduce the iron ore to iron, and to heat it up long enough, and hot enough, for it to absorb carbon from the charcoal. Thus the manufacture of iron in sufficient quantity to make a sword was a long process. The iron had to be smelted and purified, the process repeated several times in order to get some small pieces of steel. But these small pieces of steel could be welded into a larger section, and lo and behold, a sword blade! And this brings us to pattern-welded swords, Damascus and Japanese sword blades.

As with many things, we do not know who first developed pattern welding. We do know that it was in use from at least the 2nd century AD, and continued up until about 900 AD. There are at least two Roman swords that we know were pattern welded after modern spectrographic analysis of the swords. These date from the 2nd century, and the workmanship on both is quite good, so it's clear the technique was around well before that. There are many swords dating from the 10th century that were pattern welded.

Pattern welding developed when it was found that if long thin bars of iron were placed in a container filled with charcoal and heated up red hot you got a steely iron. This is essentially case hardening. However, if you do this several times, then the iron bars became steel, with a good amount of carbon. The smith would take a few of these iron bars, wind them around each other and forge out a blade. Then additional steel bars would be forge welded to the edges and the point. After being filed to final shape it would be hardened and tempered.

The forging would cause carbon migration from the steel bars to the iron bars, and if there was a sufficiency of carbon to start with, you ended up with a good, tough blade. But as you can easily surmise, a lot could go wrong. You might not have enough carbon to start with or, even if you do, it might leach out. This is where a very good smith was quite important, and why his reputation was his livelihood. A good smith did everything he could to assure that the swords he made were as good as he could make them. One thing he did was use the best ores he could get.

Iron ore comes in many forms. Bog iron was a very impure ore that contained all sorts of inclusions, such as phosphorus, arsenic and sulfur, that made it very difficult, if not impossible, to make a good sword. Other ores might contain manganese, which increased the toughness of the steel. Vanadium and titanium might also show up, and these also helped to make the sword tougher and stronger.

Pattern welding did not produce a magical sword, but if the smith was lucky, he could produce a good sword. Several of these swords have been tested, and the carbon content varied from .03 to as high as .06 percent. Rarely was this evenly distributed throughout the sword, but there was enough to produce a tough, rather flexible blade.

DAMASCUS

The term "Damascus steel" is a very confusing one. It originally referred to swords that were purchased in Damascus, then it came to mean shotgun barrels that were forged together after being wrapped around a central core. Some also use the term to mean a type of steel produced in India that is now termed "wootz." In modern knife making it refers to taking bars of steel, forging them together and etching them to produce blades with patterns. And the term "Damascene" refers to gold work inlaid on the blade. For this book the term refers to Eastern swords, both where the blade is made of one type of steel, and one where the blade is forged with another steel to produce patterns.

The Indians developed a superior method of producing steel, and they did this quite early, approximately 200 BC. This seems shockingly early to most people, but Indian steel has long been regarded as the best. This was done by heating the iron ore in a crucible combined with various carboniferous items. As the iron began to absorb the carbon, the melting point lowered, and more carbon was picked up and dispersed throughout the iron. This produced a bloom of steel with a carbon content as much as three percent.

This method of manufacture produced a bloom of steel that is called "watered steel" as the various minor impurities and crystalline structure of the steel gives a watermark effect. This could be heightened by various forging and even mechanical Damascus methods to produce swords of incredible beauty. Not only were they beautiful, they were excellent swords. This is the real source of the tales of Damascus swords that could cut through steel and do all sorts of wonderful things. European knights encountered these blades during the Crusades; much of the steel work was traded in and around Damascus, and there were even swordsmiths there. So the legend was born, but the actual source of the steel, and many of the swords, was India.

The Japanese did not have this method of turning the iron ore into steel. Although they used rather sophisticated methods of heating and purifying the ore, heating, reheating, beating the metal to remove impurities, and doing this with the usual Japanese thoroughness, the basic ore they started with was not quite as good as the Indian. But excellent techniques of manufacture, great care in the construction, and strict observance of ritual (which aided keeping to the precise time required for various operations) and the Japanese were able to produce truly excellent swords. Not the magic swords of movies, but truly fine weapons.

There is one incontrovertible fact about steel. The harder it is, the more likely it is to break, shatter, or chip. All of the efforts the swordmaker exerts are intended to minimize this. The Japanese wrapped soft steel around hard steel, and vice versa; differential tempering, with the edge left hard and the body soft, was also used. Oftimes the smith tried "packing" the edge (repeated hammering to make the edge denser and thus stronger). Most times the sword was tempered so that the whole blade had a tough spring—able to cut well and still be springy enough to absorb the shock of a blow. All of these things worked to a degree, but none of them produced the perfect sword. Since each weapon is made for a specific type of combat, each will have different requirements. There *is* simply no perfect sword.

Suggestions for further reading from the editors:

De la Bedoyere, Guy, *The Finds of Roman Britain*. B.T. Batsford, Ltd., London, 1989.

Grancsay, Stephen, V., *Arms & Armor: Essays from The Metropolitan Museum of Art Bulletin* 1920–1964, The Metropolitan Museum of Art, New York, 1986.

Spring, Christopher, *African Arms and Armour*. Smithsonian, 1993.

► 3 ◄

Design and Geometry of Swords

People have been designing swords since the discovery and use of copper. They found that copper, even with a central rib down the blade, was not really a good material for swords. With the invention of bronze, swords became more practical. But even here the material helps to dictate the shape of the sword and consequently its capabilities and usage.

Iron gave a much wider range, and steel increased it even more. But there is so much more involved in sword design than merely the material involved. How was the sword to be used? How was it to be carried? What was the type armor it was likely to face? How strong was the individual carrying the weapon? And just as important, what was the fashion of the day? These are just a few of the questions that might be asked regarding the design of the sword. So let's examine it bit by bit.

PARTS OF THE SWORD

In discussing the sword most people like to start with the blade and separate it into three parts: the forte, which is the strong section of the blade near the hilt; the middle of the blade; and the foible, which is the weak section of the point. This is fine if you happen to be talking about rapiers or nothing but straight-bladed

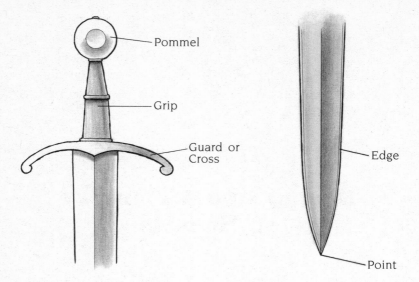

Basic handle parts include
grip, guard and pommel.

Basic blade parts include
body, edge and point.

European weapons. If you happen to be talking about a kora it makes no sense at all. (The kora is a down-curved Nepalese blade that ends in two cusps.) To me, when talking about swords and sword design it makes more sense to divide the sword into two basic parts, and then subdivide them and discuss each.

The two basic parts of the sword are the blade and the handle. The handle can be broken down into the grip, the guard (if it has one) and the pommel (if it has one).

The blade can be broken down into the body of the sword, the edge, and the point. Now it is quite possible for the sword not to have a point, as in the case of the above mentioned kora. It can also not have an edge (many thrusting swords did not have edges).

The body of the sword, the blade, governs which working part, the point or the edge, is the most important, and it also governs how the sword is to be used in general.

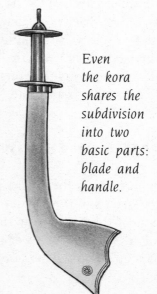

Even
the kora
shares the
subdivision
into two
basic parts:
blade and
handle.

There is some confusion about the development of fighting styles and swords. I have encountered people who believe that the fighting style was projected, and the sword designed around it, and others who believed that the sword was developed and the style evolved around it. Both of these ideas are true, and both are false. Confusing, isn't it?

The truth is that swords and fighting styles revolved and evolved around each other. This was particularly true in Europe, if less so in other parts of the world. A sword can have many purposes. It can be a cutting sword, it can be piercing sword, it can be both a cut *and* thrust weapon. It can be made to oppose lightweight armor, heavy mail, or even plate. It can be made to slice cleanly or to rip and tear, or even to crush. Japan, for instance, developed a particularly effective sword that was suited for their early forms of combat. Fighting and dueling styles evolved around this sword, and the sword remained essentially the same for close to a thousand years. Now, I know that the purist will scream that there were many differences over the years. But all of these differences are rather subtle, and to the casual observer, they all look pretty much the same.

Europe, however, seemed to revel in constantly trying new sword forms. This was due to constantly shifting and improving armor, as well as to changing tactics and concepts on the battlefield.

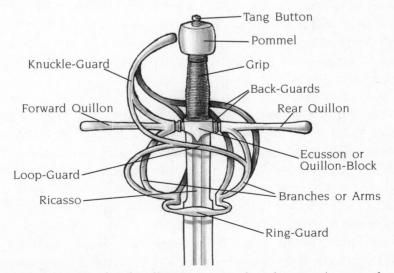

The basic parts of a handle—grip, guard and pommel—may be further subdivided, as this drawing of a rapier demonstrates.

Social changes allowed the carrying of swords during the normal course of the day, and this also caused differences in the style of swords. But it is not the purpose of this book to discuss all of the relevant sociological changes that took place. Nor, as it has been previously stated, to discuss the history of the European sword. Ewart Oakeshott has covered this better than anyone else, and I strongly recommend his books. You should start with *The Archeology of Weapons*.

THE EDGE

For a sword that has a cutting function, the working part of the blade is the edge. There is nothing mysterious about an edge, it is simply a wedge. It cuts by exerting a tremendous amount of pressure on a very small area. It will also cut when the blade is slid along material being cut. This is a result of both the wedge and the friction that the blade encounters. In addition to this, in many blades there will be very tiny teeth (when observed through a microscope), and these act as a saw by actually tearing the material.

Now, not wishing to be particularly bloody, I still have to point out that the sword is basically designed to cut flesh and bone. However, most people are rather reluctant to be cut, so they make many efforts to defend themselves with armor. So the swordmaker has to take into account the armor that his sword will be facing. This is reflected in the type of edge, as well as the shape and dimensions of the sword.

But let's look at the edge.

The edge of a sword must have support, and it must have mass to allow it to cut. The mass is achieved by either the width or the thickness of the blade, and this also supports the edge. Generally speaking a thin, flat blade will cut quite well. When a blade cuts into a substance, it must displace the substance it is cutting. Therefore, it is an advantage for the blade to be flat, and thus offer less resistance. There are problems with blades that are too thin. The temper of these blades must be exactly right. If the blade is too hard and not flexible enough, it will break. If it is too flexible, then the blade will flex during the cut, and may even turn slightly and thus not hit the object properly. In the many years that I have been playing with swords, I have seen both. I have encountered one sword that is extremely flexible and have seen a gentleman in India so skilled in its use that he could cut a lime while a friend stood on it, and not take off his friend's foot. But this takes skill and practice time far beyond that allotted to the ordinary soldier. Nor would it work particularly well in battle, as there is not the time to get set up.

Another way to overcome the resistance that the blade will encounter is the hollow ground blade. Although we usually think of a hollow ground blade in terms of a razor, many of the old blades are also ground this way. This type of grind has certain advantages. It lightens the blade, yet keeps it stiff and strong. On a double-edged blade this allows for an excellent cutting action, while keeping the rigidity needed for effective thrusting.

In Westminster Abbey there is a truly beautiful little sword that is believed to have belonged to Henry V. This sword has a flat blade with a ridge in the center, and the grind that is called hollow ground. It is a very fast sword. I had an exact copy made for me, and the little blade is unbelievably

Cross-sections of hollow ground blades.

fast. It would be quite effective against mail armor. One must always remember that not everyone on the battlefield wore plate.

But any flat or hollow ground blade will generally not be as strong as a blade with a greater thickness and more support for the edge. As with everything in life, you have a trade-off.

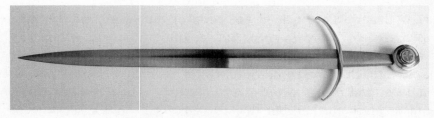

Reproduction Henry V sword. Photo by Peter Fuller.

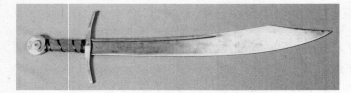

Reproduction falchion. HRC74.

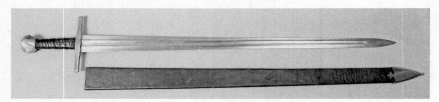

Reproduction sword; note the fuller. HRC53.

The thicker the blade the stronger, but thickness comes with an increase in resistance and greater weight. The secret is, of course, a compromise between the two.

This is why many European swords have flat grinds. The single-edged swords, such as a falchion, are almost always flat ground, with wide, flat blades. The double-edged knightly sword, if it has a fuller—a groove down the blade—will have a flat grind from the fuller to the edge.

The fuller, by the way, has nothing to do with channeling blood from your enemy. It is there to lighten the sword blade, while still leaving enough metal to support the edge.

The Japanese did an excellent job of combining cutting power and strength. On most European swords, the blade is ground almost to the edge. Then a different bevel, called the cutting bevel, is put on the final edge. The Japanese forego this last step, and grind the blade down to create a very sharp edge.

HOW THE SWORD WILL BE USED

Now that we have named the parts of the sword, we can take each type of sword in turn. But we must also look at how the sword is intended to be used, since form follows function. Swords can be roughly broken down to: cutting swords, thrusting swords, and cut-and-thrust swords. Actually they can be broken down much, much further, but that isn't necessary in a discussion of design.

THRUSTING SWORDS

In thrusting swords, and in cut-and-thrust weapons where the thrust is the dominant feature, care must be taken that the point is effective. In many swords that are designed to go up against both plate and mail, you will often have a point that is thicker than the rest of the blade. This reinforced point is excellent for splitting the links of mail, both butted and riveted. It can also find the small openings in the plate armor and force its way in. This reinforcement is found on swords, but also in spears and the spikes of

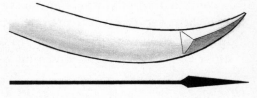

Sword with point thicker than rest of blade: top view is side-on; bottom view is silhouette as seen from above.

many polearms. The point acts as a wedge and, due to the small surface area, will exert many tons of force on a small area. But the point must also have the support of a stiff blade in order to

Reinforced point on polearm. HRC70.

exert the force needed to penetrate. Even the unarmored human body can offer a surprising amount of resistance if the thrust is not straight on or a bone is hit.

RAPIERS

The most obvious sword that one thinks of in regards to thrusting is the rapier. Hollywood has made it seem that the rapier must have a highly flexible blade. How many times have you seen the hero flexing his rapier before engaging in a deadly duel with the villain? Hollywood was so in love with fencing that it borrowed many fencing conventions and passed them off as real combat methods. Many fencers *will* flex their blades before a bout. This limbers up the blade, and it will also give it a slight set. This slight bend will allow a fencer to go over an opponent's blade, while it will also assure that the blade will bend, which you want in a sport fencing blade. Fencing swords are designed not to hurt people, exactly the opposite of real swords. A good fighting rapier needs to be stiff enough to puncture, but not so stiff as to be brittle should the sword be hit a hard blow in a parry to drive it aside. This combination of stiffness and flexibility must be achieved through tempering. Merely adding material to the sword blade to make it stiffer only adds weight, and this would slow down a rapier.

As the rapier became established as the European civilian weapon of choice, starting in the 1500s, efforts were made to improve it. This led, at first, to extremely long rapier blades, swords with a blade length of 54 inches, or even more. The idea was that if your blade was longer, then you had a chance of hitting your opponent before he hit you. This is only partially correct, as a slightly longer blade helped, but not a great deal. It was found that they were quite clumsy, and an opponent could close inside the point and then you were at his mercy. Just as bad, and maybe even worse, they were damnably hard to wear, as you were forever knocking over things and causing people to trip. Having attended some events

Spanish cuphilt rapier, circa 1750, 47 inches overall length. HRC25A.

where many were wearing rapiers, I can testify that they can be quite annoying when the wearer does not hold it close to his body.

As a fencing style of swordplay became more and more popular as a method for settling various disagreements of a serious social nature, efforts were made to improve the sword. Early in the 17th century the cup hilt was developed, and then the dish hilt. Various blade lengths and sections were tried, until the small sword was developed. This is considered by many to be the ultimate fencing weapon. Generally a hollow triangle in cross section, with a blade length between 31–36 inches, it was very light and very fast. One variation, called the "colichemarde," had a blade that thickened at the forte of the blade. This allowed it

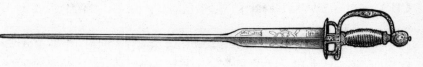

The colichemarde blade thickens at the forte of the blade.

to be used to parry cuts from heavy blades. Although, as stated, it was quite fast, it suffered from the problem of not having any edges. In a really nasty fight this made gripping the blade a viable and useful tactic.

THE TUCK

However, this was done to another kind of thrusting sword, the tuck or the estoc from northern Europe. This long, straight sword of the 15th century was intended solely for thrusting and the earlier versions were designed to penetrate armor, either mail or plate. Some of the later versions do not have quite the thick, heavy blades of the earlier models, but have blades that are almost heavy rapiers. Many think that these weapons were the ancestor of the rapier, but I do not think it is possible to know this for sure.

As an interesting side note: many are not aware that the Turks used a large number of estocs. There are many in the museums in Istanbul. Although I have not been fortunate enough to study them personally, a fellow sword lover has sent me some photos and descriptions. They are impressive, and are truly bars of sharpened steel. The blades appear to be about one-half inch in thickness, square in section, with a smooth, even taper and a very strong point. You have no doubt that in the hands of a strong man it would penetrate plate armor.

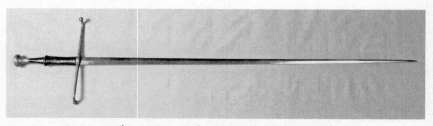

Swiss tuck, 50.25 inches overall length. HRC25C.

CUTTING SWORDS

Not all swords are for thrusting, and for many the primary purpose is the cut. Even so, there are very few who wish to do away with the point entirely. Thus cut-and-thrust swords have a point, just not as pronounced as on the thrusting sword. The blade in back of the point is somewhat wider, and thus able to give a stronger blow than the narrow blade of a thrusting sword. It is an effective sword, doing both cutting thrusting with equal facility.

But there is one type of point that has been generally ignored, and that is the cutting point. I know that it sounds like a contradiction in terms, but it really isn't.

When you cut with a sword you usually try to hit with the optimal striking point. This is the area of the blade where you will encounter the least amount of vibration. This is the same as the sweet spot on a baseball bat or a tennis racket. Swords will have two such spots, one well up the blade and one close to the hilt. To find them all you need to do is to tap the sword on a stump or something of that nature (whatever you do, don't use a piece of furniture; wives are quite unreasonable about this sort of thing). When you find the area that does not produce vibration, this is the sweet spot. When you strike with this area

The sweet spot is indicated on this reproduction cut-and-thrust sword. HRC181.

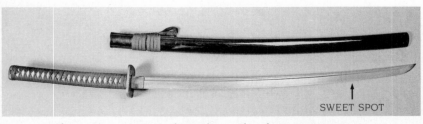

The sweet spot is indicated on this katana. HRC105.

you are able to deliver the greatest amount of force to the given area. But there is a problem with this. When you strike with this area, you are effectively shortening your sword. I have a superb recent copy of an early medieval sword. The blade is 32 inches long. However, the sweet spot is only 22 inches from the hilt. When I strike with this section, I am reducing the length of my sword. This is true with swords such as the katana, which don't have very long blades to start with. Now, the katana overcomes this problem easily. The Japanese developed a very effective cutting technique.

But we are talking about the design of swords. So look at the history and the development of the rapier to small sword, and then look at the Japanese katana.

There is no question that the katana is perfectly suited for the style of combat in which it is used. A relatively short blade (about 28 inches average) with a two-handed handle, it was capable of delivering some truly terrifying cuts, and also some perfectly acceptable thrusts. The sword was in use for close to a thousand years, and in that time there was very little change other than in materials and the skill of manufacture.

Japan, having a very stable (some might say static) culture, with very little outside contact, saw no reason to change. Whereas Europe, quite dynamic, with plenty of outside contact, was constantly changing.

If you cut with a broad-bladed strongly tapering medieval style sword you will use the optimal striking area. Should you happen to hit with the top 3–6 inches of the blade, you will not be able to deliver a very strong cut. A thickened thrusting point produces a great deal of drag, enough to reduce the depth of the cut fifty percent or even more.

The katana has a point that is rounded, and every bit as sharp as the rest of the sword. This allows a cut with no drag, as the point slices its way through the material. In most cases the katana was used so that the attacks were made with the front 6 inches of the sword. This also prevented the sword from being hung up in the body of the opponent. Remember, we are talking war and killing. People do not remain still when hit with a sharp sword, and it is possible for the sword to be trapped in the body, and pulled from the hand. This was also one of the reasons that the curved cavalry saber was popular.

This rounded cutting point is, however, also quite effective in the thrust. The edges of the curve are sharp and are able to penetrate well by simply cutting its way in. The shape of the point, almost a quarter circle, is quite strong, and with sufficient force able to cut through mail.

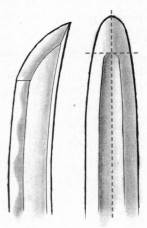

Now, I can't say that the development of the curved point was done deliberately; it could have easily been accidental. But it does work.

But the Japanese were not the only ones to develop a cutting point. The Europeans did it, particularly the Vikings. It has often been said that the Vikings and the medieval knight did not know about the thrust. This is based on the frequency of somewhat rounded points and that it is often said that the Viking and medieval sword are "far too heavy to fence with."

Katana (left) and Viking (right) points.

Well, that's true, they are too heavy to fence with. But they were never made for fencing, they were made for fighting and killing your enemy. As for thrusting, the Vikings used spears a great deal, and the sagas record many instances of someone thrusting his sword into his opponent's body.

For instance, in *Njal's Saga*, one sea battle is related that occurred between Hrut and Atli Arnvidarson, who was a pirate. When the two fleets converged and Atli found out that Hrut served King Harald Grey Cloak, battle was imminent. Atli remarked that, "your Norwegian kings have had much for my father and myself." And Hrut replied, "That's your hard luck, not theirs." Atli snatched up a spear and hurled it at Hrut's ship, where it struck a man and killed him. That was the beginning of the battle and it was quite a fierce one. The pirates had trouble gaining a foothold on Hrut's ship. Ulf the Unwashed (wonderful name, that) was laying about him with sword and spear when one of Atli's men, called Asolf, leapt on to Hrut's ship before Hrut became aware of him and turned to face him. Asolf lunged with his spear and drove it through Hrut's shield before Hrut, with a single blow, killed him. Ulf the Unwashed remarked, "That was a heavy blow, Hrut." At that very moment Atli noticed a gap in Ulf's defense and hurled a spear that went right through him. So the Vikings knew all about the dynamics of the thrust.

My own experiments have shown that a rounded sword point can be used successfully in the thrust provided that the sword is sharp. It should be remembered that mail was not worn all the time, nor was it worn by everyone, even in a battle. The improvement in range and cutting ability more than makes up for a slight decrease in cutting power.

Let me add something to the above. The rapier and the small sword were never military weapons. They may have been carried by some officers, but the rank and file used other weapons. By the time the two swords became popular in the 16th and 17th centuries, firearms had became the dominant feature of European battlefields. The katana, however, was used both as a battlefield weapon and for personal defense and dueling by the classes allowed to carry it. When firearms arrived in Japan in 1543, they were used to win major victories, then quickly banned. The Shogun wasn't stupid, and he could easily see the danger to the social order that firearms represented.

CURVED SWORDS

There are other examples, but let it suffice to say that the sword in Europe was a constantly evolving weapon, responding to styles of fighting, military needs, and fashion, whereas in the rest of the world the sword changed, but much more slowly.

A good example of this is the curved sword. Although there are curved Bronze Age swords, the weapon really came into its own with the development of iron and steel. It was widely used on the steppes of Central Asia, as the curved blade was most effective as a horseman's weapon. It gave more power to the slashing stroke and was not as likely to get caught in the body of the foe, which might cause you to lose your weapon.

The ancient Hungarians used a slightly curved saber during the period of the Magyar invasions (9th century AD). Although the Europeans became familiar with this sword, they do not seem to have adopted it. Just the reverse: after the Magyars settled down and became Hungarians they adopted the straight double-edge sword.

A Magyar type saber.

An 18th century Turkish kilij, 34 inches overall length. HRC25.

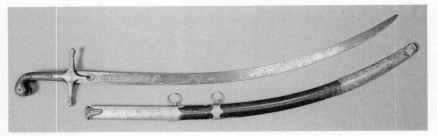

Antique shamshir, circa 1800, 36 inches overall length. HRC39.

In the Middle East the story was different. Most early Islamic swords, under the influence of the conquering Arabs, were straight and double-edged. With the Turkish invasion the curved sword found some acceptance, but did not become truly widespread until the Mongol invasion of the 13th century. Many types of curves were tried. Some were quite effective, like the Turkish kilij. It ended up with the beautiful, but ineffective shamshir of Persia.

The curved sword appears to be ideally suited for the swirling, flowing and ebbing tactics of steppe warfare. While many warriors carried, and used, lances and lassoes, their primary weapon was the bow. The steppe warrior avoided close personal combat if at all possible, preferring instead to kill from a distance. Once the battle was won, the curved sword was well suited for cutting down a retreating enemy, whether they were on foot or horseback.

But just because the curved sword was used on the steppes does not mean that it was the ideal cavalry weapon. The European

medieval knight preferred the straight
double-edged sword. The fight over which
blade shape was best for cavalry lasted
until the 20th century when both the
British Army and the US Army adopted
the straight thrusting sword as their cavalry weapon. The fight was rancorous and
bitter, and the proponents of the straight
blade barely won. I am sure that if horse
cavalry were still around, the fight would
still be going on.

The adherents of the straight blade
pointed out that the thrust was more
deadly than the cut, that many men had
continued to fight even after receiving
several saber blows to the head. Despite
bleeding badly, they were able to continue
the fight, while the man who had received
a thrust almost never continued to fight.

The curved blade proponents would
point out how often the cavalryman lost
his weapon in the thrust, the number that
had their wrists broken before the sword
could be retrieved, and the terrifying effect
of seeing a fellow soldier with large slashes
on his face and body. Rarely were military
sabers of the 18th and 19th century fully
sharpened. Usually the blade of the saber
was sharpened the last 7–8 inches below

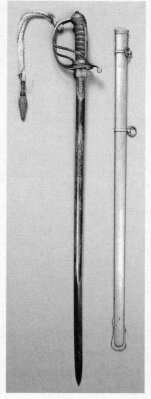

*British Life
Guards saber with
metal scabbard,
circa 1850–1880,
39 inches overall
length. HRC324.*

the point. The cavalry trooper was trained to try to strike with
the last several inches, and this was very effective and also allowed
the sword to free itself from the victim. The swords were also kept
in metal scabbards, and of course this would wear off a sharp
edge pretty quickly, but if the blade was sharpened only in the
top portion, this would be unlikely to contact the metal scabbard.

Some cavalry sabers were not sharpened much at all. The
Confederate general Nathan Bedford Forrest was roundly criticized
for having his men sharpen their sabers. The theory was that
a hard blow, even with an unsharpened blade, would split the
skin, possibly crack the skull, and do a fair amount of damage.

This is true to a degree, but there is no question that a sharper sword would do more damage.*

There is another tale that I always found interesting. During one of the numerous small wars fought by the British in India (I believe this was during the Mahratta Wars in the first decade of the 1800s), a group of British soldiers were badly cut up by native warriors. The wounds were most extraordinary. One man is reported to have been cut deep into the chest, another with having his cartridge box cut in two and he was still severely wounded by the sword blow. A young British officer was sent to investigate and see what type of mystical swords the Indians were using. It turned out they were using discarded British cavalry sabers. When questioned about their swordsmanship, one of the native troops is reported to have said, "Sahib, we run in and hit very hard!"

HOW SWORDS WORK

Anecdotal comments are all very well, but how do swords actually work? We understand how piercing works. The point is quite small, and just a small amount of pressure exerts tremendous force, several tons per square inch, and the point separates the material and enters it. The width of the blade will also govern just how much damage is done. A very thin blade can enter, and may not do much damage, whereas a large blade can cause severe damage. There are many cases of duels with small swords where one duelist received several thrusts and continued fighting. However, with a wide-bladed sword a thrust into the body will almost always cause the recipient to cease fighting. This is easy to understand as the wide blade will cause a great deal more trauma.

---

* According to *The Deadliest Men* by Paul Kirchner, page 91, Forrest was surrounded and attacked by six Federals using sabers in April of 1865. He was struck repeatedly without effect, because the sabers were dull, and eventually killed several by pistol and escaped the rest. He later remarked, in reference to one who had hit him several times, "If that boy had known to give me the point of his saber instead of its edge, I should not have been here to tell you about it."   —Whit Williams

Cutting with a sword is somewhat more complex. Swords will cut using the principle of the wedge, but it can also cut as a saw. For a sword to cut the blade must be sharp. It would seem to follow that the sharper the sword the better it would cut. But this is dependent on the materials being cut. So let's start with the edge. There is nothing mysterious about an edge, it is simply a wedge, and the thinner it is, the sharper.

The edge acts on the wedge principle same as the point. The tremendous force concentrated on such a small space will cause the edge to penetrate the material. But there has to be force. Merely laying the edge on a surface will not cause it to cut. Even a razor can be touched to the skin without cutting. But the moment you put any pressure, or if you draw the blade along the surface, it cuts. This has frequently been explained by stating that most sharp edges, when examined under a microscope, show very tiny saw teeth. This is true for only a few edges. A great many edges will be somewhat smooth. But they will cut just as well. The reason is that even a small amount of friction will cause the blade to cut into the material.

One of the most fascinating swords I've encountered was a Persian blade, I estimated the date at about 1600 AD. The blade was curved, and the edge was composed of many small teeth, almost serrated. My thought on the sword was that it would work quite well against the usual mail shirt worn in the East. The mail was generally butted, and a downward blow from this sword would catch and tear the mail, while the following portion of the blade would cut and tear flesh. Alas, this is only speculation, as I have never had a chance to try this out.

But just any edge won't do. The edge needs to be backed up and it also needs mass. The backing and strength is provided by the blade itself, and the mass is furnished by the width and thickness of the blade. A light hit with a sharp blade may not penetrate even lightweight cloth armor. However, if you change the action from a straight downward force to one that even slightly slices, the blade will cut much quicker and deeper. This action, while more effective with a curved blade, will also work with a straight-bladed sword.

For a more detailed discussion of cutting with different swords, please see Chapter 13.

Suggestions for further reading from Hank:

Oakeshott, Ewart, *The Archeology of Weapons*. The Boydell Press, Woodbridge, first printed in 1960.

Suggestions for further reading from the editors:

Ffoulkes, Charles J., *Inventory and Survey of the Armouries of the Tower of London, Vol. I.* His Majesty's Stationery Office, London, 1916.

Menghin, Wilfried, *Das Schwert im Fruehen Mittelalter.* Konrad Theiss Verlag, Stuttgart, 1983.

Seitz, Heribert, *Blankwaffen I.* Klinkhardt & Bierman Gmbh., Muenchen, 1981.

► 4 ◄

Wounds and the
Effects of Swords

The carnage of modern war is horrible, but make no mistake, the carnage of medieval battle was no less so. Although bows, crossbows, javelins and a few other missiles were used, the majority of the combat took place hand to hand. The weapons used were spear, sword, axe, mace, and variations of the above.

Until plate armor dulled the effectiveness of the sword (pun intended), it was the most popular of weapons. But axes, maces, and polearms were also much in evidence. The sword, however, due to its versatility, was the preferred close-quarters weapon.

SOURCES OF INFORMATION

There are three major sources for information dealing with the cutting power of the sword. One is archeological evidence. Although it is rare that one can say *for sure* what weapon caused a particular kind of wound, when taken in conjunction with literary sources, the second source, one can make safe assumptions. The third is experimentation. Now, while it isn't moral, legal or practical to go out and chop on people, one can test the sword against other objects, up to and including sides of beef.

Surprisingly enough, archeological evidence is fairly plentiful. There are skeletal remains that show the effects of combat, and I feel sure that many of these were inflicted with a sword.

On July 27, 1361, Waldemar, King of Denmark, attacked the city of Visby on the Isle of Gotland in the Baltic Sea. Visby had long been an important way station for trade with the east and was very wealthy. With avarice worthy of his Viking ancestors, Waldemar launched the attack, quickly overcame the city's defenses, and sacked the city.

It is doubtful that the defenders were trained warriors. Contemporary chronicles considered them poorly armed and largely peasants. Considering the percentage killed over the number taking part in the battle, it must have been a terrible slaughter. Close to 2,000 defenders were killed, and it is doubtful if they had fielded more than 4,000 in all.

After Waldemar gathered up his treasure and left, which probably took two or three days, the inhabitants started about the mournful business of burying the dead. It was July, and warm, and after a few days the bodies were not in the best of condition. This may account for why so many were buried in their armor rather than being stripped. (There were a few who were cleaned and buried properly, but it is uncertain why they were singled out.)

Reproduction Viking sword. HRC410.

The mass burial sites were excavated in the early part of the 1900s and the analytical work continued for several years. As graphic and distasteful as it may be to many, the information it has provided gives a very good picture of the horror and berserk fury that must have been a routine part of medieval warfare.

There is one skeleton of a man who has had both legs severed, and it appears to have been done with one blow! The blow landed on the right leg below the knee on the outside, and then struck the left leg slightly below and on the inside. Since it appears to be unreasonable that someone would stand still with one leg hewn

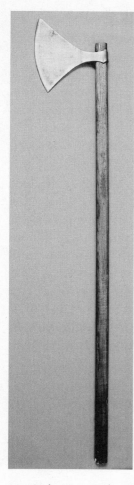

off, that one blow cut off both legs below the knee. As can be seen in another section of this book, that is not so astounding after all. There are several skeletons where a foot has been severed, and there are many with cuts to the lower leg. Indeed, this seems to have been a major target. A rough estimate is that close to 70 percent of the blows detected at Visby were aimed at the lower leg. This is quite understandable, as the lower leg is hard to protect, even with a shield. When you consider that these fighters were not well equipped with leg defenses it explains why they were targeted.

The head also took many blows. There are several skulls from Visby that received so many blows that you would think the enemy would have gotten tired of hitting the poor devils. Many of the skulls still have their mail hoods, and although the hoods did provide some protection, many of the blows cut through the mail and into the bone.

One of the most unsettling skulls is one where the victim had been hit a sharp blow right at the bridge of the nose. The blow was so hard that it cut through the upper jaw. When I visited Sweden I was able to view the skull and I could see that the deepest part of the cut was in the center, indicating that it was caused by a crescent-type axe blade, or possibly the point of a sword on a hard sweeping cut. Whatever caused the damage, it wasn't enough to kill quickly. The one good thing is that the skull also shows marks from several other cuts and one hole in the side close to the temple. One can only hope that the guy didn't suffer too long.

Reproduction Viking axe. HRC257.

But Visby is not the only archeological source. There are a great many sources scattered all over. In Ireland there is a skull from the Viking Age that has had the whole right side sheared off. In Lima the skeleton of Francisco Pizarro, the Conqueror of

Peru, showed the marks where he was stabbed repeatedly in the neck when he was murdered in 1541.* Numerous burial mounds in Europe have been opened and skeletons exhumed that show the results of many wounds. A surprising number of them show old wounds that have healed over. It is interesting to note that many of these skeletons show the wear and tear that comes from heavy physical labor.

The tomb of Charles the Bold was opened in the 19th century. He had been slain by Swiss halberdiers during the battle of Nancy (1477 AD). To quote from Oman's *Art of War in the Middle Ages*, a halberdier "struck down Charles of Burgundy, all his face one gash from temple to teeth." When the tomb was opened it was found that he had been stabbed in the side, also in the funda- ment, and indeed his skull had been split down to his teeth! All of the wounds probably had been made by halberds. It is easy and gory to visualize what happened. He was struck a downward blow by some stout Swiss with a halberd. The force of the blow would force him down and off of his saddle, and two other Swiss, seeing openings, would have stabbed with spear or halberd. Not that either blow was needed.

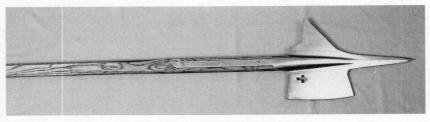

Reproduction halberd. HRC251.

Of course these blows were not struck with a sword, but it does show the amount of information that is available to a patient researcher. It is my hope that one day someone with the time and resources can gather up all of this information about ancient hand-to-hand combat and publish it. What a fascinating book it would be! This chapter can only touch on some of the rich information available.

Literary sources are another important area to explore. However, these have to be taken with a grain of salt, backed up and verified

---

* *New York Times*, August 11, 1891.

with experimentation when possible. Man has not changed any in the past several thousand years. He was just as given to hype in 3000 BC as in 2000 AD, and in England as well as Japan. When we read in "The Song of Roland" of some knight skewering a bunch of Saracens on his lance at one time we have a right to feel somewhat skeptical. When we read in early tales of some warrior bragging that the sword "Quernbiter" cut a millstone in half, we should raise an eyebrow rather than being convinced that it was evidence of some incredible new steel.

Of all the literary sources, my personal opinion is that the Icelandic sagas are probably the most reliable. They are written in a laconic straightforward style that does not allow for flights of hyperbole. When we read that a sword flashed and someone had their leg cut off at the knee, we feel that it is very likely exactly what happened. There is a pragmatic acceptance of life and its trials and tribulations that runs through the sagas, coupled with the acceptance of death that makes them very believable. Iceland has excellent historical records, and events recorded in the sagas are also mentioned in other sources. There are some sagas, such as *The Saga of Grettir the Strong*, that many consider romance rather than a tale of actual happenings. Even so, they have the feeling of, "Been there. Done that."

In *Njal's Saga*, the author tells of a warrior, Gunnar, whose home is surrounded by his enemies. A Norwegian visitor with the besiegers volunteers to go see if Gunnar is at home. As he climbs up the side of the cabin Gunnar stabs him with his hewing spear through a chink in the wall. The Easterner falls and walks back to his friends. They ask, "Is Gunnar at home?" and he replies, "As to that I can't say. But his halberd is." He then dies. Now, this is one tough man. One might think he is an exception, but this theme runs throughout the majority of the sagas. But do not think that these people were blind brute barbarians as the movies like to show. Far from it. Egil was one fierce, tough warrior. But his lament over the death of his son can tear out your heart.

As at Visby, the sagas record blows to the leg. Again in *Njal's Saga*, Gunnar and another warrior, Kolskegg, try to take a ship. Kolskegg worked his way down one side of it and Gunnar the other. Vanidil came to meet Gunnar but his sword hit Gunnar's shield and stuck there fast. With a hard twist of his shield, Gunnar snapped the sword at the hilt. He struck at Vanidil so quickly that Vanidil didn't have time to defend himself and the sword sliced through both legs.

Also in *Njal's Saga* there is the wonderful fight on the ice. This is the one where Skarp-Hedin goes sliding by and before Thrain can put on his helmet Skarp-Hedin crashes his ax on his head so hard that Thrain's back teeth spill out onto the ice. Tjorvi throws his shield into Skarp-Hedin's path, but he dodges it. Tjorvi then hurls a spear at Kari who leaps over the spear and then plunges his sword into Tjorvi's chest, killing him instantly. (Tjorvi doesn't seem to have been very good at throwing things, does he?)

And speaking of spears, that brings us to puncture wounds.

PUNCTURE WOUNDS AND HOW TO ACHIEVE THEM

There is a great deal of misinformation about wounds and their effects floating around. Most of this is due to old wives' tales that no one ever questions, and a lot is due to Hollywood and a vast number of fiction writers. If you study the subject, and check out the books on trauma, you are surprised to find out two things, seemingly contradictory: people are easy to kill, and they are also difficult to kill. Another aspect that is very important is the mental attitude of the individual. I have read of people being shot with a small caliber weapon in a nonfatal area, and then dying! Now I realize this is a book on swords, but a shot with a .22 is really not much different than a stab with a small sword. They both make nice small punctures.

I have been assured that if your leg is cut off below the knee, you can always kneel and fight on one foot! I have been assured that the reason so many stilettos were made with triangular blades was so that the puncture could not be sewn up! (I can testify personally on that one: properly treated puncture wounds are not sewn to begin with.) In short, there is a lot of nonsense out there. So let's deal with some of it.

One of the most common comments is the deadliness of the puncture wound. "Two inches in the right place is all you need!" The operative words here are "in the right place."

The rapier and the small sword were quite attractive weapons, and the small sword became a very elegant item of jewelry. No well dressed gentleman in the late 17th century would think of appearing without his small sword, whether he knew how to use it or not! They were considered, and still are today, the deadliest of swords.

But people do not die as quietly and as easily as they do in the movies. All too many times you will see the villain run through with the hero's rapier, and he staggers and falls with scarcely a moan! Now it *can* happen that way, but it isn't very likely. Rapiers and small swords make small holes. If they hit a major artery or vein, or a nerve plexus, death can occur rather quickly. But even a direct thrust through the heart can take as long as ten seconds to kill, depending on the amount of blood in the brain at the time of the strike. And a man can do a lot of damage in ten seconds! Like stabbing you before you can withdraw your blade. There are many fights recorded where both parties received several puncture wounds in the body, and both recovered. There were also many instances of fights where one man died on the spot, while another lingered for two weeks before dying from a thrust in the stomach. There are several excellent books on the subject of dueling and one can easily see that death was not the swift and easy thing that we see in the movies. (For a more comprehensive study of dueling I would suggest *The Sword and The Centuries* by Alfred Hutton, *The Field of Honor* by Ben Truman, Milligen's *History of Dueling* and *Dueling Stories of the Sixteenth Century* by George H. Powell. There are more books out there, but I think these are the best.)

One of the more unpleasant aspects of dueling in 17th and 18th century Europe was to win the duel by killing your opponent, only to be hanged for breaking the law . . . seems positively unsporting, doesn't it?

But we could talk a long time about dueling itself, so now let us get back to the wounds made by blades. Back in the 1950s, I once saw a young man who had been attacked by two brothers. They had stabbed him three times in the abdomen, then run away, leaving the Italian stiletto still in the boy. Luckily for him, the knife was not particularly sharp. It had pushed his entrails aside, and he ended up with only three minor punctures to the muscle wall. Had he been stabbed with a knife with a wide, sharp blade, the results could have been much more unpleasant. With a wider bladed sword, such as a Viking, medieval or Roman

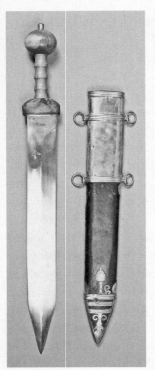

Reproduction gladius. HRC218.

weapon, the results of a thrust would be more deadly. The wider the blade, the more damage done.

Whereas it is possible for a rapier or a small sword to penetrate a chest cavity without seriously damaging the individual, and to even push the intestines aside (not likely, but possible), a wide-bladed sword will be cutting the tissue as it passes in and out, making a much larger, and much more deadly, wound.

The comment on a "stab in the right place" seems to be Roman in origin. But even then the operative words are "right place." The Roman gladius was a very effective cut-and-thrust weapon. Many think that it was *only* used in the thrust, but it is capable of delivering a very strong cutting blow. But its primary use was as a stabbing weapon. Held close to the body, the moment an opening presented itself the short sword could leap out and inflict a very deadly stab. With a blade close to two inches in width, and very sharp, the stab of a gladius was nothing like the pinprick of a rapier.

I was recently asked if the thrust was known and used in medieval times, and if so, why was it considered so innovative and dastardly by gentlemen in the Renaissance? The thrust itself has been known since Og, son of Wog, picked up a sharp stick and stabbed Ug with it. The whole history of weaponry is filled with a collection of sharp and pointy things meant to cut and stab and generally hurt people. (Also heavy things meant to crush, but we're talking about thrusting here.) Early Iron Age swords probably did not have a good enough temper for good thrusting, but they were still used that way.

For example, there is a very beautiful Celtic Iron Age rapier in the Berne Historisches Museum. The blade is a flattened diamond in cross section, perfect for thrusting, and could easily be a 16th-century rapier except for the grip. There is a whole class of medieval swords, Oakeshott Type XVII, that cannot be used for cutting: the blades are too thick, and they are obviously designed

The thick blade of an Oakeshott Type XVII sword
makes it better for thrusting than cutting.

to be used for thrusting. Jean de Joinville tells of one knight who took his sword and couched it as a lance and used it against a Saracen during the crusade of St. Louis (1248–1254).

So, the answer to the question was the thrust known in medieval times is actually quite complex and involves such variables as the deterioration of swordplay in the early 13th century, the increased use, and then disuse of armor, the growing popularity of the duel, and the effectiveness of the weapon involved.

Although the knight was primarily a horseman, and looked down on the infantry, he could, and did, fight on foot. Before the increased use of armor, the sword was the primary weapon for close combat. The actual fight itself was quite energetic, with a great deal of movement with many heavy blows being dealt and blocked.

As armor improved, and more and more foot soldiers as well as knights were equipped with it, the sword became less and less effective as a weapon. To a degree this was acceptable, because in many medieval fights between knights the object was not to kill your opponent, but rather to render him helpless so that he could be captured. After all, when ransomed he was worth a great deal of money! Another very valid reason for this "compassion" was that if you started killing others of the aristocracy, you might very well be killed yourself!

But there were efforts to improve the effectiveness of the sword. After all, some enemies just needed killing and to the devil with ransom. These swords varied. Some had very wide blades capable of cutting through mail with ease, but then use of plate armor expanded and this didn't work. So there were developed swords that were long, and very rigid, with points that could punch through any area that was thin, and could find the chinks in the plate and deliver a deadly thrust.

But armor improved as well, and soon a sword was just about useless against good plate armor. So first a knight would use a

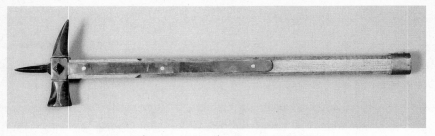

Reproduction war hammer. HRC274.

lance—a long-distance weapon—against an enemy in plate. But once the lance was shattered, a mace, axe, or war hammer became the preferred weapons.

On the ground, by the middle of the 15th century in Europe the shield had been discarded, and the weapon of choice was a two-handed one. One should not forget, as many do, that the choice of weapon during this period was based on military and tactical considerations, and not which weapon was best for individual dueling. In a large mass of men, the pike was a terror-inspiring weapon, but it was damn near useless when used by one individual. The halberd, which *was* an effective hand-to-hand combat weapon, lacked the length to be able to stand up to an armored, mobile knight, and thus became a secondary weapon.

Another and very important consideration is to look at combat at the time of the introduction of the rapier, the late 15th century. At this time the individual warrior, whether foot soldier or knight, was a man in pretty good condition. (Obviously not all of them: we know several died of heart attacks in various battles, as they weren't used to wearing their armor.)* But the real

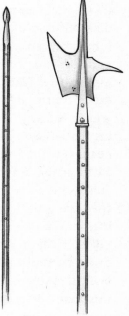

The pike (left) was only effective used en masse, but the halberd (right) was an effective hand-to-hand weapon.

---

* E.g. In 1415 at the battle of Agincourt the Duke of York died of exhaustion and heatstroke in his armor, as cited by Ewart Oakeshott, *A Knight and his Armour,* page 26. 1961 Lutterworth Press, London.   —Whit Williams

fighting man was far from a wimp. He wore heavy armor, typically weighing 50–55 pounds, and was used to dealing heavy blows in order for them to be effective. In battle he killed his enemy, or so badly injured him that he had to quit fighting. In civilian life, should he be attacked by thieves or bandits, or be challenged to a duel, it was close to the same thing. Heavy blows, dodging, ducking, parrying, and you attacked and killed your enemy any way you could: cutting, thrusting, or bashing him in the head. Generally speaking, all of the participants were fairly robust and vigorous

A *reenactor in armor.*
Photo by Peter Fuller.

specimens. There was a great deal of skill involved, but it was skill that also required a great deal of physical stamina.

Then along came the rapier. Even in its first days it meant a different type of fight. There was much more finesse, the blade was used to parry, and the primary attack was the thrust. But this was not the thrust of the sword, one that made a large and deadly wound, but rather a small hole, and one that frequently took several days in which to kill your enemy, and so he was frequently able to fight on, even after several sword thrusts. Which made it quite dangerous even to the winner. This was not the only thing found offensive by many of our Renaissance bravos. As a weapon for war it was worthless, it did not require the stamina of the swordsman, and it did not favor the forthright attacks and blows that many thought were the knightly heritage.

England probably resisted the rapier longer than any other country. George Silver, the Gentleman Scholar of the Sword, author of *Paradoxes of Defense*, hated the rapier with a passion. My personal inclination is to think he hated the Italians and French more than he did the rapier. In much of his writing he shows a clear understanding of weapons and how they were used. But in regard to the rapier he simply refuses to see any of its advantages. But the young men in other areas took up the rapier with a vengeance. It was lightweight, dressy, and was ideal for the hot-blooded fight and the duel, which was gaining in popularity.

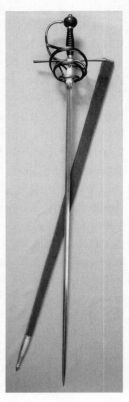

No, it wasn't the thrust that caused the indignation among the older gentlemen of the Renaissance, it was the whole idea of the rapier; useless in war, and only fit for dueling, and then using moves that looked positively effeminate! Almost like dancing!

As I have stated before: Man doesn't change, but fashion does. Within a generation the rapier was all the rage, and there were as many schools in its use as there were dances.

But I digress, as I have a tendency to do.

Reproduction rapier.
HRC14.

CUTTING WOUNDS

The cut is much like the thrust: in the right place it can be deadly, and it can instantly incapacitate your opponent. The power that a good double-edged sword can deliver is impressive, or frightening (depending on which end of the blade you happen to be).

There is the tale of Theodoric, who killed the King of the Ostrogoths by having his men hold him while he struck him at the juncture of neck and shoulder. The blow was so strong that Odovacar was split all the way down to his hip! This seemed to have shocked Theodoric, as he is reported to have exclaimed, "In truth, the wretch has no bones!"

Now, this is a pretty powerful blow and you can be easily excused if you think it is a bit of hype. After all, that is a long cut, and there are plenty of ribs in the way. But think back to the Battle of Visby, and the awful damage recorded there. And there is another factor that must be considered. Bones are very tough, but they are not as hard as many like to think. The older you get, the harder and more brittle the bones get, but live bone in a fairly young man is not much tougher than a sapling.

The other thing that must be looked at is the sharpness of the blade. Japanese swords have long been known for their sharpness, but being sharp was not something exclusively Japanese. Many European swords were just as sharp, and there are Viking era swords that *still* possess a very sharp edge. When you look at how flat and thin many blades are, you realize that in their heyday they were probably very sharp, and quite able to hew through bone.

Just as there is no way to generalize about puncture wounds, there is no way to fully comment on the effects of a cut. We have tales from the Napoleonic Wars (*Sword, Lance & Bayonet*, Charles Ffoulkes & EC Hopkinson) of soldiers receiving several head wounds from sabers who were able to continue fighting. But we also hear of one having his head cut off from the blow of a saber, so it is apparent that it depends on the blow, what is being cut, and the sharpness of the sword.

I believe that today too much attention is paid to the military sword, perhaps because many of the records that are still available detail battles and the wounds suffered. But the military saber of the 19th century was generally not a very sharp sword, and in many instances was not sharpened at all. General Nathan Bedford Forrest was highly criticized for having his men sharpen their swords, and so were the British for the 1796 Cavalry saber that was considered to be too "brutal" for war.* I think one of the reasons behind this is the modern military theory that if you wound a man it would take two to care for him, thus eliminating three men from battle. That sounds pretty good, unless you're the guy facing the enemy. You've just whacked him in the head, cutting a very deep scalp wound, so he's bleeding, but shows no intention of running away, and is also mad as hell. No thanks, I want my weapon to be as effective as possible.

Not long ago a friend of mine sent me a clipping from *High Adventures in Tibet* and in it the authors detailed a raid by some

---

* The French actually petitioned the British government asking them to discontinue its use.   —Peter Fuller

bandits in Tibet. It showed several wounded, with all the wounds made by swords. The bandits had all been on horseback and as a result almost all of the wounds were head wounds. They really were pretty ugly, showing deep dents in the skulls, but all of the people survived. The swords used seemed to have been simple single-edged blades of the saber style, with blades in the 33-inch length range with a blade width of about 1¼ inches: that is, simply not heavy and sturdy enough to cut through the hard bone of the head.

But a well made, well sharpened sword in the hands of a man who knows how to cut can do a tremendous amount of damage. We read in epics of all ages and areas of people having arms and legs cut off, and even being cut in half! The Roman Ammianus Marcellinus comments: "The heads of others were split through mid-forehead and crown with swords and hung down on both shoulders. A most horrible sight." In Caesar's *Commentaries* a Roman soldier greets him and when Caesar looks at the man blankly, he says, "It's no wonder you don't recognize me, because my helmet and face were split by a Spanish machaira."

Tibetan sword.

In the same sea battle related in *Njal's Saga* between Hrut and Atli, is an example of another limb-lopping blow. Atli leaped onto Hrut's ship, one man turned to meet him but was knocked off his feet by a thrust from someone else. Now Hrut faced Atli. Atli hacked at him and split his shield from top to bottom, but just then he was struck on the hand by a stone and dropped his sword. Hrut kicked the sword away, cut off Atli's leg and then killed him with the next blow. Such is the fate of pirates.

The question then becomes, just how well can a sword cut? Seemingly a simple question, but first we have to decide what type of sword we are talking about.

The Iron Age sword, the Viking sword and the early medieval sword were pretty close to being in

Machaira.

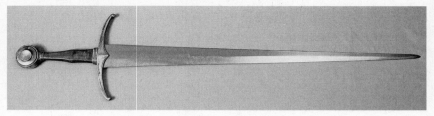

Reproduction medieval sword. HRC46.

the same broad category. Generally about 29–33 inches in length, with a width of about 2 inches, most had only a slight taper, and some no taper at all. During the later part of the Viking Age the sword assumed a slightly more tapering configuration, but this is covered better in the section on sword design.

These swords weighed in the general area of 2–3 pounds. Balance would, of course, be slightly different for each sword, but generally the balance was what the owner desired, and he might make changes to suit himself.

So what can this type of sword do? The answer is that it can do much more damage than many people think, but not near the damage as portrayed in many books and movies.

I know how well I can cut. I know how well I have been able to cut, and I know how well I do now at the age of 66 (at the time of writing this chapter). The best cut I ever made with a sword was with a Japanese-style blade I was testing to destruction. I sheared a 3⅛ inch sapling in half, and the length of the cut was 6½ inches along the diagonal. I have seen a better cut made by Jim Fikes, a blacksmith friend of mine in Alabama. But I have no illusions as to how this compares with a 10th century warrior who had grown up using a sword.

It is with this understanding that I have undertaken a great many experiments with swords on how well they cut, and how well they cut armor. But for more on how to cut, see chapter 13.

So to answer the question: could the sword make the huge cuts described in the sagas and other historical sources? Not only do the archeological data support that conclusion, my own attempts at cutting do, too. Will they make them every time? Many factors, including type of sword, strength and placement of the blow, and opponent's armor (or lack thereof) and age (and therefore bone density), enter into the equation.

Sources and further reading suggestions from Hank:

GENERAL HISTORY:

Ffoulkes, Charles & EC Hopkinson, *Sword, Lance & Bayonet*, Cambridge University Press, 1938.

Oman, Sir Charles, *The Art of War in the Middle Ages*. Greenhill Books, London, first printed 1924.

Oakeshott, Ewart, *The Archeology of Weapons*. The Boydell Press, Woodbridge, first printed in 1960.

Oakeshott, Ewart, *The Sword in the Age of Chivalry*. The Boydell Press, Woodbridge, first published 1964, reprinted 1994.

ON DUELING:

Hutton, Alfred, *The Sword and The Centuries*. Charles E. Tuttle, Company, Rutland. First printed 1901, Tuttle edition 1973.

Truman, Ben C., *The Field of Honor*. Fords, Howard & Hulbert, New York, 1884.

Millingen, J.G, *History of Duelling, Vols. I & II*. Richard Bentley, London, 1841.

Powell, George H., *Dueling Stories of the Sixteenth Century*. A.H. Bullen, London, 1904.

Silver, George, *Paradoxes of Defense*. First published 1599.

ARCHEOLOGY:

Thordeman, Bengt, *Armour from the Battle of Visby 1361, Volumes I & II*. Almquist & Wiksells, Uppsala, 1939.

Fiorato, Veronica, Anthea Boylston & Christopher Knusel, *Blood Red Roses:The Archeology of a Mass Grave from the Battle of Towton AD 1461*, Oxbow Books, Oxford, 2000.

CONTEMPORARY LITERARY SOURCES:

Caesar, Julius (102–44 BC), *Commentaries on the Gallic War.*

Caesar, Julius (102–44 BC), *Commentaries on the Civil War.*

Marcellinus, Ammianus, *Res Gestae*, AD 353–378.

Norse sagas including *Njal's Saga* and *Egil's Saga.*

de Joinville, Jean, *Memoirs*. His memoirs can be found in *The Chronicles of the Crusades*, translated by Margaret Shaw. Penguin, London, 1963.

The Song of Roland, translated by Dorothy Sayers. Penguin Books, New York, 1957.

Froissart, translated by Geoffrey Brereton, *Chronicles*. Penguin
    Books, Baltimore, 1968.
Plymire, David V., *High Adventure in Tibet*, revised edition. Trinity
    Print'n Press, Ellendale, North Dakota, 1983.

▶ 5 ◀

The Viking and Early Medieval Sword

The sword in use during the Roman period was the gladius. The barbarians they fought used a longer cutting sword. The gladius was a very efficient sword, and one that was designed to be used as part of an integrated military system. But as a weapon for single combat, it wasn't all that good. The shield the Romans carried was quite heavy, and in one-on-one combat the Romans lacked the maneuverability to be able to defend themselves properly. Like the pike, it was formidable in mass, but not too good in single combat. As the empire began to decay and more and more barbarians not only flooded the empire but enlisted in the legions, the gladius was gradually discarded and by the fall of the empire in the fifth century the spatha replaced it. The spatha was the ancestor of the Viking sword and the knightly sword of the European middle ages.

In the year 793 AD, the Anglo-Saxon Chronicles record that "heathen men" ravaged and sacked God's church in Lindisfarne. Lindisfarne is a small island off of the east coast of England and had

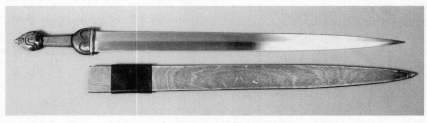

Reproduction spatha. HRC54.

a church and an abbey. This was the first recorded raid of those we call the Vikings, and marks the beginning of the "Viking Age."

For the next three hundred years a people known as being tough, hardy, adventurous, and also cruel and murderous shook Europe. The Vikings were made up of Danes, Norwegians, and Swedes. The Europeans noted little difference, and called them all Danes, Vikings or Northmen. In their time they sailed to the New World, settled Iceland and Greenland, settled and conquered parts of England and France, served as bodyguards to the Emperor of Byzantium, plundered and pillaged in the Mediterranean. Their descendents, the Normans, conquered Sicily.

Today their reputation is varied: some think of them as settlers, traders and adventurers, while others considered them merely murderous barbarians. But all agree on one thing: they could fight.

What weapons did they use in their three-hundred-year spread throughout Europe? In reality, their weapons were little different from those used by most of Europe: swords, axes, spears and bows. They also used a halberd. We are fortunate in that there are a fair number of their weapons still in existence. Many are grave finds, some are river finds, and some have shown up with no provenance known. We have good examples of all of their weapons except one, the halberd. We'll cover their other weapons and armor in the next chapter. In this chapter we'll discuss their sword.

THE VIKING SWORD

The Vikings valued their swords greatly, and would hand them down to their sons. Oft times the swords would bear delightful names like Tyrfing or Mimming, or more descriptive names like Leg Biter, or Widowmaker. The famous Viking Thorolf had a sword he called "Lang," which meant "long." His brother, Egil, had a sword he called "Viper." There was one called "Skofnung" personified by its owner King Hrolf as follows: "Skofnung bites and rings aloud in their skulls for it was the nature of Skofnung that it sang aloud when it felt bone."

The Viking sword, like the modern handgun, was a weapon that could be carried on the person all day, and usually was. Most weighed about 2½ pounds, some a little more, some a little less.

The Viking used two types of swords. One was single-edged

and was used more by the Norweigians than the rest; it was given the name "long sax." This sword is curious, as the back can curve down to the edge at the point in one sword, but in another the edge will curve up the back.

Reproduction sax.
From the collection of Peter Fuller. Photo by Peter Fuller.

The most popular was the second type, the double-edged sword. This sword was about 30–32 inches in length, with a width of about 2 inches. It was a single-handed sword, and the grip was usually of wood covered with a wrapping of leather. But since this was an entirely personal thing, there was great variation. As with most early European swords, the two edges were parallel, then curved gently to a rounded point. One thing this rounded point will do is allow the sword to be used as if it were a longer blade, as discussed below.

Viking and other early medieval swords differ primarily in decoration and style. Most Viking swords have pommels that are lobated, with three to five lobes. Many of the later Viking swords have wheel pommels, essentially the same as many early medieval swords. The Viking also had "cocked-hat" and "brazil nut" style

Lobated pommel (right).

Wheel, cocked-hat & brazil nut pommels (below, left to right).

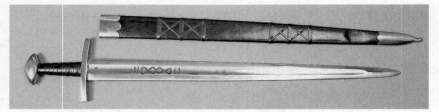

Reproduction Ulfberht sword; see page 31 to view the name inscribed on the reverse side. HRC210.

pommels. So it's basically the location of the find that indicates if a sword is Viking or early medieval; the blade shape is pretty much the same for both kinds of swords.

As mentioned above, early Viking swords had blades whose edges were parallel, with a rounded point. These early blades were pattern welded. In this process, as discussed in an earlier chapter, small strips of steel were twisted with small strips of iron. The two were forged together, and then a hard steel edge was usually welded to the pattern-welded core. When completed and polished, this produced a blade of exceptional beauty. Sometime in the early 10th century the ability to produce a large enough bloom of steel to make a full sword was developed. Although the process didn't happen overnight, all steel swords became the norm. These steel swords also had a slightly different shape. Instead of the edges being parallel, there was a defined slope to the point. The point was still rounded, but the slope put weight closer to the hand, thereby making them somewhat quicker on the stroke and on the return. These new swords all had the name "Ulfberht" engraved on the blades. It's fun to speculate how this sword was developed and who this person was.

Often the blade was polished bright, and the fuller (the slight indentation designed to lighten the blade) would have a pattern that the smith had designed beforehand. This design could look like mown hay, a ladder, or chevrons, or many other things.

MYTHS ABOUT THE VIKING SWORD

Viking and medieval swords have been the subject of many myths that are only now being dispelled. I have often heard it said that the Viking sword was a crude, clumsy weapon, suitable only for slashing and wild swings. Nothing could be further from the truth. Handled with skill, it was capable of thrusting and cuts that could easily take off a leg at the thigh.

It has been stated that Viking and medieval swords are so heavy that a modern man can barely lift one, much less fight with it. The fact that the average weight is between two and three pounds is completely ignored. It has also been stated that many Viking and medieval blades were made from steel so tough that it is superior to modern steel, and you will also hear that Viking and medieval swords were made of metal so poor in carbon content and so poorly tempered that they bent under each blow.

The truth is that some swords were poorly made, and some swords were excellent. It was impossible to be consistent in manufacture as they usually didn't have consistent ore, nor was the importance of carbon understood.

Curiously enough, the European sword appears to be the only one where the pommel acts as a counterweight to the sword. Although the evidence is too sketchy to be presented as a fact, the practice seems to have started sometime around the 7th to 8th century AD. (Although some Japanese swords have long tangs which help in the balance of the sword, there were no weighted pommels.) Weighting the pommel changes the balance of the sword and allows a heavier blade to be manipulated as if it were a much lighter sword.

Two of the more common myths, and two that are quite widely accepted, concern the use of the sword as well as its design. It has been stated many times that the Viking and the early medieval swords were not suitable for thrusting, indeed, they probably did not use, or even know, of the thrust. These statements are made in spite of numerous drawings and comments to the contrary in both medieval and Viking literature. As proof, they point to the point (bad joke intended, as I have no shame). The points of many Viking swords, and early medieval, are quite rounded and somewhat spade-shaped.

It has long been assumed that in any combat between two warriors armed with swords, all blows were struck so that the sweet spot of the weapon would be the section of the blade delivering the blow. Although the sword was sharpened for its full length, the other sections were of secondary importance to the optimal striking point. At first glance this makes sense; in a life and death struggle you want to do as much damage as you can. (Of course, it is possible to use the sword as a knife, and slice your opponent if you have the chance, but a heft cut is more effective, and what we'll discuss in this section.)

Now, if the blade on a Viking sword or early medieval sword was about 33 inches long, as it often was, then the optimal striking point will be about 22 inches from the guard (this distance can vary due to shape and size of the blade). Swords whose primary purpose was to deliver a strong and penetrating thrust have fairly narrow blades, and sharp points. This can be seen in swords dating back to the "rapiers" of the Bronze Age. A narrow blade and point allows more pounds to the square inch pressure to be applied, and not only will it penetrate flesh, it also can split the iron rings of mail.

With this information in mind, it is easy to conjecture about the use of the Viking sword. Relatively close-in fighting, strong, heavy blows with no attempts to use the point would be the norm. There would be a little "science" and tactics, but mainly the fight would be one of an exchange of heavy blows.

A little experimentation can really change your mind about some things. A careful reading of the Norse sagas will show that mail was popular, but not near as prevalent as it became in the later Middle Ages. Most duels and skirmishes were fought without mail coats. For example, at the Battle of Stamford Bridge, Harold Godwinson defeated the King of Norway, Harald Hardrade. The well armed and armored Saxon army caught the Northmen by surprise, and it was recorded that none of them had mail shirts and only a few had helmets. Before the armor could be retrieved, the battle was lost.

You can see from this that mail was an important item of defense. But this occurred in 1066 AD, in what is considered the *final* onslaught of the Vikings. But mail had been accumulating over hundreds of years, and the price was going down. Early on, it was only the wealthiest of chieftains and warriors who could afford a mail shirt. Even then many chose not to wear it, regardless of their wealth. Egil Skallagrimson and his brother Thorolf chose not to wear mail in the battle between Hring and Adils (about 940 AD). Many felt that it simply slowed them down, and on shipboard mail could be a real nuisance if you suddenly had to swim for another ship.

CUTTING WITH THE VIKING SWORD

I have been using pork shoulder roasts for testing mail for quite some time. Pigs are similar to man in many ways, though the skin is much tougher and more resistant. But for this sort of testing it really doesn't matter. In the past I had been concerned with the cutting power of various swords, and how well they would cut through a mail shirt, and the best type of backing for the mail. But this time it was different. What I was interested in was testing those myths about Viking swords, seeing what was the difference in cutting ability between the optimal striking point and the first few inches of the point. How did it work in bare meat, and how well did it cut when the flesh was protected by mail? Also of equal importance was the thrust: How well did the sword penetrate, and how was the penetration when mail was used? I certainly didn't expect a rounded point to penetrate mail or flesh with the ease of a narrow point, but was the difference great or minor? This I aimed to find out.

Original Viking swords are rare and rather expensive. But blades quite similar are available. Having been lucky enough to have examined several up close, it was rather easy to get some blades that would correspond to old ones. The most important factor was that the blades had to have a rounded point, but also that the distal* taper be very flat within a couple of inches of the point. This would correspond to the majority of Viking swords examined.

One variable over which there is no control is mail. Mail came in all shapes and sizes, some thick, some thin. Made individually, each shirt would be slightly different. So I settled on what was available to me.

From Museum Replicas, Ltd., I got a mail shirt. I can't say I borrowed it, as they knew well enough that it was going to be destroyed. So they gave it to me with a cheerful "hack away." It took me several days for the local supermarket to come up with a suitable roast, one that weighed in at twelve pounds with a good thick bone, like a man's thigh. Then it was necessary to select the proper sword. I selected a replica blade that I had lying around. I had Eddie Floyd, who has been at a lot of Blade Shows with me, to thin the blade and round the point to the proper shape and

---

* Cross-sectional   —Whit Williams

Reproduction transitional Viking sword. HRC180.

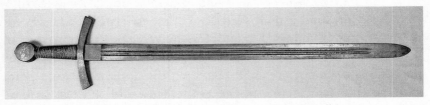

Ethiopian Crusader style sword with fuller;
37.75 inches overall length. HRC26.

dimensions. I also selected an old sword that was in excellent condition. This was a sword with a rather mysterious past. The blade, straight, with no taper, but an excellent distal taper, appears to have been made in the late 18th century. But the guard and pommel appeared older. The grip had rotted away. The blade is in excellent condition. The original pommel (which was on it when I got the sword in 1968) had been lost in a move. I had replaced it and then added a grip. This gave me two swords, both with Viking-like blade geometry.

My next task was to select the proper backing for the mail. I decided on some gambeson padding material. This is modern material, and therefore not exactly accurate, but it is close enough to give a good comparison.

Now, let me say a few words about your author. At the time of the cutting, I was two months short of 70. I have been playing with swords, and cutting with them, for well over 50 years. Even now, I can still cut pretty well. Some of you whippersnappers can cut better than I can. But frankly, none of us can hold a candle to what a 25-year-old Viking warrior could do. He spent most of his life in hard physical labor—working a farm, fishing, chopping wood, and learning to fight. So keep this in mind when you read the results of the test cuts. Also remember that I am cutting a shoulder roast on a stump. From this you may extrapolate what would happen in a real fight, though my results are not a one-to-one correlation for a historical fight.

Having all my gear ready, I journeyed forth to do battle with the vicious shoulder roast of infamous renown. The first cut was made with the replica sword. I struck with the top five-six inches of the blade. The sword cut through the mail, and deeply dented the padding. When the padding was lifted up, the flesh was split for a distance of about three inches and about one-half inch deep. The next blow was with the old sword. I tried to maintain the same force in both blows. This cut was somewhat more effective. Again the mail was cut, the padding dented, but this time the cut in the flesh was somewhat longer and deeper, about 4 inches long and three-quarters of an inch deep. I then made a control cut with each sword. This time I struck on the optimal striking point of each sword. Both were just about what I had expected. The mail was cut, the padding dented, and the flesh sustained a longer cut on each, but with slightly less depth. The cuts were about 4 inches in length, with a depth of about one quarter inch.

It was now time to try a sword with a much more narrow point. For cutting with the tip, I used a well loved Windlass blade that I have been doing demos with for several years. This was as I had thought also. The sword did cut a few links of mail, did dent the padding, but the actual split in the meat was very small, and not very deep. It did appear that there would have been some "bruising" had this been live flesh, but the cutting was not as effective as the other two swords.

Next was the penetration tests of all three swords.

This test is a little more difficult to achieve. I did not have the means to keep the roast at a proper height so that I could strike it. I tried to enlist some help from some friends, and have them hold it up for me. Strangely enough, I picked the wrong day for the tests, as they all had things to do. Oh well, the path to truth is often difficult and filled with thorns and wayward friends.

I solved the problem by simply stabbing the roast as it lay innocently on the stump. After all, this was a comparison test, and not intended to strictly mimic combat. And, anyway, I'm sure plenty of guys got stuck while lying on the ground in real combat, too.

I used my old sharp-pointed testing sword for the first blow. It split the links, punched through the padding and, not meeting any bone, penetrated the whole roast and stuck into the stump. The replica sword cut the mail and padding as well, and cut deep into the roast, but did not fully penetrate. I would estimate that the blade entered into a depth of about 4 inches. The old sword with the well rounded point was next. Frankly, I took a break. After all, killing a pork roast is not as easy as it was when I was a young man of 65. So, after manfully chugalugging a glass of ice tea, with renewed vigor I attacked once again. This time, despite being refreshed, the sword did not hit square on the mail, and skated off to the side. Alas, the shoulder roast regarded my efforts with cool disdain, again. The next time my aim was accurate, and I cut the mail, the padding, and into the roast. But not as deeply as my previous attempts. The wound was slightly wider, since the blade was wider, but the depth was only about three inches.

In summary, the series of tests that I conducted were many and varied. I used up so many pork shoulders that I'm sure I caused a spike in pork futures. I also tore up a lot of mail in the process. What I found was highly interesting, and wasn't quite what I'd expected.

The cutting done with the top few inches of the sword was the most impressive. It sheared through the mail with ease when the blow was solid. The cut with the optimal striking point was only marginally more effective. On many cuts I couldn't tell the difference. It was at once obvious that fighting at a slightly longer range did not diminish the severity of the blow enough to negate the advantage of distance.

Thrusting with the rounded point was also an eye-opener. On flesh, it was just as penetrating as a sharp narrow point. The fact that the rounded point was sharpened all along the curve easily explains this. In short, *a rounded point is not a detriment at all to the cutting sword.* It allows greater reach, while not reducing the usability of the point at all.

As for mail: original mail has such incredible variety of ring and diameter sizes that it simply is not possible to make a categorical statement. What I found with my mail was pretty much the same result as on flesh: the rounded point cut mail about as well as a blow with the optimal striking point. It was also able to penetrate mail, but swords with very narrow sharp points penetrated better.

One thing this rounded point will do, is allow the sword to be used as if it were a longer blade.

But the sword was not the only weapon available to the Vikings and their foes. The next chapter will explore in more depth what the swordsman had to face.

Suggestions for further reading from the editors:

Davidson, H.R Ellis, *Scandinavian Mythology*. The Hamlyn Publishing Group, Limited, Middlesex, 1969.

Davidson, H.R. Ellis, *The Sword in Anglo-Saxon England: Its Archeology and Literature*. The Boydell Press, Woodbridge, 1962, 1994.

Hollander, Lee M., translator, *The Sagas of Kormak and The Sworn Brothers*. Princeton University Press, Princeton, 1949.

Johnston, George, translator, *The Saga of Gisli the Outlaw*. University of Toronto Press, Toronto, 1963.

Johnston, George, translator, *Thrad of Gotu: Two Icelandic Sagas from the Flat Island Book*. The Porcupine's Quill, Inc., Ontario, 1994.

Jones, Gwyn, translator, *Eirik the Red and Other Icelandic Sagas*. Oxford University Press, New York, 1961.

Palsson, Hermann and Paul Edwards, translators, *Egil's Saga*. Penguin Books, New York, 1976.

Peirce, Ian G., *Swords of the Viking Age*. The Boydell Press, Woodbridge, 2002.

▶ 6 ◀

The Fighting Milieu in the Viking and Early Middle Ages

Although this book is mainly about swords, it is impossible to write about swords without dealing with the other weapons in use at the time. Just as you have to look at the armor that was used, you also have to look at the weapons the sword would be facing. Battles, duels, and chance encounters were not based on everyone being equally armed and armored; rather it was what each individual preferred, or just happened to have with him. Rarely did anyone have only one weapon. When working in the fields or on the farm a man might have only an axe with him, but when he felt that there was the possibility of trouble, or when going into battle, he made sure he was well armed. We are talking life, death and honor. You carried the best you could afford and the things with which you were the most comfortable and familiar.

PRECONCEPTIONS

To discuss and understand the use of the sword and combat in the Viking period (from circa 793 AD to 1066 AD), three things must be abandoned. One is all thoughts of modern fencing. Another is all forms of swordplay as depicted in movies and books, and the third is the modern concept of "fair play."

Modern fencing is a sport that was originally developed to teach the use of the rapier and small sword. Although schools of fence (from "offence" and "defense") had been around since at least the 1300s, these had dealt with many types of weapons and many combinations of weapons. In the early 16th century with the introduction throughout Europe of the rapier, greater and greater emphasis was being placed on dueling between gentlemen, the rapier being just about useless for war. As dueling continued to gain in popularity it became quite necessary for gentlemen to learn to use the rapier and, later on, the small sword. Fencing was not only a skill for self-preservation, but became a social requirement, as much as the ability to dance. With the advent of the gun beginning to replace the sword in the 18th century, skill with a sword was no longer necessary, but it remains to the present day as a sport.

Two variations of the rapier developed: the foil and the epee. Both of these "weapons" are extremely light in weight and have nothing to do with the Viking or medieval sword. The third aspect of fencing is the saber. Another weapon that is extremely light, and is based on saber play as if you were on a horse! In other words, leg cuts are not allowed. Fencing is a sport, with its origins in dueling with two types of swords. But it is a sport and has nothing to do with fighting.

Movies, and most of the books where swordplay is an important part, have obviously been written from the standpoint that all swordplay is ultimately fencing. This gives us such wonderfully wacky scenes as a twelfth-century Robin Hood fighting up and down stairs with the Sheriff of Nottingham and using all of the approved moves of the nineteeth-century fencing saber. Or men armed with sword and shield fighting with right foot forward, shield in the left hand, and doing all of their parrying with the sword blade. About the only thing I have seen that is sillier is long, thin rapiers being used as if they were cutting swords!

Abandoning all thoughts of fair play when it comes to fighting with swords is one thing that is sure to cause a stir. All of the knightly virtues, all of the tales of chivalry are bound up in the concept of fair play. If there is one national characteristic that Americans have, it is the concept of fair play and pulling for the underdog. This is true in our movies, books, sporting events, and all of our fables. It just isn't true in real life. If it were true, then one heroic cop would call out the bank robber and the two would meet in the street in the classic shootout. (Of course the cop would give the bad guy a chance to go for his gun first.) But that isn't what happens. Instead they call out the SWAT team, and ten to twelve heavily armed officers try to capture the felon, or if necessary kill him, with as little a risk to themselves as possible. Is this fair? Certainly not, but it does get the job done.

I bring up the "fairness" issue so that you will not be shocked as you read many of the incidents from various sagas. Sometimes the good guys outnumber the bad guys, and sometimes it's vice versa.

It is also important, gentle reader, that you understand that this was not a sport, nor a game, but a deadly serious affair, in which people died. It was as real then as a murder is today.

For instance, there was a fight in *Njal's Saga* involving an ambush. Sigmund and Skjold set out to kill Thord when he was on his way from the Allthing (a popular time for ambushes, either going to or from that meeting). Sigmund rode up to him and said, "Get ready, for it's now time for you to die." "Certainly not," said Thord. "Come and fight in single combat." "Certainly not," said Sigmund. "We shall make full use of our advantage in numbers." They attacked, and Thord managed to shatter both their spears. They fought on and Skjold hacked off Thord's arm. Thord still continued to fight for a short time until Sigmund ran him through and he fell dead. (Such a nice group of people.)

It is not possible to say for certain how the weapons were used in the past. It will always be a matter of speculation until such time as someone invents a time machine. Then we can go back and watch, but until then we have to rely on our ability to study, interpret and experiment. Given this, I think it is possible to come up with some pretty good ideas of the actual use of the sword and axe during this period.

As mentioned before, some of the richest written sources for studying the use of weapons are the Viking sagas. Some of them are believed to be fictional romances designed to entertain, some are believed to be relatively accurate accounts of real people. One thing that is absent from most of them is the hyperbole of many of the medieval romances. Instead the sagas are told in a laconic, matter-of-fact style. Sometimes detail is lacking, but this is understandable. The stories were being told to people who were familiar with what was involved, and did not need the detail.

Let me clarify this. If a group of boxers and boxing enthusiasts are talking about a fight, they will not go into details. "Thompson was using his left really well, kept sticking it in Hammond's face and really stinging him. But in the ninth Hammond caught him with an uppercut to the chest that bounced him off the ropes and back into an overhand right that put him away. But hell, he was out when he hit the ropes."

What they do not give is the detail of the blows. One is dancing and throwing left jabs on a steady basis. They do not mention that the uppercut consisted of slipping the feet into position, dropping the shoulder, and driving in and up with both hip and shoulder. In short, these people already know how it's done.

For instance, in *Njal's Saga*, a number of weapons are mentioned when Skarp-Hedin and his two brothers set out to avenge themselves on the writers of some lampooning verses made and sung in public, Sigmund and Skjold (the ambushers of Thord). But specifics about the weapons are left out, and while this fight is fairly detailed, even the killing blow placement is left out. Skarp-Hedin told Sigmund to gather up his weapons and waited while Sigmund armed himself. Skjold turned to face Grim and Helgi. Grim sliced off Skjold's foot at the ankle and then Helgi killed Skjold with a sword thrust. Skarp-Hedin and Sigmund fought one-on-one. Sigmund was wearing a helmet and shield, with a sword in his belt and a spear in his hand. He thrust at Skarp-Hedin with the spear. Skarp-Hedin blocked the blow with his shield then severed the spear shaft with his axe and cut directly at Sigmund. The blow struck Sigmund's shield and split it down past the handle. Sigmund drew his sword and hacked at Skarp-Hedin. The sword pierced the shield and stuck there. Skarp-Hedin twisted the shield sharply so that Sigmund let go of the sword. Skarp-Hedin struck him again; this time the axe caught Sigmund on the shoulder and cut into the shoulder blade. Skarp-Hedin jerked the axe toward himself and Sigmund fell forward to both knees, but he jumped to his feet again. Skarp-Hedin hacked once at his helmet and killed him with the next blow.

But before I analyze the use of these offensive weapons, let's take a look at the armor and defenses that were generally available at this time.

MAIL

The most important and prevalent body protection was mail. Mail was very expensive. It is very difficult to translate modern dollars into Viking or medieval purchasing power, but let us say that only the very wealthy could afford it: chieftains, kings, jarls, or very successful pirates. As time passed, mail became more and more available, but it was well into the Middle Ages before mail became common for the average soldier.

Drawing of international pattern of mail.

Mail is composed of wire formed into circles, and then linked together. The most common pattern, known as the "international pattern," is used all over the world. This pattern consists of one link being joined to four others, two above and two below. This pattern lies flat and is very flexible. Each individual link is flattened on one end with a hole punched in the end. Once linked, they are then riveted together. This is known as riveted mail. Some mail, which was rare in Europe, did not have the ends riveted, but was merely butted together. Curiously enough, this is known as "butted" mail. In slightly later periods the mail was

*Butted mail.
Inset shows detail.
HRC356.*

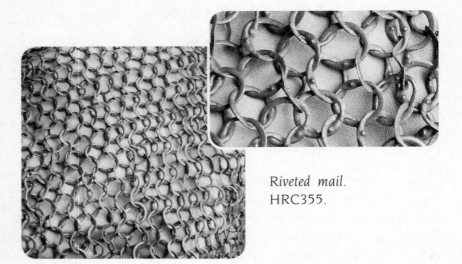

Riveted mail.
HRC355.

composed of a ring stamped out of sheet metal, and then joined with a riveted ring. This was still known as riveted mail.

Shirt length varied a great deal. Some were thigh length with long sleeves, called a hauberk, others were waist length, with long or short sleeves, called a habergeon in the Middle Ages, or a byrnie by the Vikings. Later, during the early medieval period, the legs were also protected with pants of mail or flat sections of mail that were tied around the legs.

Antique mail shirt.
HRC356.

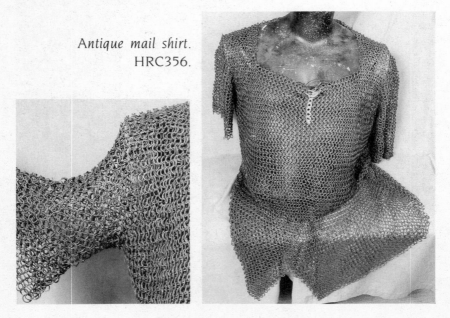

One big drawback to mail is that it is almost too flexible! If you were wearing a fairly heavy shirt and bent over, then your shirt and all its weight dropped out in front of you. This is really only annoying, but was solved by simply running leather strips through the rings and tying them so that the mail fit the body more closely, and did not shift.

The weight of the shirt obviously varied depending on the size of the rings and how tightly woven they were. There are some full shirts that weighed only about 20–25 pounds, and some that will go as high as 50. There is a shirt in the museum in Gotland, in excavated condition, that had to weigh close to 60 pounds when new. It has very thick rings, and is very close woven.

The amount of protection also depended on the size of the rings. If I had to guess at an average, I would say that the most common size was a ring thickness close to 16 gauge, and a ring diameter of about one quarter of an inch. But remember, this is only an average, and refers mainly to mail of European origin. I have a pair of mail pants with rings much smaller, of about one eighth of an inch. (And each one is fully riveted. A most remarkable pair of pants. They wear like iron also.)

Mail is very effective against a slice or drawcut. It is very effective against a strong cut, and also resistant to a stab. But it can be cut, and it can be pierced, though neither of these is easy to do. The blow has to land squarely, with a great deal of force.

In the past I have done a great deal of testing of mail, on all of the average sizes given above. I found the most effective mail was riveted and made with soft iron wire. The soft mail has a tendency to fold around a sword blade, rather than be cut. Spring steel mail and case hardened mail put up a little more resistance, but then would break or shatter and allow a sword to cut deeper. Riveted mail was much more resistant to thrusts.

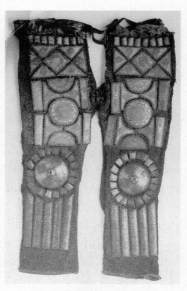

Antique riveted mail pants, circa 17th–18th century. HRC405. Photo by Kenneth Jay Linsner.

When struck with maces, hammers, or clubs, mail showed a positively gory tendency to grind itself into whatever was underneath. It did not stop the shock of the blow, and when using a pig shoulder joint, the mail cut through the leather backing and into the meat itself. A padded undergarment helps distribute the shock of the blow and improves the effectiveness of mail. A partially educated guess would be about 30 percent improvement. Not a figure to be ignored when it's your hide you are protecting.

Hank cutting mail on a pig shoulder. Photo by Patrick Gibbs.

A lot of men chose not to wear mail. It is heavy, and it does slow you down. It also feels like a radiator unless you wear good padding underneath. In the summer it is very hot, and in the winter it is very cold. You can get used to it. When I was active in sparring with sword and shield with various friends, I would put on my mail shirt. It was one I had made, and weighed in, after I learned how to tailor it, at 29 pounds and ran down to mid thigh. I had no problem moving in it at all, and made it a practice to run at least a mile four times a week wearing the shirt. If the shirt is tightly belted, about half of the weight is suspended from the hips, and it all doesn't hang from the shoulders. At times I wore a padded undergarment. But I lived in Alabama and sparring in 95-degree heat with a padded gambeson and mail shirt made me yearn for winter. As a warrior I would have demanded an air conditioned battlefield. One can also see why I envied Icelandic Vikings.

Another form of armor that was used was lamellar. This consisted of small flat plates of metal that were joined above and below so as to form a thin plate surface that was slightly flexible. It was more rigid than mail, but also somewhat lighter. It was used during and after the Roman period, but seems to have lost favor and was gradually replaced by mail. Although never fully abandoned, it was certainly not common.

HELMET

The next item of importance in the field of armor was the helmet. There is only one known helmet that dates from the Viking period. This is the Gjermundbu helmet, originally found in a burial mound in Norway and now housed in the Museum of National Antiquities in Oslo. It is in pretty bad shape, but its basic outline can be seen. The most notable thing about it is the extensive eye and nasal protection, to where the

Reproduction of the Gjermundbu helmet.

helmet looks like it has goggles. This can be seen in earlier helmets from the North, and was probably a very common feature. But this wasn't the only type of helmet worn. There were conical styles that we now term "Norman," there were helmets that we would call kettle hats, and old Carolingian style helmets. One

Photos this page by Peter Fuller.

Reproduction Viking helmet.

Reproduction kettle hat.

Reproduction Norman helmet.

thing we know they didn't wear was hats
with horns or wings. That is Victorian
nonsense. (Although I will admit I think
the wings look kind of dressy.)

As the Viking Age drew to a close, the
helmets became more uniform, with the
conical style being the most popular. By
the beginning of the 12th century, the
head was frequently covered with a full
helm. While generally providing great
protection, there were drawbacks. Despite
vision slots and breathing holes, reduced
vision and lack of air persisted, especially
if fighting on foot.

The medieval knight was essentially a
horseman, and he did most of his fighting
on horseback. He rode with a long stirrup, and when actually using his sword
he stood in the saddle, and fought from
a moving platform. Other than standing,

*Reproduction full
helm.* HRC348.

and using his knees to guide his horse, he didn't use his leg
muscles much. Now these huge thigh muscles devour oxygen at
a tremendous rate. Much, much more than do the muscles of
the back, arms and shoulders. So you can fight pretty well on
horseback, but on foot you simply do not get the oxygen that
the body requires. Like athletes today, some were better at it than
others, but even the good ones needed the oxygen.

All helmets were handmade, and even those produced by the
same smith would probably vary in thickness and weight. Sometimes this was probably requested by the owner. One might prefer
a little less weight, another would want it as heavy and as strong
as he could get it. Weights and thicknesses seemed to vary from
what we would term eighteen gauge to a heavy one that would be
as thick as fourteen gauge. But the average conical helmet seems
to have been slightly less than sixteen gauge in thickness.

Sixteen gauge is good protection; a sword really isn't going
to cut through it. But it would damn sure rattle your brains to
catch a hard blow on the side of the head. It's problematical how
much damage it would do, but it isn't something I am going to
volunteer to find out.

The great helms of the Middle Ages gave almost foolproof protection against sword blows, and a great deal against mace blows. Large axes and halberds are a different matter. Even if they didn't penetrate the iron of the helm they could drive it down on the head and crack the skull, and in some cases have been known to actually cut into the helmet.

Helmets were usually not steel, but iron. A very rich knight might have a helmet that was made of steel, or case hardened iron, but usually the helmet was made of iron. This means that it usually wasn't as hard as the sword edge, but that doesn't mean the sword could cut through it.*

SHIELDS

Probably the most important item of defensive armor was the shield. You could be in real trouble if you were caught without one. But a shield is also a nuisance to carry, so a lot of people were caught without one. It is obvious from the sagas that the thickness varied a great deal. You can read of thin shields and some that are described as thick and strong.

Vikings shields were generally round, and varied in width from 20 to 42 inches. They were made of boards glued together on the ends. The center of the shield was cut out for the hand, and the hand was then covered by a bowl shaped piece of metal

Round reproduction shield made by Peter Fuller for Hank Reinhardt. HRC401.

---

* Armorers didn't start heat-treating armor until the end of the 14th century—up until then there wasn't enough carbon in the metal used to do a proper heat-treat—and even in the 15th and 16th centuries it was hit or miss. Some armor was heat-treated and some wasn't. A good book for info on this subject is *The Knight and the Blast Furnace.* —Peter Fuller

called a boss. Often the rim of the shield would be covered by a strip of rawhide that was laced, or even glued to the edges. This was good protection, and also helped hold the boards together. On rare occasions the rim of the shield might be reinforced with iron. The shield was gripped in the center where there was a grip, usually of iron. There may, or may not, depending on personal preference, be a strap to secure the left forearm to the shield. While primarily a defensive tool, it could be used offensively, too. A punch to the side of the head with a ten-pound shield can easily break someone's neck. The shield can also be used to drive an opponent's shield in a direction that will open him up for a sword cut.

Reproduction shield made by Peter Fuller, back. Photo by Peter Fuller.

Although round predominated, it was not the only shape. You can have oval ones, and square ones, and later you will have the typical kite shaped shield that is referred to as "Norman." There is very strong evidence that suggests that the kite shaped shield originated in the Near East, and was brought back to Europe by returning members of the Varangian Guard in Byzantium. Nevertheless, there was a lot of individual preference.

For someone living in our standardized age it is frequently confusing and even difficult to grasp that nothing was consistent or standardized. Uniforms were still several hundred years in the future. The Viking Age didn't end at 12 midnight October 14, 1066, with everybody jumping around shouting "We're now in the Middle Ages." Armor and swords didn't change overnight, and a blade could be in use for well over a hundred years, and a mail shirt that belonged to grandad might just fit you. One of the hardest things in discussing this

Reproduction shield made by Peter Fuller. Photo by Peter Fuller.

subject with someone who is just getting started, is that there are no hard and fast rules. If someone doesn't have a helmet, and gets hold of one that is two hundred years old, he'll wear it. Better to be old fashioned than to have your skull split!

The kite shield began to dominate Europe by the 11th century. It was ideal on horseback, as it protected most of your left side, and on foot it gave good protection to the left leg. True, it wasn't quite as effective a weapon as a good round shield, but it could be used that way. As coverage of the body in armor increased, the shield became somewhat smaller, soon ending up in the classic flatiron shape so beloved by all. After all, it is a great way to display your arms, and looks really cool hanging in back of your high seat.

The kite shield was fairly thick, being close to an average of one-half inch in thickness. These were generally covered in leather and decorated in gesso, with a weight of ten to twelve pounds. They were very sturdy, and their primary purpose was to divert the lance of the opponent. Foot soldiers at this time carried all types of shields, but as armor improved and became more accessible, it was more important that they carry a weapon that could defeat the armor, a two-hand weapon, and so the shield began to lose favor. It never fully went out of use but its popularity did dwindle considerably starting about 1400.

Reproduction flatiron shield made by Peter Fuller for Hank Reinhardt. HRC381.

OFFENSIVE WEAPONS

A warrior who wanted to survive had to be familiar with all types of weapons: sword, axe, bow, spear, halberd. Although he may have a favorite weapon, he may not be guaranteed that he has it when he needs it. If you're attacked when you're out cutting wood, you'd better know how to use an axe. If you had thrown your spear, you needed to be able to pick up some dead guy's halberd and use it.

HALBERDS AND HEWING SPEARS

Although there are a surprisingly large number of Bronze Age, Iron Age, Dark Age and Viking Age weapons still in existence, there are also a lot of weapons of which we do not have samples. Consider the Maceijowski Bible. It shows sword-like items, strangely shaped spears and weird polearms, none with existing copies.

Reproduction of chopper from the Maceijowski Bible. HRC51.

Similarly, we read of the hewing spear, but have no remains that we can identify as the specific weapons.

So I would first like to clarify the definition of "halberd." This term is used in the English translation of the Norse sagas, as well as "bill," and both these are translations from the Icelandic for the term "hewing spear." The hewing spear was clearly a very formidable weapon, and used by many. It appears all through the sagas, and is a source of frustration for me—and tracking it down might be termed my personal quest. For I have been unable to determine what the weapon looked like, and I've been searching for thirty years or more, so far with no success. But I am convinced that in the basement of some museum there is a strange looking weapon, and no one knows exactly what it is and, alas, does not care.

We do know from written descriptions that the hewing spear is a polearm, and one that is light enough to be thrown, though probably not very far, but with tremendous force. We know that it has a very sharp point, with a blade long enough to go all the way through someone, and we also know that it has a blade capable of cutting

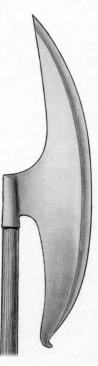

Viking hewing spear as envisioned by Hank Reinhardt.

a man in half. Thorolf kills Earl Hring by stabbing him through the body, and then picking him up and planting the halberd butt first in the ground, and leaving him there. Another time a different hero, Gunnar, cuts a man in half with one.

In *Egil's Saga* there is a description of the halberd. "The thrusting spear he carried had a blade two ells (approximately six feet) long with four edges tapering to a point on one end and broad at the other. The socket was long and wide and no taller than might be grasped at the socket by the hand, but wonderfully thick. There was an iron spike in the socket and the whole shaft was bound with iron. It was the kind of spear that is called a halberd."

I can fantasize and sketch my thoughts, but I still don't know what it looked like. But I have hopes that one day I'll run across something that will give me a more positive clue than just my imagination.

SPEAR & LANCE

The spear was by far the most common weapon. Its length gives it a definite advantage over the sword alone, and it can be hurled as well. Many people are amazed at how effective a quarter staff is as a weapon. The spear has the same capabilities, with a sharp point on the end. It was also not as expensive as the sword. But the desire to decorate one's weapon takes hold, and richly ornamented spears are not only mentioned, but have been found as well.

Indeed, grave finds have been rich in spears, with several being found in just one grave. The abundance of the weapon shows how prevalent its use was. Only rarely have the mostly wooden shafts been found, and these are usually quite decayed. But traces show the length of the shafts in many cases. Size ranges from about five feet to well over eleven feet! This longer length must have been difficult to manage. Although there is no record of the Vikings using the lance on horseback, it probably occurred very late in the period. After all, the Normans still had some ties with their homeland. But one use for a spear this long would have been when two ships were about to join for battle. This reach would have been an advantage, and once the ships were joined together the spear could have been dropped in favor of a shorter weapon.

Shafts seemed to be about one inch in diameter, with a few being slightly larger. The most common wood used was ash, although it appears that other woods, such as oak and elm, were also used. Hard, tough woods are a necessity in a spear shaft, and even using these woods it was still possible to have them cut in half. Although we have a large number of spears, we are unable to tell exactly into what class each one falls. The Vikings mention a "hoggspjot," which translates as a hewing or cutting spear; a "gaflak," which was a type of javelin; an "atgeir," which appears to be a type of halberd or bill; a "skepti-fletta," which appears to be a spear with a cord attached; a "kesja," which is somewhat undetermined; and a "snoeris-spjot," which is a string spear.

The string spear is quite interesting, and a kind that I have made and played with. The shaft has a string wrapped around the cen-

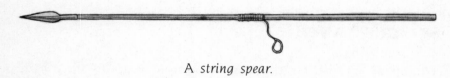

A *string spear.*

ter near the balance point, and as the spear is thrown, the string is held and as the spear is released, the string is pulled sharply, giving additional momentum and spin to the spear. This should increase the range and accuracy of the throw. In our experiments, several of my friends were able to get an additional 15–30 feet in distance, and their accuracy was much improved. It didn't help *me* at all. I'm one of those people who can't throw, not a rock, baseball, football, or spear. The only thing I can throw is an axe, but the arm motion is different.

Hooked spears were also used. Hooks can be most useful. You can pull someone off of a horse, catch their leg and trip them, or better still, hook the shield, pull it down and then thrust with

Antique *hooked spear, circa 1475-1575, head 39 inches long, with shaft 94 inches overall length.* HRC4.

the spear. In *Egil's Saga* there is the following description of Egil carrying a hooked spear:

"It was seen from the Thing that a body of men rode down along Gljufra River, and that shields glittered there. When these arrived a man in a blue cloak rode foremost; he had a gilt helmet on his head and a gold ornamented shield at his side; in his hand a hooked spear, the socket of its head was inlaid with gold; he was girt with a sword. This was Egil Skallagrimsson."

Another very popular spear was the barbed spear. From the grave finds these appear to be javelins, which makes a great deal of sense. If you're using the spear as a hand weapon, you don't want to get it stuck. But if you're throwing it, then it stands to reason that you want to do as much damage as possible, and don't want the spear thrown back at you. If the spear hits anything the barbs will prevent or delay its being withdrawn.

The head of a barbed spear.

Medieval spears were frequently pattern welded. Often a broken sword might be salvaged and re-forged into a spear, as was done with the sword "Greyflank" when it was broken. The spear was a well loved weapon, and often named, such as Odin's spear, "Gungnir." The kennings describing spears in the sagas are also delightful, and the spear was oft referred to as a serpent: the serpent of the shield, the serpent of battle, wound serpent.

The lance was a horseman's weapon, and dominated the battlefield for several hundred years. It took the English longbow and the Swiss pikeman to finally put an end to its dominance. But in its heyday it was a fearsome weapon. Essentially a stout spear ranging from nine to twelve feet in length, it presented a really frightening picture when you had to face it. I think it was in the Real De Armeria in Madrid when this first hit me. There was a fully armored knight on display, with his lance lowered as if in the charge. When I looked at it closely I thought of what it would be like to be standing in a line of infantry and seeing this coming at me. I really did yearn for a pike or a longbow. (Truthfully, I would have preferred a .50 cal., but that would have been cheating.) I felt the same way in the Tower of London looking at the suit of plate armor that is about 6 feet 10 inches!

The thought of this coming at you on a battlefield is positively disconcerting!

The Bayeaux Tapestry shows the lance being used both over-hand, being thrown, and underhand, couched. The stirrup had made its way to Europe several hundred years before the Battle of Hastings in 1066, but it took a long time for people to realize how effective a couched lance could be. Not long after Hastings it became the preferred method for using a spear or lance.

Mounted knight with leveled lance.
Photo by Peter Fuller.

BOWS & SLINGS

Because the English used the foot archer to such telling effect, many people think that the longbow was unknown except in Wales. It is frequently stated that the English borrowed the longbow from the Welsh and made it their own. Certainly Edward III used it to great effect in his wars against France. However, attributing the *invention* to the Welsh is a little bit suspect. The longbow was in use in many areas and much earlier than most people realize. The Vikings were using it a great deal as early as the ninth century and considered it a very important weapon.

The famous warrior, Gunnar of Hlildarend of *Njal's Saga*, was noted for his skill with his bow and is mentioned using it on several occasions. When he was finally overcome it was only because his bowstring broke, and his wife (a really nasty type of person) wouldn't let him use a lock of her hair to plait another. All through the sagas the bow is very prominent, again described by some really beautiful kennings. Arrows are referred to as "the rain of the string," "the herrings of the corpse," "the hail of battle," and "rain storm of the wounds."

The bow itself was made of ash, elm, witch hazel or yew, and was about 6 feet in length. We can tell from the thickness of the bow staves the draw weights were probably around 80 to 120 pounds, similar to those of the bows taken from the *Mary Rose*, a ship of Henry VIII's that was recovered from where it sank and is now on display. In many of the Viking grave excavations the remains of similar longbows have been found.

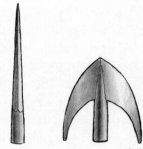

Arrow heads were pretty much the same as you would expect: thin bodkin points for battle, and broadheads for hunting. Shafts were usually about 30–36 inches in length.

Bodkin arrow point (left) and broadhead (right).

The longbow does not lend itself to ornamentation. The Eastern recurve was frequently decorated, but the longbow, being essentially a stick, was not. Of course it is possible that some of the bows were painted, but that is not known for sure, and such decoration would not have survived.

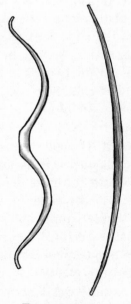

Curiously enough, the sling was also used during the Viking Age. Although not as popular as the bow, it was still an effective weapon. In *Kjalnesinga Saga* we read how the outlaw Bui, attacked by twelve men, defends himself by gathering stones, standing on a hill and killing some of the attackers. Slingers are also mentioned as being on the flanks of some of the battles. Personally, I would rather have a bow and a good axe.

Eastern recurve shape (left) and Viking bow shape (right).

VIKING AXES

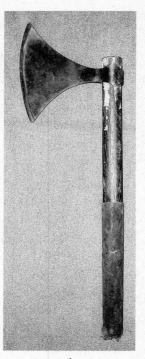

If there is one weapon that is most closely identified with the Vikings, it is the axe. Axes have been in use all over the world and at all times, and are probably the oldest weapons next to clubs. But the Vikings worked a variation that became popular all through the North, and even down into Italy, and that is the "Danish Axe."

This is a big weapon. There is no way that this can be confused with a wood axe. This is a battle weapon, and intended to lop the limbs of men rather than the limbs of trees. The cutting edge on these axes ranged from eight inches to many that are ten to twelve inches in width. Curiously, these axes are not particularly heavy, but really rather light in weight. Most weigh in at two to three pounds. The blades are quite thin, about 2mm in thickness, with the blade being thickened at the edge. This gives the edge the backing it needs without

Reproduction Viking axe.
Photo by Adam Lyon.

a great deal of weight. Generally mounted on long shafts and swung with two hands, it is quite possible for a strong man to wield it effectively with just one hand. I have been able to do it and, although I did not have the control I had with a sword, I could deal a most devastating blow with it. The light weight allowed it to be swung easily, and with great speed. The edge, even thickened, was no thicker than a sword blade, so that the axe could cut quite deeply. The very thing that makes the Danish axe a deadly weapon also kept it from being an effective tool. The blade would not be strong enough to cut into a tree, and the stress created would likely cause it to buckle.

In one battle the blow from a Danish axe was almost incredible. When the Norse under Haskulf Thorgilsson attacked Dublin in 1171, there was among them a famous berserker called John the Wode. When the Dubliners attacked and their knights penetrated the ranks of the Norse, the Norse began to fly. But John stood his ground and fought with terrible ferocity. It is recorded that he cut off the leg of a knight at the thigh, and in doing so, cut through not only the knight's long byrnie, but also through his mail breeches as well! The power it would require to do all this is almost, but not quite, unbelievable. He is also reported to have cut down ten or eleven men before he himself was slain.

Thin and thick beaten axe heads, silhouettes as viewed from above.

But the large Danish axe was not the only one in use. There were many shapes, and a large number of them were short and intended to be used with one hand in conjunction with a shield. Regardless of the profile of the axe, they were referred to as two distinct types, the "thin beaten" and "thick beaten." This seems to refer to the blade below the eye or socket hole. In the thin beaten axe, when looking at the front of the eye and blade, the axe suddenly narrows and the blade is fairly thin and flat. On the thick beaten the blade hollows only slightly as it thins down to the edge. The thick beaten is obviously more sturdy and capable of heavy duty chopping. This type of axe could be used for a multitude of purposes. It is very difficult to say that any one axe was designed for a specific purpose. A wood or carpenter's axe made a good weapon—especially if that was the only one you had. The one exception to this is the large, thin beaten Danish axe. Its only purpose is that of a weapon. The thin blade does not allow for good wood cutting, but is superbly designed for a weapon.

In the final analysis, the Vikings did not have anything really unusual in the way of weapons. Many other European warriors had similar arsenals. What the Vikings did have was a core toughness that very few other cultures ever exhibited. It is easy to consider the Northmen hard and brutal, even cruel when judged by 20th-century standards. But those were hard and tough times that called for hard and tough men.

FIGHTING WITH THE SWORD IN THE LATE MIDDLE AGES

In my opinion, skill in the use of the sword began to decline during the middle of the 13th century. At this time armor began to be increasingly effective and was available to more and more warriors. Mail, which could be penetrated by a strong blow with the sword, was now being augmented with sections of plate. The mounted knight was by this time dominant in most of Europe, and only in the out of the way places, like Iceland and some of the Nordic countries, did foot combat still play an important role; but even there it too was on its way out.

The sword remained a symbol for nobility, honor, and so on, and was a very important weapon, but in actual combat more and more the weapon of choice was a mace, axe or war hammer.

On foot the preferred weapons were bills, halberds, and polearms in general. And although carried, the sword was now a weapon of last resort. The foot soldier found it more convenient to carry a two-hand weapon, and a small shield that he could easily wear. His armor was also becoming more and more protective, but far from the complete coverage that the wealthy knight could afford. Some of a foot soldier's armor was paid for by his employer, but it was also augmented by what he could pick up from the battlefield. Generally speaking, he was expected to provide his own armor and weapons.

Reproduction transitional armor, circa 1360, made by Peter Fuller.
Photo by Peter Fuller.

This is rather easy to understand if you look at the improvements that were taking place in the field of defensive armor. Mail was becoming much more plentiful because mail was frequently repaired and reused and could be handed down. As the whole economy of Europe improved, a rising middle class could afford more and better protection. Many foot soldiers were wearing a gambeson under mail. The use of such a padded undergarment absorbed much of the shock that mail normally passed on to the wearer. Plate defenses were also being added, and this made it more and more difficult for the sword to do much damage.

As the armor improved, the shield became less and less important, and was gradually phased out. However, it was still used by the knights: not only was it quite dressy, and showed off the coats of arms, but it had a real use in that it helped deflect the lance. Which, after all, was the main weapon of the mounted knight.

There was also a more subtle social change taking place. It became much more advantageous to capture a knight than to kill him. After all, dead he was worth what you could get for his armor and horse, but alive his ransom could be a great deal of money. Several knights gained extreme wealth by being good enough, or lucky enough, to capture enough enemies to set themselves up for life. In England Falstaff was one and so was William Marshall.

These are the basic reasons that I feel that skill with the sword began to decline in the mid-13th century. Of course it didn't stay that way. As soon as the social and military conditions warranted it, swordplay came back, and skill was once again brought to the fore.

Suggestions for further reading from the editors:

All Norse sagas, especially *Njal's Saga* (aka *The Saga of Burnt Njal*), *Egil's Saga*, *Eirik the Red* and *Grettir the Strong*. The editor is particularly fond of the Penguin editions with the Magnus Magnusson translations.

Bradbury, Jim. *The Medieval Archer.* The Boydell Press, Woodbridge, Suffolk, 1985.

Delbrueck, Hans, *History of the Art of War Vols. 1–IV*, translated by Walter J. Renfroe, Jr. University of Nebraska Press, Lincoln, this edition first published 1982, original German edition published 1923.

Fiorato, Veronica, Anthea Boylston & Christopher Knusel, *Blood Red Roses: The Archeology of a Mass Grave from the Battle of Towton AD 1461*, Oxbow Books, Oxford, 2000.

Jones, Gwyn, *A History of the Vikings.* Oxford University Press, London, 1968.

Manjno, Guido, M.D., *The Healing Hand: Man and Wound in the Ancient World.* Harvard University Press, 1975.

Oman, Sir Charles, *The Art of War in the Middle Ages, Vols. I &
    II.* Greenhill Books, London, 1991, first published in this
    form 1924.

Schaal, Dieter et al., *Vermisste Kunstwerke des Historische Museums
    Dresden.* Staatliche Kunstsammlungen Dresden, Dresden,
    1990.

European Swords: The Rapier and the Smallsword

The rapier is the most romantic of swords. In spite of the recent popularity of the katana, the rapier remains the dominant sword in all romantic fiction. It is a slim, elegant, and oh so deadly weapon. Who has not thrilled to the duel in rhyme in Cyrano de Bergerac, to D'Artagnan and the Three Musketeers fighting fiercely for the honor of the Queen? The very name evokes morning duels, with the mists lending an air of mystery to a deadly confrontation, or moonlight glinting off blades in a desperate midnight encounter.

Books and movies have contributed to most of this romanticism, and I feel the reality was not quite like that. Your "adventure" is always someone else's terrifying problem. It is easy to ask how many of us would actually engage in that sort of thing if we could, and the answer is best kept to our secret selves.

Still, for all-time popularity, the rapier has an advantage that other swords lack: play and contests can be held with a practice sword that can be made to feel very much like a real weapon. Heavier epees are on the market,

Antique Spanish cup-hilted rapier, 47 inches overall length. HRC25A.

and there are "schlager" blades as well, and these mimic the feel of many real weapons. Alas for the katana, the shinai still feels like a stick.*

But enough of romanticism.

ORIGINS OF THE RAPIER

Although considered a weapon of the Renaissance, the origins of the modern rapier really go back to at least the 15th century. But there are swords that can only be called rapiers that go much further back. As mentioned in the chapter on bronze, there are Bronze Age Mycenaean swords that can be called rapiers, and in the Berne Historisches Museum in Switzerland there is an unusual iron sword that is most definitely a rapier. The blade is narrow, slightly over a half inch in width, four sided with somewhat shallow faces, and it tapers to a sharp and deadly point. The hilt is

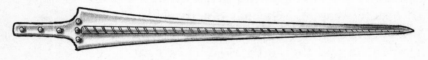

Bronze Mycenaean sword.

knobbed. This sword dates from about 2nd century BC. No one knows how these weapons were used. While it is unlikely that a form as sophisticated as modern fencing was used, I feel sure that some form of fencing was developed and used with these weapons. But nothing can be proved either way.

The first of the "modern" reincarnations of the rapier was the "estoc," also called a "tuck" by the English, and this is what we will call it. This seems to have developed in the first part of the 15th century and became quite popular. The tuck was a long, straight tapering sword whose primary purpose was the thrust. The cross section of the sword varied, some triangular with deeply hollowed faces, some flattened diamond, some square, without hollowed faces and edges that were for all intent and purposes

---

* Hank was working on changing that. He developed a curved sparring
  sword and patented it; but the manufacture was done after his death and
  no royalties have been paid to his estate.   —Editor

useless. These are not "fencing" weapons in the common sense of the term. They are heavy, and the balance and size of many of them lend themselves to a two-hand use.

Still, as with most everything in this field, even that statement must be qualified. I have in my possession a tuck with a rather light blade that would lend itself to fencing except that it has no protection for the hand other than a wide crossguard.

However, they were stout swords, and unlike the rapier, were intended for war. The tuck seems to have been an offshoot of an earlier sword, an Oakeshott Type XV. These had thick blades that narrowed quickly to a sharp point. It was probably an earlier forerunner of this style of sword that the Sire de Joinville used at the Battle of Mansourah (1250 AD).

There De Joinville was attacked by a Saracen who struck him a hard blow on his back, pushing him forward in his saddle, and then tried to hold him there. The Sire de Joinville broke free, grabbed his saddle sword, couched it under his arm like a lance, and ran the Saracen through. (He was an interesting man. I would suggest reading his Chronicles.)

Ewart Oakeshott considered the rapier to be a development of the arming sword, and has presented some excellent arguments for this. And while I have no wish to even try to counter his arguments, and am not even opposed to them, I do feel that there are some things that must be noted. Any sword development has so many contributing factors as to be almost impossible to detail in depth, let alone describe in a neat linear progression. For instance, consider that improvements in armor led to lessened use of the shield. This in turn led to the sword being used for defense as well as offense. Make no mistake, this had been tried before, and we read of it in the Norse sagas. But the shield was very much in use then and no effort was made to further develop this style of combat.

When using the sword in any defensive movement it becomes necessary that you control the sword with more dexterity than previously. This was achieved by hooking the forefinger over the guard. This also led to losing a forefinger, and very quickly a bar was added to protect the finger. This, in turn, led to greater and greater hand protection, which reached its peak in the basket hilts of the Scottish broadsword and the Venetian schiavona and, to a lesser degree, in the swept and cup hilt rapier.

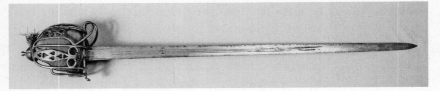

Antique basket hilted claymore,
38 inches overall length. HRC28.

In passing, I'll note that the crossguard of the classic medieval knightly cruciform sword was there to protect the hand from hitting the shield, and not from a blade sliding down the sword. Should two edges meet, there is almost no sliding that I have found in my experiments. Instead, the blades grip as the edges are nicked, and hang together. Should the blow be parried by the flat of the blade, and the opposing sword slide down, the guard offers no protection, as it extends in the wrong direction. Japanese, Korean, and Chinese swords are frequently used to parry with, and their guards extend in four directions on a plane at right angles to the hand.

Although this section is devoted to the European tuck, rapier and small sword, it is interesting to note that the Turks of the Ottoman Empire also possessed and used tucks of their own. These appear to be similar to the European but on closer observation they are heavier and thicker. Of course the use was the same as the European. However, the rapier itself was never used in the East.

By the 1400s the tuck had become a distinctive sword style of its own, and remained in use until well into the 17th century. One of the most telling differences between a tuck and a rapier is the usage. The tuck would work well in battle. It could be used with one or two hands and deliver a powerful thrust.

The rapier, although worn at times as a mark of rank, was essentially useless in combat. George Silver, the English gentleman who wrote on swords and sword play, called it a "birdspit, that cannot harm our enemies in war, and only harm our friends in peace." Today, many enthusiasts look down on Silver, and say that he was trying to defend an out-of-date fighting style, that he was merely xenophobic, or that he just didn't understand the potential of the rapier. Having played with a lot of weapons, and having met a lot of people, I feel that George Silver would have been a lot to handle, regardless of what weapon was being used. And I feel that he did understand the rapier, probably all too well.

Most telling are contemporary comments. In his excellent book *The Rapier and the Small Sword,* A.V.B. Norman quotes a bill from Robert Selkirk, cutler to James IV of Scotland, for the wrapping of a rapier, a riding sword *and* an arming sword. Even earlier, the rapier is described as being a cutting weapon, and a tuck as having three or more edges.

There is also the question as to the origin of the word "rapier." Many think of it having descended from the German word "*rapper,*" meaning to tear out, or the Spanish word "*raspar,*" to scratch. Claude Blair offered another source, the *espada ropera,* or sword of the robe, i.e. civilian wear. To be quite honest, I really don't care. In many respects it's like questioning the number of angels that can dance on the head of a pin. If I had to choose, I would choose the Blair explanation. My reasoning is quite simple. (Many have said that I am simple as well, so don't waste your time thinking it.) The rapier is an excellent weapon for dueling, (though for multiple assailants, it leaves something to be desired—more on this later), but is useless in war. Since it is worn with civilian dress, the *espada ropera* seems to fit.

THE TYPES OF RAPIER

It is confusing to read that one of the earliest mentions of the rapier pertains to a cutting sword. One has to remember that not only were our ancestors somewhat lackadaisical about spelling, but had the same carelessness regarding terms. This is a very confusing area because there are no hard and fast lines that can be drawn. We live in an age where everything must be compartmentalized. It is a Ford, or a Chevrolet, it is a 21-inch TV or a 33-inch. A copper-jacketed round nose .45 caliber bullet leaves the barrel at 830 feet per second and develops a specific amount of muzzle energy. Well, it's not that way with swords, and it sure would be a lot easier if it were.

But the rapier itself is a confusing weapon. Just what is a rapier? I have seen rapiers with blades that will cut, although not too well. And these are not sword rapiers, but rather regular rapiers with slightly wider blades. I can see why our ancestors were careless about terms, as there is no specific set of rules to determine what is a rapier, a sword rapier, or just a narrow sword. There are rapiers with blades that are very thin, with no discernible edge, and yet, to my mind, the blade shape and function should indicate that it is a specific type of sword. Alas, this does not seem to work with the rapier. However, for convenience sake, I will define a rapier as a sword with a long, thin blade that is primarily used for thrusting.

Those swords which can also be used for cutting we will term "sword rapiers," and will deal with them later in the chapter on straight-swords. The term itself is quite confusing, as no one is really sure what it means.

Ewart Oakeshott offered the best way to distinguish between a sword and a sword rapier: if you pick up the sword and you think you could cut off a man's arm, then it's probably a sword rapier; if you don't think you can, it's probably a rapier.

If I am facing someone with a sword rapier, with a heavier cutting blade, and he is foolish enough to hold the sword in an "en garde" position, the moment he lifts the sword for a cut I will attack. And with the balance of my sword, it should be quicker to enable me to avoid a defending left hand that might be trying to block my attack.

Like everything else in life, it's a trade-off. If you make the sword blade wider and heavier to facilitate cutting, you make it somewhat slower and less able to "fence" should that be required. If you keep the weight the same, but shorten the blade to achieve the same purpose, you lose length. If your rapier is lightning fast due to a thin deadly blade, you can't cut, nor do you have the strength to block a heavy cut from a heavier weapon. You also stand in danger of having your sword blade grabbed by an opponent. Make no mistake, gloves were made with mail lining in the palms for just that purpose. Later, as the rapier blade became almost totally without a functioning edge, it could easily be grabbed by the left hand. A strong man could grab the blade and bend it until it was useless, or in some cases even break it. That, of course, depended on how strong the man was and on the temper of the sword.

A cutting sword has to have a relatively flat blade in order to cut. A thick blade prevents the sword from cutting deeply, but the sword also has to have a certain amount of mass behind the edge in order for it to cut at all. Machetes, with their thick backs, are excellent for light chopping, but are not as efficient as swords in combat. However, if you add just a little mass to the blade by making it only *slightly* thicker, then you can have a devastating weapon, and one quite similar to Chinese swords.

From the above, you can see that categorizing these swords is very chancy indeed. It is a constantly shifting set of values, but no set rules. Finally, add into the equation the very real fact that much of the sword's use will depend upon the wielder.

There are several things that can be considered. First, the guard: the hilt of the rapier is quite attractive, and does provide some protection for the hand. The rapier was lighter, quicker, and easier to carry than many of the standard swords of the day. Another factor is that the rapier was a lousy weapon of war. So attempts were made to solve all of these problems, and obviously they solved none of them. (Well, maybe the fashion one, as there are sword rapiers that are quite attractive).

Early rapiers were generally only a little lighter than the tucks. Many were made with wider blades that did have edges. But it was also found that these blades were slower, and that a purely thrusting blade was much quicker.

By the middle of the 16th century, the rapier had reached the form given above and lasted until it was supplanted by the small sword. It was also realized that a somewhat longer blade gave one a slight advantage over an opponent armed with a shorter sword. This led to a rapid increase in the length of the rapier, and pretty soon it reached absurd lengths. I have handled and seen many with blades as long as 54 inches. I have been told of one in a private collection that reached a full 5 feet in blade length!

Blades this long were incredibly annoying to the average person. It would be difficult to walk around without having someone's long rapier rapping you as they passed by (another source for the term rapier—something that's always rapping other people?). Good Queen Bess responded to this by issuing an edict in 1562 that all who wore these long rapiers should have their swords broken to a yard in length. I have often wondered if wearing of the long rapier did not have some influence on the design of many buildings and plazas during the Renaissance. Certainly they are spacious and airy and you could wear a reasonable length sword in such places without creating much of a disturbance.

But I wander (as I am given to doing). The extra long rapier blade presented a more deadly problem: it really didn't work all that well. Its great length made it slow and awkward and, once an opponent got past the point, there was great difficulty in gaining control of the thing. Remember, they were *not* fencing, and there were no rules for combat. A long blade would be slow and, with almost no edge, it is relatively easy to grab the blade with the off hand. So rapiers quickly dropped back to what many considered an ideal length.

Some rapiers do have edges, but the mass of the blade is so light, and the blade is so thick, that any cut will act more as like a slash with a whip than an actual cut. Even if the actual edge is sharp, the angle of the wedge would be too great to allow the sword to penetrate. True, a wound from a sword like this would be unpleasant to receive, but it wouldn't be deadly, and it leaves the wielder of such a sword open to a killing thrust.

A very few rapiers were made with points that were spade-shaped, flattened and sharpened. This allowed them to be used in a slashing cut called the "stramazzone." This was usually directed at the face, in the hopes of a head cut that would blind the opponent. It doesn't seem to have worked very well, as there aren't a lot of them around.

Various forms of the swept hilt were used for the rapier until well into the 17th century. In the first quarter of the 17th century a new hilt form emerged, the cup hilt. This is the hilt form that most think about when the word rapier is mentioned. It is a very practical form, and gives great protection to the hand, as mentioned above.

Many years ago I purchased a rapier from Ewart Oakeshott with a cross cross-section. To digress a moment, I was at my first visit to Ewart and Sybil Oakeshott's home and I was a little nervous. Ewart had written what I consider to be the best and most informative book on arms and armor that I had ever read, *The Archaeology of Weapons*. I read it when it first came out in 1960, and even today it still stands head and shoulders above anything published before or since. I wasn't sure that he would want to spend time with a potzer like me, but he had extended the invitation so I accepted. I shouldn't have been worried. Two more delightful and wonderful people you will never find. Within five minutes I was completely at home, and every visit was a total joy from that day on.

We were having a great time talking about swords and Ewart was allowing me to examine his collection. He was a great one for "hands on" experience. He said that he had a rapier he wanted me to look at, and handed me this beautiful sword in almost perfect condition. The gilding was worn, but the fighting capabilities were still there. I took it from him and immediately started looking for someone to duel. (I had this experience only one other time; see the chapter on Japanese swords.) I knew that whoever had owned this weapon had not died in a duel, for who could lose with such a sword in hand? I had a hard time relinquishing it, and Ewart gave me his word that should he ever sell it, I would get first crack. From that day on he referred to it as "Hank's sword," and a few years later I did become the proud owner.

To this day I consider it the finest rapier I have ever seen. There are many rapiers that are more decorative, with beautiful hilt work, gorgeous sheaths, and some can be traced to notable figures. But of all the rapiers I have been lucky enough to hold, this is by far the best. The blade is 43 inches in length and at the ricasso the blade is 1¹⁄₁₆ inches wide and ¼ inch thick. There is a maker's mark, a crown over a T. The blade is deeply hollow ground, so that it is almost a cross in the cross section. Quite rigid, the blade has a slight curve, which I think happened in use. (Rapiers are not intended to be flexible like a fencing epee—that is movie nonsense. It has to be stiff in order to punch through the torso of the enemy.) The hilt is the "standard" swept hilt, and the weight of the sword is 2 pounds, 7 ounces. The balance is right in front of the hilt, so that when you grip it with one or two fingers around the ricasso, it seems to float in your hand. Ewart believed it dated from about 1600 AD, and I have no reason to doubt it. Although to my personal taste the sword is about 3 inches longer than I like, with a main gauche in the left hand, I'd feel it was a very formidable weapon. A few years later, Simon Fearnham of Raven Armoury was kind enough to

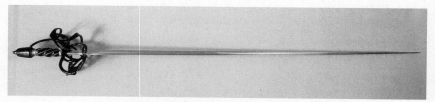

Reproduction Oakeshott rapier. HRC24.

make me a close copy (even I am reluctant to play with a four-hundred-year-old antique). This allowed me to handle the rapier in a defensive mode. Alas, I had to assure my friends that I would make no thrusting motions with the blade, but would only parry. I am convinced that it is the sword I would choose if ever challenged to a rapier duel.

The rapier quickly became the sword of the gentleman, and although other weapons were used on occasion, the rapier was the weapon of choice for dueling. It was admirably suited for this, but alas, for little else. Oh, it might defend against thieving footpads provided one had time to draw it, but as for war, it served no purpose. In the maelstrom and raging hell of battle, the little rapier was ineffective. Unlike the Roman gladius, the long rapier required more distance to thrust and stab, and the thin blade would break under the pressure of battle. Against wheel lock, polearm, broadsword and axe, and having to face armor, the rapier was insufficient.

MAIN GAUCHE

The rapier was often accompanied by a dagger termed a "main gauche," for the hand it was used in, *gauche* being French for "left," *main* for "hand." Back then, people were pretty serious about their fighting, and saw no reason to limit it to one hand. The left hand was used to ward off a thrust by slapping the blade, or to grab your opponent's blade. If that happened, you could stab your enemy, or even try to bend the blade if it were a thin-bladed weapon.

Our ancestors were far from stupid, and could easily see that having a dagger in the left hand made a lot of sense. At one time a very few swashbucklers carried a pair of rapiers. The idea being that if one sword was good, then two swords were twice as good. Alas, that was wrong, and I am sure a few people learned of their mistake, but I doubt seriously if they lived long enough to correct it.

Reproduction main gauche. HRC121.

In single combat the most serious problem facing a rapier is that it is a distance weapon. Once the opponent has broken past the point, it is impossible to turn the hand and then stab him. The sword is simply too long, and its main advantage becomes a deadly disadvantage. This problem was solved by using a dagger in the left hand. Blade length was important. It is very easy to choose a dagger with a long blade, as this will allow you to reach your opponent quicker, but then you can end up with the same problem, of your dagger being too long. A blade of about 14–16 inches seems to be pretty close to the ideal, but this does depend on the arm length and physiology of the person using the dagger.

Reproduction main gauche with thumb ring. HRC116.

The main gauche was designed for this type of fighting. Often the left hand holding the blade is protected by a thin shell and a crossguard. Sometimes the crossguard will have a ring projecting out of it at right angles instead of a shell. This is called a "thumb ring" and I haven't the slightest idea as to why. It is on the opposite side of the dagger from the thumb, and the people who think you put your thumb through it have no concept of swordplay. The ring is there to protect the hand from a sword sliding down the blade. All parries are made to the outside. Certainly you don't want to parry the sword across your body, and if you put your thumb through the ring, you are quite likely to get it lopped off.

The usual way of holding the main gauche was in the same fashion as you held the sword. However, there are illustrations and comments that some held the main gauche with the "icepick" grip. I tried this several times in play, using fencing swords and dummy flexible daggers. I managed to stab myself several times, and was also able to lose all of the fights. I went back to the old way.

Many of the left hand daggers are designed to trap an opponent's blade. Sometimes the guard will be lifted up out of the plane of the blade. When a parry is made the hand can be turned, catching the blade, if only momentarily. This can be a great advantage, and in the fraction of a second, allow you to stab your opponent in any area that happens to be open. Another method is to have two small projecting blades coming up about an inch from the main blade. These will have little hooks that can also catch a blade. Some blades will have these same hooks. Many times these

A *main gauche* with *"blade breaker"* hooks.   HRC130.

are referred to as "blade breakers," but that is wishful thinking. They are there for the sole purpose of catching and holding the blade.

The left hand dagger was an important weapon, and it seems to have been first fully appreciated and used in Spain. There is a small amount of argument about this, but no one has been able to offer definitive proof for any one location. At any rate, the use of rapier and dagger lasted longer in Spain than in any other European country, well into the 18th century.

But the main gauche was not only an important adjunct to the rapier, but to the sword, and sword rapier as well. It is always better to use both hands, and if you don't have a shield or a good buckler with you, then a good dagger is quite nice.

THE RAPIER'S FORM

The cross-section of most rapier blades was a diamond shape, although there are triangular cross sections as well (in the forerunner of the small sword), some square, some square with deeply hollowed faces. All of the blades were straight. However, there was one variety that is quite interesting.

This is the rapier that is often called a "flamberge rapier." The sword has a blade that is a series of S curves that gives it a serpentine look. These types of blades are found a great deal

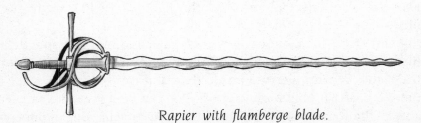

Rapier with flamberge blade.

in two-handed swords, in straight swords, sword rapiers and, of course, daggers. It was thought that the curved blades inflicted a deeper and more serious wound (more on this in the section dealing with the geometry of swords). A few years ago I got a good copy of a rapier that had one of these curved blades. In playing with it with some of my friends I made a rather interesting discovery: when you first lunge, and your sword is parried by a flamberge blade, it can cause you to lose your concentration if you're not careful. The parry causes your sword to vibrate, and although the effect is slight, it is still disconcerting. After a few times you get use to it, and it no longer matters. Of course, the reverse is also true, that it takes a short while to get used to using one of these rapiers. So hey, anything to gain an edge or, in this case, a point.

In popular works, such as the movies of *Cyrano* and *The Three Musketeers*, the rapier is shown with a cup hilt. It is surprising how long it took for this eminently practical hilt to be developed and used. Most authorities believe that the cup hilt was developed in the first quarter of the 17th century. (Still, there is a cup hilt in the Spanish Naval Museum in Madrid that is listed as belonging to an admiral who died in 1571. In this, I am inclined to believe the authorities rather than the museum, as the museums in Spain have frequently mislabeled some of their weaponry.)

Many of the cup hilts possess a turned over lip around the cup called a "rompepuntas." If a strong thrust is aimed at the cup, it is possible for the blade to slip over the cup and strike the arm or even the body of the swordsman. This lip is designed to prevent that from happening. In play with blunted fencing weapons we found that this works. A hard thrust to the top of the cup can frequently cause the blade to slide off and into the arm of your opponent.

Aside from the rompepuntas, the majority of the early cups also had a great deal of pierced

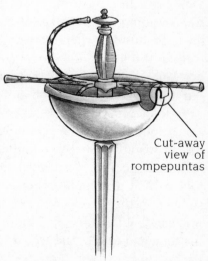

Cut-away view of rompepuntas

Cup hilt with rompepuntas.

work. This is really beautiful work, often
cut steel. This open work serves the same
purpose of the rompepuntas, as it provides
many opportunities for any thrust to the
hilt to be caught.

The cup hilt quickly spread throughout
Europe and was quite fashionable, but of
course, the swept hilt remained in use.

By the middle of the 17th century, the long
rapier was undergoing some changes. The
blade was getting shorter, somewhat lighter,
and the hilt was also being simplified. In
Spain, the long rapier remained popular, and
this reduction in size was less notable. At the
same time, due to many factors—and fashion

*Reproduction
rapier with swept
hilt. HRC14.*

most assuredly played a part—the main gauche was being used less
and less. Single combat was taking more and more of the aspects of
pure fencing, and the small sword was coming into its own.

I find it hard to understand why the main gauche was abandoned.
In any dueling system you can set up whatever rules you wish,
and duels were frequently fought under some really absurd rules.
Consider the duel fought in Europe (France, I believe), where the
two men did not possess any weapons other than helmets with
sharp beaks, and were required to butt and peck at each other. Or
a man put in a pit to his waist having to fight a woman who was
free standing. But as a self-defense item the rapier alone leaves a
lot to be desired when confronted by more than one attacker.

Take the death of Pizarro, the Conqueror of Peru. He and his
brother were attacked at dinner by a group of assassins. Pizarro
did not have time to put on any armor; instead he seized his cloak,
wrapped it around his left arm and attempted to fight off his attackers. He and his brother were doing pretty well when Pizarro stabbed
one of his attackers. As he attempted to withdraw his sword, one
of the attackers in back pushed the unfortunate pierced assassin
forward. Pizarro could not clear his sword in time and was himself
stabbed in the throat. We do not know exactly what sword Pizarro
was using at the time, but more than likely it was a type typical of
the time and origin, and would be a straight-bladed sword, relatively
narrow in blade width and excellent for thrusting.

Not that I think he would have survived, but I do think he would have been able to take more of his assailants with him had he an additional weapon. Pizarro was far from a nice man; in fact, calling him treacherous, murderous scum might be harsh. Accurate, but harsh. However, there is one thing he was, and that was tough.

My point (maliciously intended pun) is that with a long weapon a thrust can penetrate too deeply, and present problems in the withdrawal. A second weapon, such as a main gauche, still allows you to be defend and attack while regaining use of the weapon.

SMALL SWORDS

In the third quarter of the 17th century, the small sword gained great acceptance and dominated the field of civilian swordplay almost exclusively. It also became a very necessary item of male jewelry, and some of the hilts of these weapons are incredible works of art! You can find examples with cut and pierced work, tiny granules of gold and silver, and incredibly detailed figures, some holy, some erotic, all beautiful. It would seem almost a crime to use one of these swords in combat, but they did. Of course they were also worn by men who really had no idea of how they were used, nor any desire to learn. Although there were duels aplenty, there really weren't as many as books and movies seem to suggest.

Many have considered these early small swords the most deadly sword ever developed. But these are people who consider classic fencing as the only "proper" method for fighting with a sword. I hear the same thing from devotees of the katana, who think that small swords and rapiers are silly effeminate sticking toys. Sigh. I also do a lot of shooting, and hear pretty much the same thing about the different calibers of handguns.

I'm a heretic in both fields. The best weapon is the one that you have with you at the time you need it.

But back to the subject at hand.

The wearing of the small sword as an item of male fashion was beginning to fade by the

A gaudy small sword.

mid-18th century, and soon was to pass away completely except for ceremonial occasions. By the time of its passing, the blade had degenerated into a small, thin and unimpressive sword very similar to the swords such as those of the Knights of Columbus and other modern fraternal orders.

At its peak, say from 1660 to 1720 for rough dates, the sword was long, slim and quite light, with very little hand protection. The most effective of these small swords had beautiful triangular blades, with very deep hollow facings. This made for a stiff, light, and really quick sword blade. There was an interesting development, called the colichemarde, which came close to turning the small sword into an actual military weapon, although I do not think that was its purpose. The colichmarde blade was triangular, quite wide for at least a third of the blade, and then tapered abruptly to the standard triangular cross section. The wide blade, being deeply hollowed, had a balance point close to the hilt, which allowed the blade to be exceedingly quick. However, its width

Colichmarde.

allowed the blade to be used to block cuts from heavier swords such as a saber. Since there is a real possibility that a normal blade might break under the impact, this allowed the sword to be carried in circumstances where a heavier blade might be called for. It really is an attractive weapon, and I must confess, it's the only small sword that I like.

The colichmarde was supposed to have been invented by Philip Von Konigsmark (1656–1694), a Swede of German origin. He was quite the adventurer, and was reported to be the lover of Sophia Dorothea, the wife of George, Crown Prince of Hanover, who later became George I, King of England. Von Konigsmark was murdered when the affair was discovered—and I think we can safely assume it was German Georgie who had it done—and Sophie Dorothea was shut up in a castle. Kings can be hard to get along with.

It's a great legend about the invention, but probably untrue, since small swords with this shape were showing up before Philip was born—but I have no doubt about his affair. All women love a good swordsman.

FENCING

Rapier and small sword play are the forerunners of modern fencing. I first encountered fencing in the mid 1950s at the Atlanta YMCA. At the time I was wrestling, boxing, rope climbing, and I wanted to learn to fence, too. The instructor they provided us was Professor Morenus. He was retired from Georgia Tech, and was about 70–72 at the time. He was a disengage fencer, and he always reminded me of a large white spider. He informed me once that I might make a good swordsman, but that I would never make a good fencer. Now, I do not know how good a swordsman I have ever been, considering that it has to all be in sport or play, but I do know that I was a lousy fencer.

The truth was that I was never really interested in fencing, I was interested in fighting, and learning how to use the sword as a weapon. Fencing is a sport.

Originally fencing was used to teach the use of the sword for the duel. It rapidly became a sport/pastime, and a very upscale one at that. It was a gentleman's sport, and more emphasis was placed on how you behaved and moved, rather than winning. In the early days, there were a lot of sneering remarks aimed at those fencers who were considered "just stabbers" who had no form, but merely attacked repeatedly. This could be a just criticism in a sport, but in actual combat it would be a meaningless remark. Real combat is only concerned with whether you win or die.

When I first started playing with saber, it was explained to me that the saber was used mainly on horseback, and so there was a convention of not attacking the legs. However, the weapon was much lighter than any antique saber I had encountered. It weighed about 12–13 ounces compared to two and a half to three pounds for real sabers. The blade was more like a buggy whip than a sword blade, but Professor Morenus did not allow cut overs to count (this is where the blow was parried, but due to the flexible blade the attacking sword would still bend over and touch). Much of the work was done with wrist and fingers, and I didn't know anyone who could do that with one of my real swords. I still don't. When many fencers actually pick up a real saber, they are shocked by its weight and consider it useless. For sport fencing, it is.

The epee was developed as a training weapon for the dueling sword, and I feel that in many respects it would work pretty well.

But the blade is too light, and the conventions and rules prohibit many of the things that did occur in real fights. Since the whole body is a target, that does reflect a much more realistic approach than the other two forms. Even so, counting a hit to the calf the same as a hit to the chest or face is not realistic.

In the old days there were squabbles about who hit first, and the contestants had to rely on the sharp eye of the judges. To rely on the honor of the contestants was simply not practical. Not for reasons of honor, but simply because in many cases the heavily padded individuals can't tell who hit first. Many times he wouldn't even know that he was hit at all!

The introduction of electronic scoring stopped that and, in my opinion, ruined fencing and removed all pretense of it being a martial art. For those of you who may not be familiar with it, the sword is equipped with a wire that registers a hit and time. When two hits are registered, the point is awarded to the first hit. The result of this innovation has been ignoring defense completely.

The last match I witnessed was several years ago and between two world-class epee fencers. They both stood at the end of the strip, both tapping their blades on the floor, a picture of intense concentration. Suddenly they both leapt forward and clashed, both blades bent under impact, and both turned to the scoreboard to see who had hit first. The whole match consisted of this sort of "swordplay."

Another result of electronic scoring is the "coupe." (I have heard that some places have banned this, but I can't say for sure.) The coupe is a flick of the blade that will merely touch your opponent. However, it will close the circuit and register as a hit. Using a real sword, all you would have achieved is *possibly* a very small nick.

Now, I may be old-fashioned, or I may just be old and wimpy. But my idea of a successful sword fight is for me to stick my enemy, and for him not to stick me. It certainly doesn't include getting stuck by him, even if I hit a fraction of a second quicker. I recall reading of one historical duel where the adversaries were so angry that they rushed upon one another doing nothing but stabbing. They were both successful and both fell dead. A bystander remarked that they were "two silly people, skewering each other on the first pass."

As of this writing, there is a great deal of squabbling regarding swordplay. There are new kids on the block, holding up as a shining beacon the fight manuals of old, all claiming to provide the secret of historically accurate swordplay. There are many other groups, all of them trying to come up with swordplay that is more realistic, and closer to being a combat art. Except for a very few, most realize that safety is an important consideration. The need for safety does, however, always interfere with the goal of being as realistic as possible. This is the nature of the beast, and I have no desire to change it. Failure to employ safety rules could easily leave me bereft of readers, which I would hate. With this in mind, many groups are achieving a modicum of success. I haven't seen all of them, so I won't make any comments regarding any of the individual groups, but I wish them all well.

Then there are sport fencers who will assure all and sundry that sport fencing is the apex of swordplay and it is what all swordplay has been aiming at for several hundred years. Lest that sound a little harsh, let me quickly say that there are plenty of swordsmen in both camps that have a full appreciation of the realities of actual swordplay and fun, whether the fun be sport or re-enactment.

I have read that Aldo Nadi was the greatest fencer who ever lived. I am not able to comment on that. But I have also read that he had two duels to first blood, and lost both of them. When the tips are off, and you are looking at a man with a weapon who desires to hurt you, many things go right out the window.

Many will think that I look down on fencing. I don't. Fencing is a highly disciplined and rigorous sport. It requires great reflexes, balance, coordination, and endurance. And it has all sorts of rules, and the rules provide enjoyment to the participants. It has nothing to do with killing people and it does not teach you to fight.

Fencers fight in a straight line. This makes sense when you are a fencing master with a fair number of students. You can't afford to have them circling each other, they would get in each other's way. But in real life you *would* circle, and would try to take advantage of any features of the terrain that might make your opponent stumble, or distract his attention.

The foil, the epee and the saber are all lightweight weapons designed with the two purposes of being fast and not harming the opponent. Now, they can really hurt when used as a whip, much as a radio aerial will if ripped off a car and used in a street fight. The bad news is when the whippee closes with the whipper. In short, a small sword is about as light as you can reasonably get with a sword blade. It is deadly, but it has its weaknesses.

Still, learning to fence can be fun, and it will familiarize you with having a sword in your hand, and with moving while learning to defend and attack. It is an excellent sport, but it will not teach you how to fight with a rapier or a small sword. There are other groups out there who will do a better job. But also remember that they have rules as well. Rules are necessary for safety's sake and that must be of paramount importance.

There are several books recounting many of the duels in the past, describing fights with rapier, small sword, sword and buckler, polearms, etc. They are entertaining and informative, but they do not go into the necessary details for the reader to fully understand what has taken place. "Wounded many times," "fighting furiously," "desperate encounter": there are general terms given, and the reader is allowed to use his imagination to picture the duel. It can be fun, but not an effective teaching tool except that you realize that it is a killing that is being recounted.

FIGHTING WITH THE RAPIER

A look at the differences between fencing and fighting can be instructive. In fencing you are taught to stand with your sword arm and leg presented to your opponent. The off hand is held well back, and is often extended backwards when the individual lunges. This is an interesting stance, and is pretty much the same as used by individuals in pistol duels. The body is presented sideways, as it furnishes less of a target, both for sword and pistol. There is one problem here: almost any hit that penetrates the torso will usually be fatal. When being struck face on, there are areas where the blade or ball might be able to pass

Fencing stance.

through without giving a fatal wound, but sideways, it is very difficult to find a path that would not hit a vital organ.

In the old days, men fought face on, with the sword arm and leg only slightly extended. The off hand was held generally about shoulder height. This allowed the arm to be used in blocking a thrust, slapping it aside, grabbing the blade, or even punching the opponent (obviously, I am talking about single weapon combat). Some rapiers were made with a thick center ridge, with actual edges. These swords were not good for cutting, as the ridge would prevent any deep wounding. However, it could make grabbing the blade somewhat problematical. This was offset by the use of mail gauntlets.

The main gauche was an important weapon in both dueling and in rough brawls and confrontations. Since there were no rules on wearing the dagger, people pretty much let personal preference dictate where it was worn. Some

Whit Williams of the Reinhardt Legacy Fight Team in fighting stance. Photo by Adam Lyon.

wore it behind the back and pretty much horizontal, others had it canted and wore it on the right side. This allowed both sword and dagger to be drawn simultaneously. (This was another reason for the demise of the long-bladed rapier: it took way too long to clear the scabbard.)

It is generally agreed that the dagger was used to parry with, and the sword was the attacking weapon. However, in play I have had a great deal of success using the rapier as the parrying weapon, closing and attacking with the dagger. This will catch many by surprise, but after they have fought with me several times, it becomes a fight of taking advantage of any opportunity that presents itself.

There is one neat trick that I have had work for me several times in play. If a dagger gets too close to the rapier, or the rapier to the dagger, it is possible to move against one or the other forcefully, and tie up both blades. This only lasts for a fraction of a second, but it is enough to land a blow with the dagger. Obviously this will work in reverse, tying up both weapons with your dagger and striking with the sword. There is a more unpleasant reverse of this, when your opponent ties up your blades.

Generally, the dagger was held with the thumb on the flat of the blade, and any other position was what the individual preferred. It could be held at shoulder height with a bent elbow or fully extended. There are historical drawings of fighters holding the dagger in an icepick grip with the point down. There may have been individuals who could fight this way, but I am not among them. I can say that I never lost a bout when my opponent was holding his dagger like that.

Hollywood has often shown Our Hero fighting a Dastardly Villain with rapier. He makes a sudden, very mysterious move, and the villain's sword goes flying off into space. Ah, would that it were so! But there are two disarms that are effective, and amazingly simple. One is to parry a thrust to the left side, and as the blade passes beside the body, the left arm is locked to the side, while the forearm is brought under the blade then up and out. This forces the man to relinquish the sword or risk having his fingers broken. The other is even simpler. A lunge is parried, again to the left of the body, and the the left hand is shot out, grabbing the swept hilt or the cup, and yanking it out of the man's hand. There is a counter to this, where the other fellow replies by grabbing the hilt of his opponent's sword. There has been some speculation that this is the way the swords were intended to be exchanged in the climactic duel in Shakespeare's *Hamlet*.

Rapiers became slimmer and slimmer, usually cup hilted, usually Spanish, until they were nothing but long thin rods of steel. These are pretty fast, as it was found that the lighter the sword, the faster it became. (It followed the same silly path as rapier length did, so that today you have fencing "swords" that weigh 13 ounces or less.) This quickly led to the development of the small sword. In the hands of a knowledgeable swordsman, it can be quite deadly, especially when facing an opponent who has only a single heavier weapon. However, let your opponent add a small shield, cloak, or dagger, and things change.

Two things to consider here: it has been stated, and proven, that a light, fast thrusting weapon is much quicker than a cutting weapon. This is true provided that both start from the same position! But what happens when the man holding the cutting sword has it in a ready position over his head? The cutting sword may have further to travel, but it is moving much faster! If the left hand is held out to ward off a thrust, or it has a dagger or shield, then there are real problems for the small sword. It can only thrust, and a thrust is not all that hard to parry.

Let me repeat a theme that occurs throughout this book. The main consideration is the men behind the weapons. If you look on a man as an army, and his mind as the general, then you can apply Talleyrand's comment, "I had rather face an army of lions led by a sheep than an army of sheep, led by a lion." In short, it doesn't matter how physically imposing an individual happens to be. What is important is how tough, strong and smart his head is.

Suggestions for further reading from Hank:

De Joinville, Jean. His memoirs can be found in *The Chronicles of the Crusades*, translated by Margaret Shaw. Penguin, London, 1963.

Hutton, Alfred, *The Sword and the Centuries, or Old Sword Days and Old Sword Ways*. Grant Richards, London, 1901.

Norman, A.V.B., *The Rapier and the Small Sword: 1460–1820*, Arms and Armour Press, London, 1980.

Silver, George, *Paradoxes of Defense*. First published in 1599.

FICTION:

Dumas, Alexandre, *The Three Musketeers*. First published in 1844.

Rostand, Edmond, *Cyrano de Bergerac*. First published in 1897. Hank preferred the Bryan Hooker translation. The Modern Library, Random House, New York, 1923.

Sabatini, Rafael, *Scaramouche*. First published in 1921.

Suggestions for further reading from the editors:

Bryson, Frederick Robertson, *The Point of Honor in Sixteenth-Century Italy: An Aspect of the Life of the Gentleman*.

Publications of the Institute of French Studies, Inc., Columbia University, New York, 1935.

Franzoi, Umberto, *L'Armeria del Palazzo Ducale a Venezia*. Canova, Treviso, 1990.

▶ 8 ◀

European Swords:
The Saber

The saber is another of those swords whose very name generates confusion. Like the rapier, the form is so varied as to render meaningless the term "saber." It can mean a sword straight or curved, single- or double-edged, with a wide or narrow blade. You have cavalry sabers, artillery sabers, and infantry sabers. I feel sure that if underwater "SEAL" type warriors had been developed in the 18th century, you would have had an "underwater saber."

Originally the term meant a curved sword used on horseback. It gained great popularity beginning in the late 16th century and by the early 19th was the weapon of choice for that most romantic of dashing soldiers, the cavalryman. This was also the period of some of the most flamboyant uniforms ever worn on a battlefield. The German Landsknechts were possibly a little more florid, but they didn't wear uniforms, they

A *Napoleonic uniform.*

were just wildly dressed individuals. I could appear cool and aloof and make some disparaging comments about the many styles of uniforms worn by the various groups before, during and right after the Napoleonic Wars, but I'd be lying. Frankly, I think they all really looked sharp! When you were being bayoneted, sliced with a saber, stabbed with a lance, or torn apart by cannon shot, at least you looked good while dying!

The saber had its origins on the vast plains and steppes of Asia. From horseback, a slightly curved sword offers a definite advantage when dealing with infantry. You can cut down easily and quickly and usually the sword won't get stuck in the enemy. If you have a good seat, you can reach down and stab someone lying flat on the ground. While possible, it was a technique rarely used, as a horse does not like to step on people, as they're all soft and squishy.

The development of the stirrup (usually guessed at about 300 AD and somewhere in Central Asia), gave much greater security to the rider. But it not only allowed him to feel more secure in his seat—it let him strike a harder blow with his sword, and even to thrust with it. This led to varying degrees of curvature, and over fifteen hundred years later, a heated debate in the military halls of the United Kingdom. But I get ahead of myself.

Many consider that the saber has to have a guard to qualify as a saber. It doesn't matter whether it is a simple D guard, or a full or half basket. But then, what do you call a shasqua, which is a saber pure and simple in use, and has no guard whatsoever? I will leave this up to the reader. I have given up trying to get all things to fit into a nice clean and simple pattern. (Fifty years of study, and I still can't get people to write "mail" rather than "chainmail." Oh well, they still say "La Brea Tar Pits" which, equally redundantly, translates to "tar pits tar pits.")

One of the first true sabers to make it into Europe came in the hands of a wild, conquering horde of horse archers that called

Modern shasqua, 38 inches overall length. HRC322.

themselves Magyars. These were Finno-Urgrian peoples who originated somewhere deep in Asia, possibly Siberia. In the Imperial Treasury in Vienna there is a sword that tradition says was a gift to Charlemagne from Haroun El Rashid. It is no such thing. It is a very typical Magyar saber that they used from their first incursions into Europe and until much later when they had settled and ceased being nomads and horse archers. We know them as Hungarians, and they were a tough, bloodthirsty bunch. They gave Europe a foretaste of what was to happen in a few hundred years when the Mongols came on the scene.

The Hungarian was a lightly armed horse archer whose specialty was the bow. He frequently carried a light shield, one or two bows, obviously arrows, knife, small axe and sword. The sword is of primary interest in this book.

The blade of the Magyar sword was slightly curved, ending in a good sharp point. The last third of the blade was always double-edged. Blade length varied, but on average was about 35–36 inches long,

Magyar saber.

with a width of one and a quarter inches. This allowed for easier penetration in a thrust and made backhand slaps also effective. The grip was short, with small projections ending in small knobs. This short grip was down curved, with a metal cap and secured to the tang by small rivets.

This is an excellent design for a sword used in the hit-and-run tactics of the horse archer. The Magyars rarely had to engage opponents who were heavily armored. If faced with a knight in full armor they always tried to avoid closing. However, as they settled into what is now Hungary, they gradually abandoned their nomadic life style, and this necessitated changes in both armor and weapons.

A few years ago a sword was discovered in what is now Iran. The sword dates from about the middle of the 13th century and is in excellent physical condition. It was displayed at the Metropolitan Museum along with many other artifacts and can be seen in the book *The Legacy of Genghis Khan*. (It was promised that something would be printed on this sword in the near future, but to my knowledge it has not been released.) This is a very beautiful sword, and looks to be an improved version of the Magyar sword. The blade is slightly curved and somewhat wider with a serviceable point. The grip is missing, but the tang is slightly inclined toward the edge of the blade, and is pierced by rivet holes. The guard appears to be a forerunner of the type of guard so popular in the Near East, with two small langets extended from the crossguard, one toward the blade, which would secure the sword in the scabbard, and the other into the grip which would make both grip and guard more secure.

Mongol sword.

The sword is very similar to swords excavated over the years, all of which are considered to be Cuman sabers. It should be noted that although curved swords show up all over the world at various times, they were not prevalent in the Middle East until *after* the Mongol Invasions. The primary swords used by the Arabs in their expansion and conquests were straight double-edged swords, wide-bladed, flat and capable of delivering a fearsome cut. I know it hurts to think that Hollywood has lied to you all these years, but the classical scimitar didn't come until later.

Antique cutting sword, 37 inches overall length. HRC29.

The Magyars did not simply fade away or blend in with the rest of Europe. Although they abandoned their nomadic ways and settled into a sedentary existence, they still maintained an interest in cavalry. By the 15th century they had developed light cavalry which they called "Hussars." (No one knows for sure where the name came from, but the most logical etymology seems to indicate that it referred to the number of peasants needed for the nobleman to supply one horseman.) This cavalry unit was quite effective, and in a few years most all of the countries in Europe had groups of

Hussars, though not all were lightly armed. It should be noted that the sword or saber was either the primary or secondary weapon for these units. If the unit of cavalry was armed with firearms or lances, then the sword was secondary. But often the sword was primary. Sometimes the lance would break, or the gun misfire or run out of ammunition, and then the cavalryman had to rely on his sword, so great attention was paid to the weapon.

One group that I have to comment on is the Polish Winged Hussars. This is probably the most flamboyant of any group of fighting men. You could find them with steel breast and backplates made of overlapping lames of steel, heavy and made to try to withstand musket balls, lobster-tailed helmets, steel shoulder and arm guards, and—fashioned to the back of the backplates—huge curving pieces of wood with feathers projecting like wings! This must have been quite a frightening sight to see this group coming at you, and it wouldn't matter whether you

Karabela.

were infantry or cavalry. Regardless of the fear factor, there is one thing for certain: they could fight. For about a hundred years they dominated Northeastern Europe, defeating many armies, some when they were heavily outnumbered. Interestingly, they carried two swords. One was the karabela, a broad-bladed single-edged curved sword that was an excellent cutting weapon. The other was a long stiff-bladed sword very much like a tuck, and really excellent for use against armored units.

By the beginning of the 18th century, firearms, both hand-held and field pieces, had improved to such an extent that the sword and lance were being relegated to second-class weapons for the infantry, but in the cavalry they still were quite important. Eighteenth-century battles were frequently set pieces and waged on open land. Hills and woods were still used for flank protection, but space was needed for cannon. The relationship between cavalry and infantry is curious. Good, solid infantry pikemen whose pikes were longer than the lances of the cavalry could never be broken if they held firm. Should the lance be longer than the halberds, such as happened with the Swiss at Arbedo in 1422, then it becomes a near run thing.

The advent of gunpowder changed this equation, but only slightly. The development of the British square, with successive ranks firing while others reloaded, could easily withstand a charge of horse. The withering firepower, coupled with the horse's reluctance to charge into a line of men, made the square a ferocious defense. But let the square be broken, for whatever reason, and then there was hell to pay. An accurate cannon shot of grape or chain, or just one or two men who lost their nerve and ran—and once the square is broken the infantryman stood very little chance.

During the Napoleonic Wars a battle occurred when French cavalry came upon a square of Prussian infantry. It was a very wet, ugly day. The ground was muddy, and the gunpowder of the Prussian infantry was damp. The French could not charge, but could only walk to the square. The Prussians fixed bayonets and held them off

Reproduction Polish saber. HRC369.

repeatedly. The horse was no advantage in those conditions, and the sword could not reach the Prussians, but the Prussians could reach the horse and the man. This went on for a spell, and then some French lancers showed up, drove a wedge into the ranks, and that did it for the Prussians.

Sitting comfortably in a well padded and well used chair, it is easy to conjure up ways of defense to withstand the most awesome of attacks. However, if you use your imagination and think of being the warrior or soldier facing a charging horseman who is armed with a sword or a lance, you can sense that it is a most terrifying event. It is not just the imminence of death, but that you can see and feel the sword or the lance as it kills you.

As the 18th century wore on, more and more the swords became standardized and mass-produced. Hilt forms varied from full basket hilts that gave full hand protection, to simple stirrup guards. Blade shapes also changed on an almost yearly basis. There are a few general officer's swords in Great Britain, as well as some French Hussar swords, that are so deeply curved as to be almost useless. They are often wide-bladed, but are obvious copies of the Persian shamshir.

During the Napoleonic Wars two types of swords were quite popular. One, used by German and Polish forces as well as the British, surprised me quite a bit when I first encountered it back in the late 1950s. It was the 1796 Pattern Light Cavalry saber. The sword had a simple stirrup hilt, a nice curve, a wide blade that ended in a rather rounded point. What amazed me at the time was that the blade thinned all the way to the point, so that the last 5–6 inches of the blade was quite thin and very flexible. So flexible that should you bend that section of the blade, it would stay bent. But it was rather simple to straighten it back out. This was rather puzzling to me at first, since I was of the opinion that a spring temper was essential to a sword. But the more I thought about it, and the more I played with the weapon, I began to see the logic. The sword was quite light and quite fast. It was a light

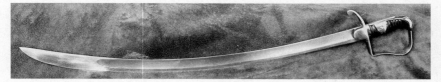

Reproduction British 1796 cavalry saber made by Windlass Cutlery. HRC224. Photo by Charlotte Proctor.

cavalry weapon. Light cavalry was used to harass troops, to engage other light cavalry, to charge troops making them form a square and thus delaying them, and in other movements requiring quick action. The sword was perfect for this. Armor was not worn by the infantry, so for penetrating heavy cloth and flesh this was excellent. One of the problems facing a cavalryman is getting his sword caught in his victim. When slashing at an opponent the sword may not cut through and can be caught in the body. On a running horse this can result in a lost or broken sword. However on the 1796 pattern, it was easy for the sword to simply bend and then be pulled out. If the tip was bent, it could be easily straightened with the hand. (If you worry about handling a bloody blade, then you shouldn't be in the cavalry to start with. And those gaudy uniforms did include gloves.)

The other sword was the 1796 heavy cavalry sword. This has been described as a "butcher's blade" and a rather apt description it is. It has none of the grace and beauty of other swords. It is straight, heavy, single-edged, with a good solid point, and the weight of the blade makes it an efficient cutter. Heavy cavalry was used to charge and hit the enemy with great force. Armored with breast and backplate and a stout steel helmet, they were a formidable force if they closed with the enemy. Although this is a book about swords, it should be mentioned that not all heavy cavalry wore breast and back plates. The Austrians wore only a breastplate, and that caused them much grief in several encounters. Keeping your front to the enemy sounds nice, but it is easy to bring a sword back around to strike the back. And once you try to retreat, you leave yourself open with almost no protection. The sword was almost never used for defense, but to hack and stab whenever the opportunity presented itself.

French heavy cavalry sword.

The French heavy cavalry was armed with a very similar sword. The arrangement of the fullers was slightly different and the guard was three branched, but in essence it was the same sword.

Slightly before the Napoleonic Wars, the swords began being sheathed in metal scabbards. Now, it is possible to keep a sword sharp in a metal scabbard, but it is difficult. You have to be careful each time you draw or sheath the sword. Once the edge encounters the steel of the scabbard it becomes dull. But metal scabbards are cheaper, and the military powers that were decided that you didn't need a sharp edge anyway, that the force of a three-foot piece of steel striking a person was enough to split the skin and probably severely wound or kill. This became such an entrenched dictum that it was considered downright mean to sharpen your sword. So much so that Confederate General Nathan Bedford Forrest was highly criticized for having his men sharpen their sabers, this in the Civil War in the 1860s.

This led to many heated debates regarding the cavalry saber. One side insisting on straight-bladed swords and the other on curved blades.

The substance of the two arguments went like this:

Straight Blade—An enemy combatant, stabbed with a sword, is highly unlikely to continue fighting. Even if the wound is not fatal, if it is in the arm it is likely to render the opponent ineffective. The straight blade can be used to cut with, if needed, and it can be used to reach down and stab an enemy lying on the ground.

Counter Argument against the straight blade—The thrust is harder to master than the cut. There is a strong likelihood that the blade can be lost in a thrust, wedged in the body, or broken as the horse moves past quicker than the blade can be withdrawn, or almost as bad, the wielder's wrist can be broken before the sword can be released if caught. In an encounter between units of heavy cavalry, the cutting sword is easier to use than a thrusting one.

Curved Blade—The curved sword is easier to use since the cut allows the arm to move in a very natural motion. With a properly curved sword it can be used to thrust as well. Aside from the hooking thrust, by turning the wrist over, you get a "natural" downward motion of the arm. By cutting an opponent, the sight of blood is likely to cause him to withdraw and tend his wounds.

Counter Argument against the curved blade—Numerous references are cited of soldiers of both sides receiving numerous cuts about the head and shoulders and continuing to fight. (No mention was made about dull swords.) Also there were rare instances of a soldier in the heat of battle striking his horse, which he was unlikely to do with a straight sword. (Although there was no PETA at the time, this was still looked on as not being proper. Even killing your opponent's horse was considered not very sporting, and something a real gentleman would not do, but okay for rankers.)

There was a small amount of logic on both sides. (Personally I prefer a curved sword, but I would also keep it quite sharp.) The arguments raged on and on, with first one side winning, and then the other.

The 19th century saw the introduction of a really nice saber design, and one that I quite like, the quill back, or pipe back, blade. This

Quill back blade;
silhouette view from above shows rounded spine.

blade had a round back, with the edge extending downward. The thick round portion of the blade extended almost to the point, but several inches from the point is a back edge. This gave you a slightly curved blade with excellent rigidity for thrusting, yet great strength of cutting. It had two flaws. The round back edge would prevent the sword from cutting very deeply, and it was expensive to make. Other than that it would make a fine weapon for unarmored combat.

The final saber issued for combat was a single-edged straight-bladed sword with a thick back, and really useless for cutting. To many people this signaled that the straight-bladed thrusting sword was the ultimate cavalry weapon. I would like to point out that this was also the group that sent the cavalry charging machines guns—and that was the end of the saber as a weapon of war.

This leads us to modern saber fencing. Saber fencing is based on the use of the cavalry saber. Since a cavalry saber is used on a horse, and it doesn't make much sense to cut at a man's leg when he's on a horse (except to be mean and spiteful), leg blows are not allowed. Sabers were heavy swords, usually the weight ran between 2¾ to 4 pounds. Now, the reality of combat dictated that a man had to be a good horseman and his horsemanship was actually more important than his skill with a sword.

Modern sport fencers use sabers that weigh 13 ounces and fight on foot. Go figure.

THE SHORT SABER, THE HANGER, THE CUTLASS

The advantage of a short close combat weapon has long been known. Although called by many names, the above swords are all basically the same weapon. None of the above-listed swords was ever intended to be the primary weapon of the individual. The closest would have been the cutlass. Even on the confines of a small ship the preferred weapon would have been the short pike

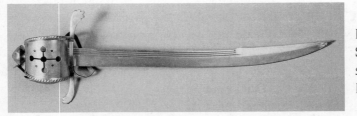

Reproduction Sinclair saber. HRC44.

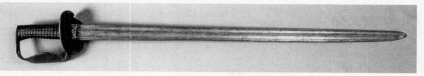

*British naval cutlass from the late 1700s,
33 inches overall length. HRC40.*

or a brace of pistols. But going into combat with one weapon is foolish, so there was always a backup.

The hanger was a favorite infantry weapon as well as a civilian one. Anytime there was a chance of miscreants or rascals being about, the knowledgeable gentleman might have a small pistol, plus some type of edged weapon. In the narrow streets of the European cities the small sword was favored. However, in the wilder regions of the world a good stout hanger was preferred. The very sight of such a weapon could put off an attack. Thugs are not interested in fighting for fighting's sake, they're interested in plunder. A few coins, even gold ones, are not worth a split skull or a severed limb.

From a military point of view the short saber was also a useful tool. It could be used in pioneer work and building fortifications. It was so popular that one version was made with a saw back, and issued to engineering and pioneer troops. It did cause some outcry, as it was really mean looking (just like mean looking "assault rifles" today) and it was rumored that any soldier found with one of these swords was shot on the spot. Since it was used in several armies, Russian, French, German to name a few, the rumor could have been just wartime propaganda.

Hanger.

Some of these swords are really ugly, and some are quite beautiful. In the Tower of London there is a particularly nice short saber and Museum Replicas, Ltd., made a superb copy of the sword. I grabbed the first one, and still have it. It is a very effective and attractive sword. The American

*Saw-backed
short saber.*

Cutlass, model 1862, is another sword that is really attractive. You can compare it with the last issued cutlass of the US Navy, the 1917 Model. No comparison in looks.

Reproduction US Navy 1917 model cutlass.
Photo by Mike Stamm.

Suggestions for further reading from Hank:

Komaroff, Linda, and Stefano Carboni, editors, *The Legacy of Genghis Khan: Courtly Art and Culture in Western Asia, 1250–1353*. The Metropolitan Museum of Art, New York, 2002.

Suggestions for further reading from the editors:

Farwell, Byron, *Eminent Victorian Soldiers: Seekers of Glory*, WW Norton & Co., New York, 1985.
Farwell, Byron, *Queen Victoria's Little Wars*, WW Norton & Co., New York, 1985.

► 9 ◄

European
Two-Handed Swords

Of all of the two-handed swords in the world, none are as impressive as the European two-hander. Although the Japanese no-dachi is fearsome and most impressive, it is not quite as awesome as the Swiss or German two-hand sword.

In many of the action films dealing with swords that are not rapiers, the combatants are shown using their weapons with two hands. This is fine if it's appropriate to the country and period, as for instance when they show the Japanese katana or the larger European versions. But this does give a skewed version of history, as the sword and shield were the preferred weapons for most of the time when swords were used. Still, it is easily understandable when you realize the difficulties in choreographing a fight with sword and shield.

But just how popular were these two-handed weapons in reality? When did they start to be used and how effective were they?

No one is able to say for sure just how early the two-handed sword began to be used in Europe. It seems only logical that in battle when one has lost his shield to continue to fight using both hands on the sword. Given the wide range of individual preference, I feel certain that there were a very few people who actually preferred a two-handed sword. But these early medieval swords appear to have been merely outsized versions of the standard sword blade of the various periods. Rather than two-handed swords, these are called "bastard swords" or a "sword of war."

Great sword, early 15th century, steel, 68 inches overall length.
From the collection of Glenbow Museum. R1945.285.

These were swords that could be swung with one hand, but had space in the grip for an additional hand should the user feel it was needed.

Although the two-handed sword had not gained any great popularity, there were still very large two-handers in existence. There is one in the Glenbow Museum in Calgary, Alberta, Canada. This is a huge sword, well over 6 feet long, and weighing about 12 pounds. It dates from the early 15th century and I would consider it an important sword in the history of arms.

Two things brought about the development of the two-hand sword in the 14th century. One was the improvement of armor. As mail was superseded by plate armor, the sword became less and less effective. When an infantryman of the period was forced to face a fully armored knight, a two-hand crushing or cutting weapon was needed: a halberd, a bill, or a two-hand sword. This was also true for the fully armored knight when fighting on foot. With no need for a shield, then a two-handed weapon was the most practical. While a staff weapon was impractical to carry on horseback, a two-handed sword could easily be strapped to the saddle. All of these weapons could deliver tremendous blows capable of crushing the new steel armor that was spreading across Europe.

The second was the development of new tactics and a new appreciation for infantry. The Scots Schiltroon and the Swiss pike phalanx both utilized the long 12 to 16 foot pike as their major

Reproduction two-handed sword. HRC64.

weapon. This would stop cold the charge of the knights and, once demoralized and in confusion, the men armed with shorter, crushing weapons, the aforesaid halberd or two-hand sword, could rush in and dispatch them. When pike formation fought pike formation, the two-hand sword was used to break the pikes of the opposing force. This use brought about a redesign in the two-hand sword.

Whereas the knightly fighting weapon was a big sword, shaped much the same as the smaller version, this weapon was different. The guards were quite large,

Parrying hooks on a two-hand sword.

sometimes as wide as 16 inches, often with steel rings on both sides as additional protection for the hand. The most unusual feature was the added parrying hooks that projected out from the blade about one foot or so below the guard. The hooks not only provided additional resistance from a blade cutting down the sword, but were the main protection for the hand when the sword was shortened. This was a favorite tactic when the fighting got to close quarters. The hand could be shifted to the unsharpened portion of the blade below the hooks, called the "ricasso," and thus the sword could be used for short cuts and as a short spear.

This was quite an impressive sword, and very popular with the Swiss and their arch foes, the German Landsknechts, in the later Middle Ages. These swords quickly spread throughout Europe and also became a favorite dueling weapon, and whole schools developed on the use of the two-hand sword in duels.

The soldiers that carried these swords in war were called "double pay" soldiers, and usually wore half armor. They were invariably big strong tough types. Although these swords are not as heavy as they look—most weigh between 6 and 8½ pounds—it still requires a strong man to swing and control the weapon for long periods of time. During the engagements of the pikes, their job was to rush between the lines of pikemen, and when they reached the front they were to swing and smash the pikes of the opposing line. You almost never sheared the tough oak or ash staff, but you could splinter and break them. Once the

A double pay soldier.

shaft splintered then the point became useless. Of course you can imagine what would happen should the Landsknechts send their double pay soldiers forward at the same time that the Swiss sent theirs! A brutal battle royal, between the two double pay units, huge swords flailing about and blood and limbs all over the place. Not the clean puncture wound of a pike, but a ghastly harvest of body parts, blood and brains. But then war has never been pretty, and as that Yankee general Sherman put it properly: "War is Hell!"

SWISS/GERMAN TWO-HANDERS

The designation "Swiss or German" is frequently used to denote the uncertainty of geographic origin, as well as a specific style of sword. This is a very large sword, often over 6 feet in length, with a wide crossguard, long grip, and a long ricasso that extends from 8 to 15 inches. At the end of the ricasso there are two large horns or parrying hooks that project toward the point of the blade. From here the blade proper extends to the point. The blade is usually about two inches wide, sometimes even wider. Often the blade was composed of a series of half circles and this type of sword was often referred to as a "flamberge." (Rapiers with these

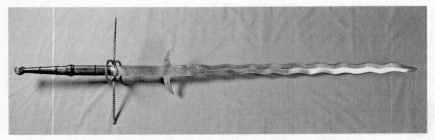

Reproduction two-handed flamberge. HRC66.

styles of blades were also at times called a flamberge. It was easy to distinguish the two once you saw them together.)

The weight of a sword depends on its size. A good plain fighting weapon for the ordinary soldier weighs about 7–9 pounds. But here confusion really starts. It also made a most impressive display when being carried by the guards of some noble or very rich person. To be even more impressive, some of them began to grow in size!

These bearing swords were not really intended for use. They were intended for display and ornamentation. It still took a big strong man to carry one, but he wasn't really expected to have to fight with it. So there are a lot of "bearing" swords found throughout Europe, about which more below.

But what about a sword made for a really big man? There is a common and mistaken belief that the soldier of the Middle Ages was quite small. Well, he wasn't a giant, but he also wasn't tiny, either. Full grown, the average guy was in the range of 5 feet 7 inches to 5 feet 10 inches. Henry VIII (1491–1547) was 6 feet 4 inches. Most of the German Landsknechts were big burly men, so it is in the realm of possibility that some of these big swords were actually used by big men. Remember, diet plays an important role in growth and they ate well then.

As you might have already expected, once the swords became popular for display, they also became popular for dueling. By the 16th century there were schools dedicated to the art of dueling and not only with the rapier, but with the hand-and-a-half sword, the halberd and the two-hand sword. There were fencing blades developed for both the hand-and-a-half (also known as "great sword" or "long sword"—names being much more variable then than they are now) and the two-hand sword.

Although over the years I have played and sparred with many types of swords and weapons, including halberds and pikes, the two-hand sword is one that I have been unable to play with. I've cut things with them, but have never been able to actually spar with a dummy two-hander that would behave like a real sword. The reason is weight. Even a padded staff that weighs 7 to 8 pounds will do a great deal of damage, and can possibly break bones or inflict some severe bruises. I have found that most people are quite reluctant to be hit with one, even in the pure pursuit of knowledge of real swordplay.

Swinging a real two-hand sword can give you an idea of how strong and tough some of these guys were. Of course, infantry walked most of the time, and they didn't have cars to use to run to the store, nor did they smoke or sit about watching TV. What I did learn was also how fearsome a weapon it could be in the hands of a strong man. The one drawback is that if you should miss, recovery can be time consuming. A full arm swing could brush aside a shield and crumple armor, including the guy inside it. When shortened with the hand grasping the ricasso it becomes a formidable short polearm. The very weight gives great authority to a thrust, making it hard to turn aside. Overall, I think I would prefer a halberd or a bill, but they do not look nearly as impressive.

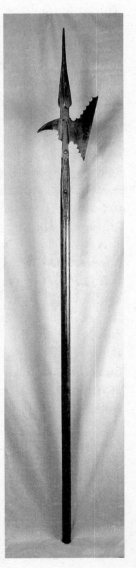

Like a halberd, the two-hand sword was rarely fully tempered. Only the Swiss were known to always temper their halberds, many of the others were forge tempered, or slack tempered. The same with the two-hander. The very size of the sword made full tempering difficult. Once the blade had been forged, and still while it was quite hot, it would be cooled, pulled out of the cooling medium, letting the residual heat build up, then cooled again. This is not as slipshod as you might think. A weapon that size, with that much mass, is quite destructive even it if wasn't tempered at all.

But there is another mystery about these two-hand swords. Why are there so many of them? They abound in private collections, museums all over Europe and the US and Canada have large numbers of these swords, and dealers have no problems in finding

Antique halberd, circa 1600, head 17.5 inches, with replaced shaft 91 inches long. HRC9.

them for sale. True, they are rather expensive nowadays, but they are still available. (I had a chance to buy a beautiful Swiss two hander in Zurich in 1957. But I didn't have the $150.00. I saved the whole time I was in Germany, finally got the money, and never was able to get back to Zurich before I rotated back home. One of the swords that got away.)

I can't say that this is the answer, but consider this. They were quite popular both for looks and for use, and they remained in use until well into the 17th century, even being in use during the Thirty Years War (1618–1648). There were a lot of fakes made during the Victorian period when collecting of arms and armor became a status game of rich people. These fakes are now difficult to distinguish from older swords unless you are really well versed in their identification. They may have been made in 1860, so now they have 150 years of time to age them even more!

There is one way that can help in distinguishing a Victorian copy from an original. Most all of the original swords I have seen have a ricasso that is thick, sometimes as much as ⅝ of an inch. Modern copies, and in these I include the Victorian copies, always have ricassos of the same thickness as the blade. It is simply too expensive to forge one in the old manner.

CLAYMORES

The Swiss/German style swords were not the only two-handers in use. This same period saw a rise in the use of other two-hand swords. Many of the other two-handers were quite effective, and they did not weigh as much as the big German types. Even the Swiss and the Landsknechts might carry one of these. These swords are quite varied, some are purely two-hand estocs, while others are pure cutting swords. In general, these swords reflect

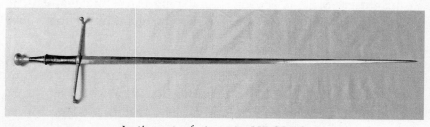

Antique tuck (estoc). HRC25C.

what you might consider the standard European sword, a broad slightly tapering double-edged blade.

The name "claymore" comes from the Gaelic, *claidheamh-mor*, and means "great sword." This has caused some confusion, as the term "claymore" is also used for the classic Scottish basket hilted sword. Sir Guy Laking, with no knowledge of Gaelic, proceeded to call the basket hilt "claybeg," meaning "little sword."

Claude Blair did an excellent article on this in the book *Scottish Weapons and Fortifications*. He showed that both weapons were referred to as "claymores" by the Scots themselves. Since it is a Scottish sword, and it is their language, I will abide by it. However, I will try to make it clear when I use the word "claymore" to which sword I am referring.

There were two varieties of two-hand claymores. One is the lowland variety, which is actually nothing but the standard two-hand sword: long blade, long grip and long straight crossguard, often with ring guards as well. But the classical Highland claymore is quite distinct. It has down sloping guards that end in quatrefoils. This seems to be typical of the Highlands, as older one-hand swords also have the down sloping guard.

A note of warning about the large claymore. This sword was romanticized in the 19th century. As a result, as with other two-handed swords, there were a large number of Victorian copies made. Now that over a hundred years have passed, it is difficult to tell which are actual originals and which are Victorian copies. I doubt if there are more than two dozen originals still in existence, but there are large numbers of copies.

It is easy to believe that these swords also had specialized uses and even "secret" techniques, but such was not the case. When used in single combat, they were used much the same way as the hand-and-a-half, or the "long" sword of the period. Often the blade was grasped and used to parry, sometimes to shorten for a strong thrust, or as is shown in the some of the old manuals, to actually strike with the pommel. The actual utility of that move I doubt rather strongly.

These regular size two-handers were lighter and could be moved with a lot of speed. They were also quite intimidating. Even a knight in full plate, when faced with a whistling sword that weighed between 5–7 pounds, knew that he had problems. A sword of that size, swung hard and fast, could deal a deadly

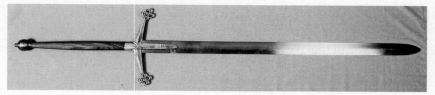

Reproduction two-hand claymore. HRC68.

blow even to a man in armor. True, it did not have the force of a halberd, but dead is dead, whether cleaved in twain or merely cut halfway through.

The two-hand claymore is not as impressive a weapon as the Swiss/German two-hand sword. It does not have the wide guards nor the parrying hooks. But it does have that quite distinct crossguard. Generally the guards are bronze or brass, and usually the pommel is a steel sphere. However, there were other metals and pommel shapes used. One thing always present is the distinct guard.

The origin of this guard is not fully known. There are a few Scottish medieval swords with down-sloping guards but none of them end in quatrefoils. All of these swords are single-handed swords.

Blade size varies, but all the others can be classed as two-hand weapons. Some of these are large swords, with blades up to 50 inches, while there are smaller versions with blades of 36 inches. I have heard that many preferred their sword pommel to reach eye level. But personally I think this is a modern idea. Certainly I have never seen it sourced anywhere but in someone's imagination.

Curiously, this is one of two swords that *was* actually carried on the back.

Hollywood is in love with warriors carrying their swords slung across their backs. There is a problem with this. If you have to draw the sword in a hurry, your arms—if you are human—are simply not long enough to draw a sword of any length. (In Ceylon, Sri Lanka, the ayda katti was worn slung on the back. But it has a blade only about 17–18 inches.)

The Scots never worried about this. The sword was in a scabbard, and the scabbard was slipped off of the back, belt and all, the sword drawn—then all hell would break loose. If the Scotsman won, then he had time to look for his scabbard, and if he lost . . . well, he didn't need it anyway.

This is a very effective sword. I have had a chance to play with a really superb copy that I had made several years ago. The blade is 41 inches and the guard is well over 17 inches. A young strong man can move and swing this with terrifying speed. The weapon is not designed for defensive work, but on the offense, it is scary.

Scotland always seemed to be about a hundred years behind the Continent when it came to weaponry. The two-hand claymore is recorded to have been used at Culloden Moor in 1745. It was a fearsome weapon for the Scots—but it just couldn't stand up to a loaded musket.

BEARING SWORDS & EXECUTIONER'S SWORDS

There was another development of the two-hand sword that really had nothing to do with war, and that was the bearing sword. These are often confused with fighting weapons, and have given rise to the fiction that two-hand swords were very heavy, since these bearing swords can weigh up to 15 pounds!

These are very big swords, with some exceeding 6 feet in length. But these are processional swords, and used only to impress the populace during parades, gatherings, civic investments, and at times to surround a person of high nobility. They were never intended for use, and frequently are not tempered.

There is an easy way to tell if the sword was intended to be used in battle. If you pick it up, and you think that if you were in shape to swing it, it would make a nice weapon, then it was a weapon. But if you pick it up, and wonder about someone so strong he could actually swing this, then it was never intended to be used.

There's another telling clue: if the sword was inscribed, and the inscription can only be read if the blade is held point up, then it is a bearing sword.

There is another two-hand sword used a great deal in Europe, and it has a less than savory reputation. That was the executioner's sword. This sword had a blade of roughly 30 inches in length, and was wide, usually about 2½ inches. The blades were flat, or a flattened oval in cross section, and never had fullers. The blade was never made with a point, instead it was cut straight across and often three holes were drilled close to the end, so that the sword could never be made into a fighting weapon. These swords are frequently engraved with gallows and wheels, and words like "justice" and "mercy." This method of execution was favored on the Continent, with the condemned having to kneel upright and hold his head up. Anne Boleyn requested a headsman from Europe when Henry VIII had her executed.

On that cheerful note we will leave the European Sector and go East.

Suggestions for further reading from Hank:

Blair, Claude, *Scottish Weapons and Fortifications 1100–1800.* John Donald Publishers Ltd., Edinburgh, 1981.

Suggestions for further reading from the editors:

Blair, Claude, *European Armour circa 1066–circa 1700.* B.T. Batsford, Ltd., London, 1958.

Ffoulkes, Charles J., *Inventory and Survey of the Armouries of the Tower of London, Vol. I.* His Majesty's Stationery Office, London, 1916.

► 10 ◄

The Katana and Other Japanese Swords

The sword that we call the katana was the primary sword of the Japanese warrior from roughly the 11th century on into the 20th century. Although the firearm was the principal weapon in modern times, many Japanese officers led charges with the katana during the Second World War.

Japanese officer's saber from World War II, 35 inches overall length. HRC323.

Prior to the 11th century the sword in use seems to have been a straight, single-edged blade with a curious down dropping pommel. Even as far back as this the sword seems to have been quite important to the Japanese. But little is known about this weapon, and we are more concerned with the katana.

The katana seems to have been developed sometime in what is known as the late Heian Period, which is usually listed as 1100–1230 AD. The early Heian Period, 794–1099 AD, obviously saw the beginnings of the katana, but exact information is not known. As you will find stated throughout this book, do not take these dates as hard and fast. These are merely reference points. I can assure you that at the end of 1099 AD (or whatever date the Japanese used), warriors did not say, "Okay, that's it. Throw away these boring old swords and take up these new ones."

The katana is a beautiful weapon, single-edged, two-handed, with a gently curving blade, and a point that is most distinctive. Instead of tapering to a point, the katana curves abruptly to its point. This curve is just as sharp as the body of the sword. This produces a point that is excellent for cutting, with no drag on the point at all, and yet, because of its sharpness, one that will penetrate in a thrust as well as a much more pointed weapon.

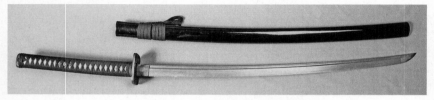

Reproduction katana. HRC105.

The Japanese sword—no, *all* Japanese weapons—are interesting and quite attractive. The Japanese sword alone has spawned many books, and one can devote a lifetime to its study and not know all there is to know. (Of course, that is true of weapons in general.) But to study the Japanese sword, you need a very good memory. The Japanese are fanatics about detail, and they have a name for every thing you can think of. Even the most minute detail of decoration will have its own name. This does have one advantage: a katana can be perfectly described and visualized by a person without ever having seen it. I have deliberately refrained from using the Japanese terms in this book. There are too many, and I don't feel the reader should have to have a translator to figure out what I am talking about. If the early Japanese had had beer bottles, and one had ever been broken and used in a brawl, they would then immediately decide on the technique for breaking the bottle, and how to get the properly jagged edge. And they would have had names for the different kinds of edges, strikes, and all of it.

The Japanese sword is one of the most studied in history. It is probably the most renowned, and certainly it is the most hyped. The tales told about the sword are many and varied, but all emphasize the incredible sharpness and power of the blade. And most are utter nonsense. The one that I have encountered the most often is that during WWII a Japanese officer cut a machine gun barrel in half with his sword. I was even consulted on an episode of the TV show *Mythbusters* about this. (I've often pointed out that it would have made more sense to cut down the gunner rather than the barrel, but that wouldn't have been as impressive). Several cousins of a person someone met, or some distant relative who also had it from a friend witnessed this incredible feat. It occurred on Guadalcanal, Bougainville, Iwo Jima or someplace in China.

But it just isn't true. The human body simply can't generate enough speed and force to slice through tough tempered steel. If you can generate enough speed, you can drive a straw through a telephone pole, but a straw is still a straw. Like the legend of the Saracen scimitar cutting through a floating silk handkerchief, it's really impressive, but it isn't true. You cannot generate enough force to cut through a machine gun barrel, nor can you get a blade sharp enough to slice through floating silk.

But don't let the reaction to the hype fool you. The Japanese sword is a superb sword even without the hype. Certainly no weapon in the history of man has had as much care, attention and love devoted to it as the Japanese katana. Old heirlooms are treasured and kept, and have been throughout the history of Japan. As a result there are swords extant that are over a thousand years old still capable of being used in combat.

I have had a chance to examine one of these rare treasures, and will relate the anecdote. I have to admit the anecdote is rather flattering. (If it were unflattering, I wouldn't mention it.)

Back in the mid 1970s, I was attending a weapons show with a close friend who is a knife maker, and can produce Damascus blades of exceptional beauty, toughness, and sharpness. While chatting with a dealer who had a few modern katanas, the subject of the old Japanese swords came up. It turns out that the dealer was also a collector and had just recently sold an old katana to the Japanese government for "over $150,000" and was delivering it that evening to their rep. The sword had been dated to the 13th century and authenticated to the name of the maker (which I have forgotten). He asked if I would like to see it, and I immediately agreed. From under the table he took out a box, opened it, unwrapped a sheathed sword and handed it to me. Not wishing to be gauche, I went through the usual formalities of unsheathing a sword, but as the sword started to clear the sheath I was unable to contain myself, and fully unsheathed the blade and held it in both hands.

Let me say up front that I am not a metaphysical type. I am a hard-nosed realist, and I don't believe in crystals, spirits or magic. I will, when frustrated, curse an inanimate object with great venom and originality, but I really don't think it works.

I held the sword in my hands, glanced around the show, and realized that I could cut down everyone in the place, and no one could stop me. I held the sword in my hands; I did not make any silly passes or poses or any of the nonsense that is designed to impress the onlookers. Instead I held the sword, and I felt a strange power course through my body. It was with great reluctance that I handed the sword back. Had I had $200,000 in my pocket I would have paid it even if it meant starving for months. Alas, I did not have the money. We continued talking, and he commented that my friend's Damascus knives were incredibly good, and shortly I took my leave.

At last I fully understood Ewart Oakeshott's comment about "a sword that woos you to strike!"

Shortly afterwards, the blacksmith friend (Jim Fikes of Jasper, Alabama) came back from talking to the collector, and he was laughing. I asked him what was so funny and he wanted to know what I did when I held the sword. I told him that I didn't do anything.

"Waal," he said in his Alabama drawl, "he said you had a touch of the samurai about you. I told him you *were* crazy as hell, and asked him what he meant. He said that when you picked up the sword, it looked like you thought you could cut down everyone here without any problem, and would really like to do it."

I hadn't realized it showed. . . .

But how good is the Japanese sword, and what is the truth about it?

The Japanese are a most meticulous people. A great deal of their handiwork is not merely excellent, but actually borders on genius. Metal serpents, with each scale articulated, birds of steel, with wings that hold whatever position you put them in, and so lifelike that you expect them to fly: in so many areas the handiwork is incredible.

So too with the sword. The Japanese sword makers created truly beautiful weapons, and it is easy to see why the Japanese sword was traditionally regarded as the "soul of the samurai."

HISTORY OF THE KATANA

A brief history of this sword is in order.

Early Japanese weapons were directly descended from swords from the mainland. We know this because there are many excavated swords that are very similar to Chinese swords of the same periods. Aside from the single-edged swords mentioned above, there are swords that are straight, with parallel double edges and a sharp point. Modern terminology would call them cut-and-thrust weapons, since they were capable of both. These early swords are of iron, and do not appear to have been of layered construction. However, I have not been able to find any reports of any metallurgical analysis of these blades in the various books and papers on these early swords.

While the Japanese will admit to the influence of China in the early blades, they feel that the later developments are strictly their own. This is particularly true in the manufacturing process (which we will deal with a little later in this chapter).

Sometime between 400–500 AD the Japanese increased the use of both horse and bow, eventually combining them to produce horse archers. This is a little strange, as the majority of Japan is quite mountainous. But there are central flatlands, and it is probably there that the Japanese horse archer developed. This adoption and reliance on the horse could easily have been a contributing factor toward the development of the katana. Regardless of how effective the horse archer is, there are times when combat comes down to swordplay, whether afoot or on horseback, and curved swords have been preferred by horsemen all over the world.

This is not to say that horse archers were the only force, but only that they were the dominant one. The spear was also used on horseback, not in the European mode of couching the lance, but rather in stabbing and cutting on both sides of the rider. But the horse archer was favored, and even today they still practice the art of the bow while on horseback.

The samurai class began to develop in the early Heian period.

The social forces that combined with both religious and economic forces are not fully known, and it is not in the province of this book to go into this type of detail. Suffice it to say that the samurai class developed into the upper crust of Japanese society, and remained that way until the 19th century. But do not think that all warriors were samurai, or that all samurai were warriors. This varied greatly both with time and location.

TYPES OF JAPANESE SWORDS

Japanese swords present a unique contrast when compared to European swords. Whereas the Europeans tried very many types and styles, straight single-edged, straight double-edged, curved cutting swords, thick butcher-type cleavers, wide and sharply tapering swords, slim thick bars of steel to punch through armor, and later, long thin rapiers, the Japanese adopted one type of sword and stuck with it. It is quite easy to see a sword and tell whether it is Japanese or not.

To the untrained Western eye, all Japanese swords look the same. One might notice that in some the grip is curved and the blade straighter, or that this blade has a little more curve than the other, but that is about all the average Westerner can tell. However, to the trained eye there are many differences, and many experts are stunned to hear someone say that they all look alike.

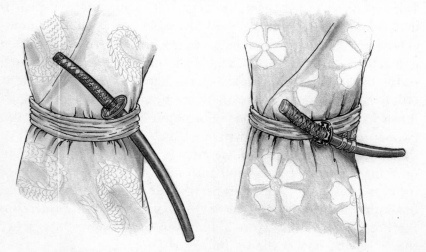

Samurai with katana (left) and samurai with tachi (right).

But then I have heard some say the same thing about Viking swords and later medieval ones.

The Japanese sword can be classified in two ways. When worn thrust through the waist sash with the edge up the sword is called a "katana." When strapped to the waist with the edge down it is called a "tachi."

Generally speaking, the tachi is usually longer, and often somewhat more curved than the katana. The usual katana has a blade length of about 27 inches, while the tachi has a blade length of 28 inches. But this is a most general statement, and meant only as a rough guide.

For instance, the great duelist Kojiro Sasaki had a katana about five feet overall, which he called his "clothes pole." He was a contemporary of the most famous Japanese duelist, Myamoto Musashi. Interestingly, I have encountered several versions of Sasaki's duel with Musashi. The most common version has Musashi arriving late to the island. He rows up to the island, out of the rising sun, with a very long oar on his shoulder. He then marches up to Sasaki, who cannot see the length of the oar, and promptly bashes Sasaki in the head. This was perfectly acceptable behavior in ancient Japan. It would appear that equal opportunity was not important as far as dueling was concerned.

Another important sword was the wakizashi. The wakizashi was a proportionately smaller katana, and made with the same painstaking and loving care that was lavished on its big brother. This was a short sword with a blade length of about 16–20 inches. In the later years, when worn with the katana, the two in combination were called "daisho." Only the samurai were allowed to wear the two swords.

The wakizashi was a very convenient item to have. In the low-ceiling rooms favored by the Japanese it was a formidable weapon. It was the custom for a samurai to remove his katana when entering a dwelling, but he continued to wear the wakizashi. In sudden

Reproduction wakizashi. HRC104.

encounters, the wakizashi could be quicker out of the scabbard, particularly when the action was close. Musashi, observing the Portugese play with sword and dagger, developed his famous two-sword school, with katana in his right hand, and the wakizashi in his left. (The Portugese first arrived in 1543.) This can be a formidable combination to face under any circumstances and, when the wielder happened to be Musashi, it was really bad.

Another formidable sword was the "odachi," or as some have it, the "no dachi." In the wonderful film *The Seven Samurai* this is the sword carried by the Toshiro Mifune character. It is a really long sword, and often they were wider than normal as well, sometimes as much as 1¾ of an inch. Sometimes these swords reached lengths of over 5 feet 6 inches. More about these in the following chapter.

There is one example of a double-edged katana, a very famous sword called "Little Crow." The blade is double-edged for about half its length. It was probably made in the 10th or 11th century. It is a beautiful sword, but the style never gained much favor. I feel that this could been due to two factors. One is that it would be more difficult to produce, and two, the steeper angle required by having two edges would affect some of its cutting power.

"*Little Crow*" *Japanese sword.*

PHYSIOLOGY AND SWORD DESIGN

To most Americans original katanas feel somewhat short for a two-handed sword. But the Japanese people were quite short back then. Most of their suits of armor are designed for people with a height range of 5 feet, rarely over 5 feet 2 inches. It is reported in several sources that Musashi was a giant of a man, right at 6 feet tall.

It is interesting to speculate on how much of their societal development was governed by the food supply. It seems that the food and the food supply not only influenced their politics, but their height as well. Modern Japanese are much taller, and before long will equal the height of the average Westerner. This is due to better quality and quantity of the food supply. I feel sure that many of their fighting techniques were governed by their size and agility. Studies of some of the armor indicate that the leg and arm length were slightly shorter in proportion to the torso than Western armor. This would cause a more closed fighting style, which is what I see in many forms of kendo and kenjutsu. With the average Japanese being more compact, with slightly shorter arms and legs, the movements are shorter and somewhat more controlled. This is why Westerners always look somewhat awkward and ungainly performing the katas associated with Japanese swordplay. In Western fencing, advances are made with strong positive movements of the front leg, usually the right, almost a kick and a stomp. The Japanese advance is just as quick, and maybe even quicker, but the foot is lifted only slightly and almost slid forward, so that the body seems to glide to the attack.

I feel that this is a subject that could use a lot more study. Is there an ideal way to attack and move based on body type? Leg length, arm length and the type of sword all would have to be considered and taken into account.

Another curious aspect of Japanese swordplay is their refusal to recognize right- and left-handed forms. All swordplay is taught with the right hand forward in a standard right-handed grip. This is the way it was taught, and if you wish to learn it, this is how you would learn it. It wasn't like you had a choice. I'm not sure that it would make much of a difference, either. Given the

A *suit of Japanese Late Edo period armor.* HRC540. Photo by Kenneth Jay Linsner.

nature of Japanese swordplay and the concepts behind it, you do not have some of the problems faced with sword and shield or with fencing.

With a sword and a shield, the blows from a left-handed fighter will fall on the unguarded side of a right-handed fighter. In fencing, the parries must be handled differently since the attacks are coming from a different angle, and you must always parry away from the body. With the katana, the basic attacks from left or right are received equally. In the sport of kendo, there are no attacks to the leg. Obviously this wasn't true in battle, as leg armor was worn. But in battle it was rare that two individuals would actually "duel," though this would happen before the battle was joined. Usually a battle was a madhouse of hacking and cutting anything that you had a chance to cut.

In individual dueling, the legs were not ignored as the formal rules would lead you to believe. This stems from the kendo teaching of ignoring a cut at the leg, and immediately cutting at the head. This technique works fine when the attack is being made with a bamboo sword, but when it is a real blade, then it's altogether different. In many respects this is similar to modern fencing practice, to attack and not guard, but to hit first. This works in sport, but in actual combat gets you killed quickly. One should always remember swordplay has a very strong Christian Principle: It's better to give than receive.

The early Japanese warriors loved the pomp and ceremony of battle, and each battle would begin with a large number of individual duels. Champions from each side would ride out and announce their heritage and standing, and challenge the champions from the other side. This type of challenge and response has been popular all over the world. It usually was initiated by a ritual verbal exchange, along the lines of "Your mother wears Army boots, your father sleeps with sheep, and I will rip your head off of your shoulders!" But the Japanese have always valued politeness, and I am sure that the exchanges were more of the, "I am so and so, and I would be greatly honored if you would be kind enough to shoot arrows at me, and I will undertake to do the same." But make no mistake, this politeness only slightly masked a homicidal intent. Such was the Japanese way for war from earliest records to the 13th century. But an event was about to happen that would make great changes in the Japanese world.

THE MONGOL INFLUENCE

In 1274 AD, Kublai Khan, grandson of the great Ghengis Khan, and Emperor of China, decided that he wished to conquer Japan. The Mongols were undoubtedly the world's finest horse archers. They were also highly disciplined and utterly ruthless warriors.

Kublai launched a fleet containing about 30,000 troops, mostly Mongols, with some Korean and Chinese auxiliaries. The first encounters between the Japanese and the Mongols were quite eye-opening and shocking for the Japanese. Used to individualistic forms of warfare, they were not prepared for unit combat. The samurai rode out, announced his heritage and challenged the individual Mongol to fight, and was promptly surrounded and stuck full of arrows fired by whole groups. The wholesale killing and use of terror was also unfamiliar to the samurai, and they were stunned by this. It just wasn't kosher.

But luck was on their side, and a great storm arose, tearing the Mongol ships from their moorings, sending the ships all over the sea, and consigning many of them to the bottom. With food and support gone, the invasion was effectively destroyed, and fewer than half of the Mongols returned home.

The Japanese were not stupid, and knew that an invasion could happen again, and made efforts to prepare for it. They were right.

In 1281 a much larger fleet appeared. This one was reported to have contained over 200,000 men. The Japanese opposed the landing, sent their own ships out, and there was a lot of fierce hand-to-hand combat aboard ships. The Mongols felt they owned the Earth, while the samurai, pugnacious to say the least, were fighting for their homeland. However, the Mongols were able to force a landing, and there matters stood for a day.

Meanwhile, all of the monks and monasteries and the common people had been praying like crazy for the gods to intervene. Something did. Whether it was the gods or just chance, I can't say, but during the night a mighty wind arose, and a truly terrible storm followed. This time the Mongol losses were much worse, with less than a third of the force reaching home. The Japanese mopped up the few left, and the *kami kaze*, the Divine Wind, saved Japan once again.

But the invasion had shown that much of their fighting style

was outdated. Many of their swords failed against the heavier
armor of the Mongols. As a result, swords became slightly heavier
and slightly wider.

A little over fifty years later, a civil war between the Ashikaga
and the Emperor Go-Daigo broke out. Most of these battles were
fought in mountains and wooded areas, where the horse archer
was not effective. The spear (yari), naginata and sword proved
their worth, and the bow was relegated to a less important role.

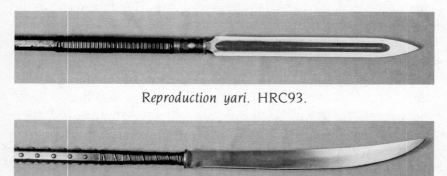

Reproduction yari. HRC93.

Reproduction naginata. HRC94.

The naginata was a polearm. It had a wide slightly curving blade,
and was quite destructive at about 7 feet in length. Another
polearm, the nagamaki, was essentially a long katana on a pole.
The blade was usually straighter than the naginata. The use of
the bow remained an important martial discipline, but not to the
degree that it had once been. Also a part of this decline was the
role of horses. Horses were expensive and hard to maintain in a
very mountainous country. Only the wealthy could afford them,
and only the wealthy had them.

After this, the spear, naginata and the sword became the principal
battle weapons, and as much care and skill went into the making
of the spear and naginata blade as did the sword. The Japanese
are rightly proud of the forging techniques used in making the
sword. I doubt if any other group of people took as much care
and time as the Japanese in the making of their swords.

HOW JAPANESE BLADES ARE MADE

Once a certain level of technology has been achieved, all sword makers are faced with universal problems: How to make a sword hard enough to cut effectively, without it being so brittle that it is liable to break with a hard blow? How to make sure that the steel is the same quality throughout the blade? This is particularly difficult when you remember that no one really knew why soft iron would turn into hard steel. Often hard steel blooms might be combined with softer iron, and the two would be combined into a single piece, which was then folded, flattened, refolded, etc. This would be done numerous times. Properly done, with a proper fire, this would result in a piece of steel which was homogenous in regards to carbon. This could be turned into a very hard sword, and tempered back, could produce a tough springy weapon. The Japanese carried their efforts a little further. This very hard steel could provide a core, with milder steel wrapped around it. When tempered, a very hard edge was produced, with a softer body that was capable of handling the shock of a hard blow.

But this wasn't the only method the Japanese sword makers used. At times the hard steel was sandwiched between softer metal, rather than being wrapped all the way around. At other times the soft steel would form the core of the blade, with hard steel wrapped on the outside. All sought to achieve the same thing: a very hard edge with a tough resilient body.

The tempering process was critical, and every smith had his own set of rules for it. In the West and in the East it might consist of saying so many prayers over the metal, or other ritual activities, such as washing the hands in a prescribed manner, actions that were unknowingly designed to produce the right amount of heat for the right amount of time.

The Japanese had an interesting method of obtaining the right edge hardness. They would coat the blades with clay. After the clay dried it would be scraped off of the edge in various patterns. The sword would then be heated and quenched. The coating of clay would delay the cooling of the body of the blade, but allow the edge to be cooled very quickly, thus making the edge much harder. The differential cooling also created a different color to the edge than the rest of the blade; this temper line was quite obvious and very beautiful when polished. The various patterns

Sword blade with temper line.
Hank used this sword to cut with at demonstrations. HRC15.

used in creating the temper line are there for a purpose. They are attempts to prevent any crack or chipping of the very hard edge from going up into the blade body. After all, it's rather easy to continue to fight when your sword blade is nicked. In the midst of a really hot fight, I don't think you would even notice a small nick. I wouldn't. But I can guarantee you that I would notice a broken sword. Frankly, I think I would be quite upset!

In part because of the temper line, Japanese swords have a distinctly different look to the blade than do European swords. But the most striking difference is due to the polishing process. In fact I cannot think of any sword that has the same beautiful sheen as does the katana. European blades were polished using buffing wheels and polishing compounds. Finer and finer grits were used until the desired finish was achieved. Sometimes this could be mirror finish, sometimes right below that, and, not infrequently, a very dull finish. After all, mirror polished blades show scratches quite easily. Mirror polishing literally consists of smearing the surface of the steel in such a way as to reflect light evenly. The Japanese took a completely different approach. They used stones for their polishing. The small stones, attached to the end of the fingers, created a surface that was quite flat. They did not smear the surface of the steel, but rather cut and smoothed the granular structure of the metal. This provides a truly beautiful finish, and it brings out the grain structure, and allows one to see the temper line clearly. Another aspect of sword polishing this way is that it actually sharpened the blade. Due to the cutting angle of the blade, when you polished completely, you also sharpened it. Swords were used only in battle and in duels, they were never, never used as merely a cutting instrument. Despite movies and books to the contrary, the samurai did not engage in deadly duels on a daily basis. The sword point was always sharp, and so were the thrusting weapons, the spear and naginata.

A word of caution here. Not all sword makers were good, not all sword makers were honest. Just because a katana is old does not make it a mystical sword, or even a very good one. In this it can be like a European sword. It can be very expensive, not because of its worth as a sword, but because of its age and maybe the name of the man who made it.

Japanese swords are usually quite sharp, and some of them are extremely sharp. This is achieved by very careful polishing and an almost non-existent cutting bevel. Most swords will have a wedge shape until very close to the edge, and then they will narrow abruptly. This produces a sharp edge, and the abrupt cutting bevel gives it strength. On many swords the cutting bevel is removed, and the resulting edge can be as sharp as the proverbial razor. This is a really terrible weapon when used against flesh and bone, and even padded armor, but it does have some problems when going up against some armor. The samurai were aware of this, and many battle swords were given an "appleseed" edge. This type of edge is popular today, and it is also called a "channel" edge, a "Moran" edge, or a "rolled edge." In this kind of edge the two flat sides of the blade are curved gently to the edge. This provides a very sharp edge, but one that is quite strong. (It was also used in China.) From the drawings you can see that the rolled edge and the abrupt cutting bevel are almost identical. With modern mechanized equipment a rolled edge is easy to attain. But without the use of modern equipment a rolled edge is somewhat harder to achieve.

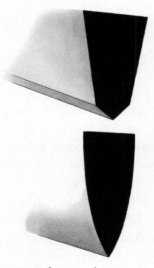

An *abrupt edge* (top) and an *appleseed* or *rolled edge* (bottom).

BLADE VS. ARMOR

But how effective was the new appleseed edge on a katana or tachi against Japanese armor? Well, remember not all armor was uniform. One thing that must be kept in mind is that the richest warriors got the best armor. For all of you egalitarians, I'm sorry, but that simply is the way it was.

In general, Japanese armor was lighter and more flexible than European plate armor. It was usually of lamellar construction and, although single steel plate breastplates were known, they were rarely used. Leather lamellae were not infrequent in Japanese armor. Leather, properly hardened and lacquered, is a pretty tough substance. It can resist a sword blow fairly well; not as well as steel, but then it is lighter and not as expensive as steel. Mail was also used. Japanese mail can follow the normal international mail pattern, but it also has many variations, with some being connected and frequently using double rings of butted mail. As the old saying goes, "you makes your choice and you takes your chances!"

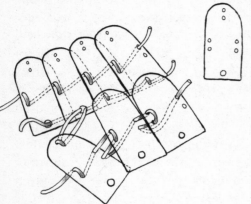

Lamellar armor construction.

A katana with a rolled edge could cut mail if the blow was solid and square on. One that strikes at an angle is likely to skate or slide off. It is unlikely that a katana could cut through a steel plate, but that also depends on the thickness of the plate itself.

There are a few paintings that show a helmet being split by a katana. While I will grant the possibility, I will also add that it is highly unlikely. I have only examined a few original Japanese helmets. As with most metal helmets across the world, one of the helmets I examined had quite thin plates, but I was unable to determine if the plates had been tempered hard. If not, it would be possible to cut through. There was one that had to be close to ⅛ inch in thickness, and there was no way that anyone was going to cut through that helmet. These were the two extremes that I have been able to actually pick up and look at. The remainder fall between these two. It might be possible to cut *into* the helmet, but not through the helmet.

Since the samurai did not carry a shield, he relied on the armor for protection. Since he did not carry a shield, he was able to use both hands on the sword, and also to train to hit specific points on the armor that were areas of weakness. These areas of weakness would vary with the style of armor, but a warrior would be able to see them immediately. This might consist of an area protected only by mail, or a gap between sections of armor.

Remember also that the katana, while primarily a cutting sword, still has a very effective point, a point that could penetrate mail and possibly even thin plate. Certainly I have done this, and have seen other demonstrations of the effectiveness of this rounded and/or angled point.

There are good indications that after the Mongol invasions, the Japanese made their swords slightly heavier. The Khan's army was known to be heavily armored, and such armor would be more resistant to sword blows. Whether admitted or not, the two invasion attempts were quite scary for the Japanese, and they made every effort to see that they would come out on top if it happened again.

Combat without armor is a different issue entirely.

COMBAT WITHOUT ARMOR

"Kendo" is the Japanese version of fencing. Proper kendo requires the attacker to call the target: wrist, throat, etc. The calling of the target is to sharpen the reflexes, and to put you in mind that you are fighting an armored warrior. Cuts to the leg are not used, as they are considered invalid in the use of the katana, as mentioned earlier.

Whereas European fencing contains attacks, blocks, parries, counterattacks and deceptive moves, and some nice sneaky tricks as well as set-up moves, Japanese fencing has very few of these. They do have their blocks and parries and deceptive moves, but the essence of combat is lightning swift strikes and full commitment to the attack. When two trained and competent samurai fought, the duel was quite brief. Movie fights, which show cut and parry, cut and parry, and all sorts of fancy and acrobatic moves, are there to entertain and to forward the plot of the movie. The reality was a quick and bloody fight. Very quick, and quite, quite, bloody.

The Japanese were great ones for testing their swords, but the way they did it would not be politically correct in today's world.

One of the favorite methods was testing it on the bodies of the dead. The head was removed, and various cuts were made on the body to ascertain the cutting ability of the sword. There are written instructions on how to position the body for the various cuts. There were special handles for the swords, and specialists who did the cutting. Curiously, they would not do this if the body was tattooed. I have no idea why, but I have a feeling that had I lived in those times I would have been quite heavily tattooed.

If that method of testing your sword strikes you as a little strange, you ain't heard nothing yet. Testing on live criminals was rather common. There are instructions and drawings as to how the criminal is to be held for which particular cut. In *The Sword and the Same* the author tells of the chapters in the Yamada School of Tameshigiri. How to catch a live man and cut him through, how to position the body for various cuts: all rather straightforward, if rather unpleasant. Simple beheadings were not done. No, there were diagonal cuts to the left and right, horizontal cuts across the chest and abdomen, and even one across the hips.

There is the story of the puppet master who entertained by day and stole by night. When he was caught he was condemned to death. When he saw the executioner approaching with a sword, he asked him if he was going to test the blade on him. When told that he was, he replied. "That is too cruel, to test a sword on a living man."

"Nevertheless, that is what is going to happen," the executioner responded.

The prisoner answered, "If I had known this, I would have swallowed some rocks and ruined your fine sword."

No further comment is mentioned.

Some of the samurai had a disconcerting habit of testing their swords on simple peasants who happened to be passing by at the wrong moment. Frankly, I think that this is a little much. But nevertheless, it happened, and it happened more than once. There is the tale of the martial arts master who noticed a samurai lying in wait. He suddenly turned several back flips. As the samurai stared in astonishment, the master thumbed his nose at the samurai, and went about his business. But it wasn't just peasants. Sometimes the samurai made a mistake. The story is told of the master sword polisher who was found dead one morning. He'd been cut down by a samurai who was testing his sword. It created quite a stir, and I'm sure that the samurai were lectured and told to be more careful.

Not all of the Japanese approved of these practices. Many Japanese were opposed to this, and protested quite vigorously. After all, this is not a type of behavior that will win hearts and minds and influence people.

For those of you who wish to pursue the study of Japanese warriors and weapons, I have listed some books below. For a broad overview of feudal Japan there is no better book than *Secrets of the Samurai*. Don't let the title fool you. This is a scholarly work filled with vital information. It also contains some of the finest line drawings I have seen. I cannot recommend it highly enough.

Suggestions for further reading from Hank:

Bottomley, I. & A.P. Hopson, *Arms and Armor of the Samurai: The History of Weaponry in Ancient Japan.* Crescent Books, New York, 1988.

Hakuseki, Arai, translated by Henri L. Joly and Inado Hogitaro, *The Sword Book in Honcho Gunkiko and the Book of the Same Ko Hi Sei Gi.* Holland Press, London, 1913.

Joly, Henri L., *Japanese Sword Fittings.* Holland Press, London, 1912.

Knutsen, Roald M., *Japanese Polearms.* Holland Press, London, 1963.

Nagayama, Kokan, translated by Kenji Mishini, *The Connoisseur's Book of Japanese Swords.* Kodansha International, Tokyo, 1997.

Ratti, Oscar and Adele Westbrook, *Secrets of the Samurai: The Martial Arts of Feudal Japan.* Castle Books, Edison, 1973.

Robinson, H. Russell, *Japanese Arms and Armor.* Crown Publishing, New York, 1969.

Sato, Kanzan, translated and adapted by Joe Earle, *The Japanese Sword.* Kodansha International and Shibundo, Tokyo and New York, 1983.

Sinclaire, Clive, *Samurai: The Weapons and Spirit of the Japanese Warrior* The Lyons Press, Guilford. First published 2001.

Turnbull, Stephen, *Battles of the Samurai.* Arms and Armour Press, London, 1987.

▶ 11 ◀

Eastern
Two-Handed Swords

JAPANESE SWORDS

In the Far East there is always some confusion about what constitutes a two-hand sword. The Japanese katana is almost always used with two hands, but is essentially a single-handed sword. Although the medieval Japanese were quite small in stature, usually in the area of 5 feet 2 inches, the katana is certainly light enough to be used easily with one hand.

The great Japanese swordsman Miyamoto Musashi (1584–1645), perfected his two-sword school, using the short waskazashi in one hand and the katana in the other. So you can see that even then it was known that the katana was not a true two-hand sword.

However, the Japanese did have a true two-hander, and it was quite a ferocious weapon! This was the no dachi, as mentioned in the previous chapter. The sword shape is the same as the katana; it is just really big, with an overall length of from five-and-a-half feet to well over six feet in length. It was carried in a scabbard, but never worn, just carried. The scabbard was thrown aside when the action started, and like the Scots and others, the feeling was that you could always find the scabbard if you survived, and if you didn't, who cared?

I have read of a sword in a Japanese museum that is so large that the owner needed a companion to help him unsheathe the sword! I don't think that qualifies as a two hand-sword, but rather as a two-*man* sword.

The Japanese referred to these swords as "field swords," or usually, "horse killing swords." Certainly they would be big enough to kill a horse and rider if it hit the two right. Both names strike me as pretty accurate. Certainly in the wild melee and confusion of battle, a large cutting sword could be most effective. There are reports of these swords with blades over 4 feet in length and grips of 3 feet! That is seven feet of sword! These are pure battle swords, and from what I have been able to gather, there was no real "technique" in using them, other than swinging hard and fast.

What I find interesting, and have never been able to get information on, is the forging and tempering of these swords. I have been able to examine two of these swords, both in the area of six feet in length, and the blades were as attractive and well finished as any of the old katanas. The temper line on both swords was a soft wave pattern, and was quite distinct. Both were quite beautiful. Obviously these were not cheap, readymade swords, but had been well made, and to even my untrained eye, made for a high-ranking individual.

Curiously, the Japanese never seemed to have used hand-held shields. They have shields, what the Europeans would have called mantlets or pavises, upright shields for archers to protect them from enemy arrows. Even in the proto-historic age of Japan the warriors seem to have developed armor more and excluded the shield. This would explain their devotion to the two-handed weapon.

CHINESE SWORDS

The Chinese were not reluctant to use shields, both for their foot soldiers and their cavalry. As a result, they had many one-handed swords, both sabers and what is now referred to as the "tai chi" sword. But a large number of their swords have grips that were easily long enough for two hands, but were light enough for use with one hand. Unfortunately there has not been a serious detailed study of Chinese edged weapons. This is a shame as many of their swords are quite beautiful.

Original Chinese late Qing dynasty sword,
31.5 inches overall length. HRC553.

After the Boxer Rebellion in the early 19th century, many Chinese swords were brought back to the US and Great Britain. These are wide-bladed swords with almost no point, but terrific cutting weapons. With a two-hand grip they have the power of a good hefty axe when they connect. There is some confusion with Chinese names for these blades, which happens with a language as complex as Chinese and with so many dialects. Over here they are frequently referred to as "war swords."

Chinese beheading swords were always two-handed, and were much larger than the European version. The average is a very large and scary sword. The total length was often about five feet, evenly split between blade and handle. I had one many years ago, and in holding it you could easily see that it was only good for a downward blow, and far too clumsy to be a fighting sword.

KOREAN SWORDS

One of the most ignored swords of the area is the Korean sword. Now, I do not think anyone can say for sure whether the Japanese influenced the Koreans, or the Koreans influenced the Japanese, and they seem to argue about it incessantly. But the two swords are very close and hard to tell apart.

The Korean sword usually has a smaller tsuba (guard) and the blade is often slightly less curved than the katana. Each has devoted adherents and each country had many schools of sword play (and still has a few). The katana has so dominated the modern sword scene that the Korean sword is either ignored or considered just another katana. This is another sword that I would like to see studied more thoroughly.

INDIAN SWORDS

India made and used two-handed swords, but not to a great degree. Since the left hand was often used to carry the shield, two-handed swords were fairly rare. But they were used, and are rather strange looking swords. Not at all like you might expect, given the Indian preference for the curved sword. These are straight, double-edged swords with a blade well over 2½ feet in length, and a handle length about 20 inches. What is curious about these swords is that

Indopersian shield, circa 1850. HRC534.

the grip is often separated with two additional pommels that create three grip sections. This allows you to extend the sword's length, and also to close up on it and use it as a shorter weapon. These globular pommels are usually fluted brass and are brazed to hollow steel grips. A common practice in India was to put a small pointed knife into these hollow pommels.

The Nagas of Assam, located in the eastern part of India, had two-handed swords that were also somewhat strange. These were slightly shorter, generally about 4 feet total length, with blade lengths just over 2 feet. The grip was divided into two sections, each with a crossguard. The blades were slightly curved, single-edged, with good sharp points. The Nagas are considered an aboriginal race and their swords were rather primitive in construction and not near as finely made as most of the Indian metalwork of the period.

There is a lot of discussion regarding two-handed swords among sword nuts. Is a two-hander better than a sword and shield? Which

Curved Indo-Persian talwar, circa 1850,
33.5 inches overall length. HRC509.

is the best sword—katana, Swiss/German two-hander, etc.? This is one of those endless arguments. In this day and age of .45s and .223s it may be foolish, but it sure is fun.

Assam two-handed sword.

Antique Indopersian helmet,
circa 1850. HRC525.

Suggestions for further reading from the editors:

LaRocca, Donald J., et al., *Warriors of the Himalayas: Rediscovering the Arms and Armor of Tibet.* The Metropolitan Museum of Art, Yale University Press, New Haven, 2006.

Rawson, P.S., *The Indian Sword.* Arco Publishing Company, New York, 1969.

➤ 12 ◄

Exotic Blades

AFRICAN SWORDS

Properly this subject needs to be dealt with in two sections; North African and sub-Saharan African. Although there is some overlap both in weapons and geography, there is enough of a distinct difference to warrant this.

North African work is frequently confused with work from Arabia, but this should not be so. Prior to the conquest of North Africa by the Arabs, and the destruction of the Christian societies, there was a lot of European influence and many of the weapons in use were of common shape with European blades. These were generally long straight swords, with some of the more curiously shaped Egyptian weapons still around. The actual knowledge of these swords, from written and excavated sources, is quite spotty.

You will often hear that the swords used in parts of North Africa—the Sudan, Ethiopia, Somalia, etc.—are not only descended from the sword of the Crusaders, but that many are even actual Crusader blades. This is sheer nonsense,

African musele short sword, 20 inches overall length. HRC555.

and arose from the erroneous concept that all Near Eastern swords were curved. Although curved swords were known and used at times, the vast majority of Near Eastern blades were straight and double-edged. The Arabs carried large double-edged straight swords, sometimes quite long, and this was the primary sword in use during the Arabic expansion under Mohammed and his immediate successors. It was not until the influx into the Middle East of horse archers from the steppes of Central Asia in the 13th century that the curved sword became popular, eventually just about completely replacing the older straight sword. (Arab weapons will be dealt with later in another section.) [Editor's note: Hank never got a chance to write that section, even though those swords were some of his favorites.]

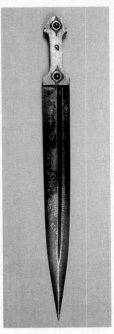

Islamic sword, quaddara, 22.5 inches overall length. HRC517.

One of the most curious of swords is the flissa used by the Kabyle Berbers. There have been many suggestions as to the origin of this sword, from the Egyptian kopesh to the Turkish yataghan. Although it bears some resemblance to the yataghan, it strikes me as being a very inferior weapon.

The sword is quite long, with a straight single-edged blade that is about 36–39 inches in length. The sword does not have any form of crossguard, is frequently octagonal in shape, and has a small rear projection to secure the hand. Although the blade is straight, the edge undulates slightly, and ends in a very long point. The point is so long that it almost forbids the use of this sword

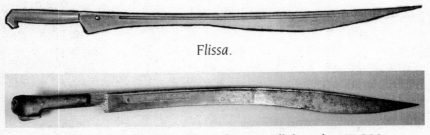

Flissa.

Yataghan, circa 1800, 33 inches overall length. HRC32.

for cutting and it appears that this sword is much more suited to thrusting. Whether it was actually used in this fashion I can't say. I've only handled two of them, and both were originals and I was unable to actually play and cut with them. But from this brief association I left with the opinion that the sword was ill balanced for thrusting, and not very efficient as a cutting weapon, with a great likelihood of usage bending the point. I would also advise the reader that I could be mistaken in this, and that it is an opinion formed by only a brief association.

The time span of this sword in North Africa is simply not known. There is no mention of it until quite late, sometime in the 19th century. It is obvious that the sword was in use before this, but there are no other references that I have been able to find.

Another sword, the nimcha, is believed to be of Arabic origin, but was very popular in North Africa. This sword is best described by the hilt rather than the blade. The hilt is wood, with a rear projection that is large and offers firm support for the hand. The guard is composed of two forward projecting quillons, top and bottom of the blade, and another quillon that turns back into a knuckle bow. The blade is always single-edged, and usually slightly curved. However, I have seen these swords with straight blades. As is to be expected, many of these swords are made with European blades.

These swords appear to be quite effective whether used on horseback, camelback or afoot. Although not having a counterweight in the pommel, these swords are not quite as heavy as many European cavalry swords and the few I've handled gave a favorable impression.

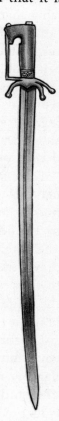

Nimcha.

THE KUKRI

The western world learned of the Gurkhas in the late 18th-early 19th century. Some fifty-odd years previous, the tiny state of Gorkha, located in the Kathmandu valley, had started on a war of conquest that eventually led to the formation of the nation of

Nepalese kukri,
16 inches overall
length. HRC545.

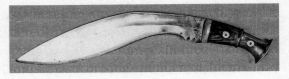

Nepal. The first king, Prithwi Narayan, was a fierce and brutal ruler, and his descendents were not much different.

Smaller tribes, towns and villages were assimilated, and inevitably that brought the Gurkhas in contact with the British East India Company. War was declared in 1814, and there were two years of bitter conflict before the British were able to enforce a peace on the warlike Gurkhas.

By this time the main battle sword of the Gurkhas had been replaced by firearms. Granted that those who could not afford them used spears and swords, but the majority used firearms, and with a telling effect. But they also carried another weapon that inspired fear in all who faced it: the kukri.

Basically a jungle work knife, the kukri also made a superb fighting weapon. The forward angled blade gave it great cutting power; in combat the edge could be used for thrusting merely by turning the wrist and allowing the blade to enter sideways. The single edge allowed the blade to be gripped and used as a drawknife and with the back of the blade being held rather than the grip, a surprising amount of fine work could be done with the knife. The Gurkhas, being inventive, also kept a very small knife, a file, and a bit of fire-starting punk on the sheath.

Of course the fighting ability of the Gurkhas was the main contributing factor to the awe in which the kukri was held. A fighting race, they have maintained their ability and reputation even today, as witness the wave of fear generated when they embarked for the Falkland Islands to battle Argentina. And they still carry the kukri. . . .

But where did the kukri come from, and why is it such an effective cutting instrument?

The origin of the forward-angled blade (for such is the technical term for the kukri) has been lost in dim recesses of prehistory. The first of these blades show up in Greece as early as 500 BC. Some are found in the Caucasus only slightly later, about 400 BC. The Iberian Celts were using them at least by 400 BC if not before.

The term most used for the forward-angled blade is "kopis," which is used to describe the Greek sword, and is derived from the Egyptian word "kopesh." It is not clear if this relationship is purely linguistic, or if there was a real relationship between the actual swords.

Many describe the Egyptian kopesh as the original of these blades. However, this is one opinion that I totally disagree with, for several reasons. The term "kopesh" is used for several blades with different shapes, not just the forward-angled one. The most common shape for a kopesh is that of a sickle, with the blade sharpened on the inside edge. However, there are others where the edge is on the outside curve, and several where the sword is double-edged! One version is simply a wide-curved blade, handle offset, and sharpened on the belly of the curve. Most telling, though, is that the cutting action of all of these swords is completely different from the cutting action of the kukri-shaped blade. (We will examine that cutting action below.)

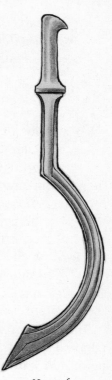

Kopesh.

So, if not derived from the Egyptian curved swords, where does the kukri come from? Now this is pure conjecture, but here is one suggestion as to how this very effective shape was discovered. Once, while studying some bronze swords, I ran across a leaf-shaped blade that had been badly battered in use. One edge was heavily dented and broken, and the whole blade had been bent near the waist of the sword. The other edge, although not nearly as damaged, had definitely seen service. Consider a blade badly damaged on one edge, but the other still in good shape. The sword was turned in the hand, and suddenly it cuts even better! Perhaps this was how some undocumented warrior created this short, effective fighting knife.

We do have archeological evidence that the forward-angled blade, called variously the kopis, the falcata, and the machera, was used quite successfully in Europe for several hundred years between about 300 BC to about 200 AD. It is very probably the weapon that caused the reinforcement of the brow on the Roman helmet.

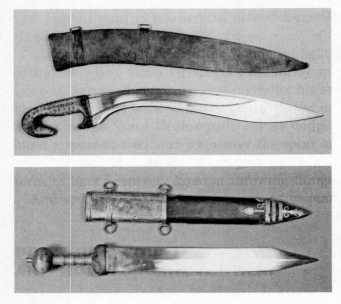

Reproduction falcata. HRC360.

Reproduction gladius. HRC198.

The Romans were impressed by the Iberian Celts, and quickly adopted one of their swords, a waisted short sword with a long point that was then known as the gladius Hispanicus. They did not adopt the falcata, as it was used in a fashion that was not suitable for the Roman soldier. The falcata was mainly a chopping weapon, although it could be used for thrusting. The shorter gladius was a stabbing weapon that could be used for cutting. This was much more in keeping with the Roman idea of tactics. However, it is believed that Scipio Africanus armed his cavalry with the falcata, and this weapon was used extensively by the Roman cavalry until replaced by the longer spatha around 200 AD.

Both the kopis and the falcata were much bigger than the average kukri. The kukri is basically a 10–13 inch knife, while both of these are swords, with an average blade length of about 20–23 inches.

It is easy to assume that the kukri shape arrived in India via Alexander the Great, and his conquest, which stopped at the Indus River. While this is a reasonable conjecture, it may not be the case at all. There is no evidence to support a direct Greek influence, and it had been used in Western Europe many hundreds of years before the shape shows up in India.

Information on early Indian swords is not readily available, but there are rock carvings, drawings, paintings, writings, and a very few archeological finds. None of these show a forward-angled blade until about 400 AD. After this period they appear quite frequently, and indeed, seem to actually proliferate, driving out many of the older, straight-bladed swords that were previously used. We do know that there was a lot of contact between Rome and the Deccan area of India, and it seems logical that the Romans introduced it there.

Once introduced to the subcontinent, the Indians adopted it as their own, and did so with a great deal of imagination. The forward-angled shape was tried for so many swords that we don't have room to show all of them. Indeed, many of them were not practical fighting tools, but they sure did look mean.

The forward-angled blade made its way throughout India as one warlike tribe after another adopted the shape, and through conquest spread it farther and farther afield. We do not know the early history of Nepal, nor do we know the weapons they used. Early art plus a few archeological finds indicate that they used the leaf-shaped short sword a great deal, plus the Chinese straight sword. There is no evidence that the Nepalese used the curved sword. Sometime well after the 10th century AD, the

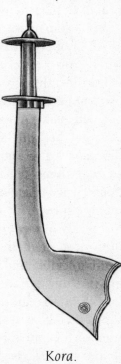

forward-angled blade appears. The primary weapon of the early Gurkhas and the other warlike tribes in the area was the kora. This was a sword, length ranging from 18 to 28 inches, with the blade sharpened on the inside edge. The tip curved forward and flared out and down. Although completely useless for a thrust, the power in the cut was awesome! However, technology invaded and the firearm assumed the place of principal weapon. The kukri, which had many uses, was kept as the kora was discarded.

The kukri has since become the national weapon of Nepal, and particularly the Gurkhas. But the Indians were the first to use the kukri and in the Royal Nepali Museum, almost all of the old kukris are of Indian workmanship. Actually there are very few old kukris in the museum, and the oldest only dates to about 1750 AD. It is identical

Kora.

Nepalese kukri,
18.5 inches overall length.
HRC42.

to the kukri shown in the photo here which, judging from the design and manufacture, I feel dates from about 1750–1800 AD.

One of the more interesting, and amusing, aspects of the kukri is the notch at the base of the blade. It's amusing, because even the Gurkhas don't know for sure its exact meaning. The notch is of two cut out semicircles side by side, leaving a small projection. It has been described as intended to catch the opponent's blade (a sure way to lose a hand should it be attempted), a symbol of the female sex organ designed to give the blade power, a representation of a cow's udder (Gorkha—old spelling—means "Protector of Cows"), or the Trident of Shiva the Destroyer. No one really knows, so feel free to choose whichever you like. I know which I prefer.

But what makes this blade so effective?

All chopping weapons have an optimal striking point, the area where the greatest force is generated with the least amount of vibration. The sweet spot on a kukri is extremely large, in fact just about the entire blade is the sweet spot. The same depth of cut will result if the blade hits close to the front of the knife or close to the back. Only at the extreme front is there a noticeable difference. The forward-angled blade helps dampen the vibration, so that there is no energy lost in the blow, but it also arrives quicker, so that you get the effect of "cutting through" without much effort. With a wrist snap just as the blade hits, much more force can be generated than most realize, enough to lop off the limb of a small tree or a small man.

All warriors and soldiers need to be familiar with their weapons before they are effective with them. The same is true with the kukri. In the mountains of Nepal, the Gurkha grows up using the kukri, and he also grows up with a warrior tradition. His weapon becomes part of himself.

The old kukris were handmade. There were several styles that

The three basic forms of the kukri:

a) the Sirupate kukri favored by the Limbu tribe,

b) the Bhujpore style favored by the Rais,

c) the standard kukri favored by the other tribes.

were popular. The Limbu tribe favored the Sirupate kukri that has a blade somewhat long in relation to its width. The Rais prefer the Bhujpore style, which has a wider blade, while the Gurungs, Thapas and Magars prefer what could be called the standard kukri.

But no two old kukris are alike. (The only kukris that are identical are those issued by the various countries that employ Gurkhas: Great Britain, India and Nepal.) Original kukris are as individual as the *kami* (the village kukri maker/blacksmith) who made them, and many of them are works of art. The knives were frequently given as gifts to officers and high-ranking people who happen to please one of the ruling classes of Gurkhas. These can be very elaborate, with ivory or silver grips and mounts, and beautiful, highly polished blades.

One of the more interesting tales about the kukri is the trouble the British ran into once they had established a presence, and then a railroad in Nepal. All too frequently the track was stolen. The English couldn't figure why, until it was realized that this is an excellent source of steel, and the kami did not have to worry about purifying the iron.

The history of the kukri is very long, and in this chapter I could only cover the basics. I wish it were only possible to go back in time and see its development. Since this is not possible, I will have to be content with speculation. I've been playing with the kukri for over fifty years, and I still am fascinated with it. And it's still my knife of choice on a lengthy trip in the wilds.

Suggestions for further reading from the editors:

Burton, Richard F., *The Book of the Sword*, originally published 1884, reprinted by Dover Publications, New York, 1987. *For his discussion of the kopesh.*

Farwell, Byron, *The Gurkhas,* W.W. Norton & Co., New York, 1984. *A good popular history of the Gurkhas.*

Haider, Syed Zafar, *Islamic Arms and Armour of Muslim India.* Bahadur Publishers, Lahore, 1991.

Rawson, P.S., *The Indian Sword*, Arco Publishing Company, New York, 1968.

Reid, William, *A History of Arms*, Barnes & Noble Books, New York, 1997, first published in Sweden 1976.

► 13 ◄

Basics of Cutting

The cutting power and the mystique of swords has been a much misunderstood subject for quite some time. The desire of the warrior, from whatever culture, for a sword that will not break, bend, nick, or get dull and that will cut steel, is easily understandable. Alas, such a blade only exists in myth and legend. Charlemagne had Joyuese, Roland had Durandel, there was the Viking sword Tyrfing, that could do all of the above, and the sword Quernbiter, that cut a millstone in half with one blow.

I confess that I would also like such a blade. But steel is still steel, and is subject to the same strains and stresses of any other piece of metal. Some of the strains can be lessened by the addition of various trace elements, but they all have limits. Some will be better than others, but none will be magic.

It should be noted that knowing how to cut with a sword does not mean you know how to fight with one. Knowing how to fight with one does not mean you know how to cut. Cutting with the sword is not nearly as easy as it looks. But it certainly isn't as hard as many would have you think. We live in a world of Hype. Everything is made out to be much greater than it is, much harder than it is, more important than it is. In short, just about everything in this society is hyped a great deal. I can't change that, but what I can do is give you the facts about cutting with the sword.

Although cutting with a sword, and doing it well, requires some basic skills, the main part of any cutting is the sword itself, and the working part of the sword is the edge. The basic geometry of the blade is also important, as curved blades have different cutting potential than straight blades.

I don't wish to be particularly bloody, but it should be noted that the purpose of the sword was to cut flesh and bone. Now, most people are rather reluctant to be cut, so they immediately started to try to protect themselves with armor. Thus was begun an arms race, as sword makers tried to make swords that would cut through the armor, while people continued to be stubborn and made thicker and better armor.

The edge of a sword must have support, and it must also have mass to give force to the blow. This mass is achieved by the width or the thickness of the sword blade. A thin, flat sword blade will cut quite well, but there are other things that have to be taken into consideration.

Anyone can swing a sword, and anything struck with a sharp edge is going to be damaged. How much damage depends on the sharpness of the steel, the mass of the sword, the speed and precision of the blow, and the ability of the man swinging the sword.

Let me switch over to something that is much closer to swinging a sword than you might think: carpentry. No, I'm not talking of building a house, but of driving a nail. I have known and seen carpenters who could set a nail with one tap, and then drive it home with two more. That was something that I couldn't do. I was able a few times to drive it home in three, but not often.*

---

*I used to work as a framer back in the day, and all the guys on my crew (including myself) could drive a 2½ inch spike home with one hit of the hammer. It took very good timing—you held the spike with your off hand, and swung the hammer, letting go at the precise moment (hence the good timing). Before the spike fell over, you drove it home with a single blow. A framer's hammer has a long handle, so centrifugal force did most of the work, but dexterity and timing was crucial. Speed was important because time was money for the contractor, so using this method, we could pound a dozen nails in as many seconds. I'm proud to say that I never once hit my hand with my hammer. This skill actually translated well when I became an armorer; my dexterity was developed to the point where I can hit the same spot the size of a pinhead a hundred times in a hundred tries.   —Peter Fuller

Now these carpenters were not big brutes. Most were not as big as I am, or was at the time. Nor were they stronger—but they knew how to hit. The force of the blow was concentrated to gain maximum force on the head of the nail. This concentration of force can also be done with the sword.

How well can a sword cut? How do you practice? Is it necessary?

I will attempt to answer all of these questions in this chapter.

HOW DIFFERENT SWORDS CUT

Curved swords, particularly those with deep curves, are very effective in the drawcut. The drawcut is essentially a slice, with the blade being drawn across the material. This will produce a long and deep cut in flesh, but is not very effective against many forms of armor.

Swords with more shallow curves, such as the katana, are still quite effective in the drawcut, but are also effective in a slash or chop. One of the most effective cutting strokes with the katana is the hard cut with a slight drawing motion. This is the motion generally used in cutting through people as well as tatami mats.

Straight swords can be quite effective in slashing and hacking cuts. They do not do drawcuts very well. However, they do have the added advantage of being capable of effective stabbing or thrusting.

The rapier is primarily a thrusting weapon. Although there were attempts to make the point and the cut equally effective, none worked very well. When attempts were made to increase the cutting power, either the point or the weight was changed, which also changed the characteristics of the sword.

A quick look at some cutting swords is in order.

Until the early 10th century, Viking swords were broad-bladed swords, usually about 2 inches wide and about 32 inches long and usually pattern welded. There was almost no taper to the blade, and the point was generally somewhat rounded. After the early 10th century all-steel swords began to appear, and usually these swords had a slight taper to the blade. This put more weight in the hand, and allowed the sword to be quicker in both strikes and returns, and yet did not sacrifice cutting power. The point was still somewhat round.

Generally speaking, European swords were not quite as sharp as many of the Eastern swords, particularly the Japanese katana. This reflects the type of combat more than anything else. Although mail was not worn at times, shield and helmet were the two most common methods of defense. A sword with a thin razor edge simply wouldn't last very long when used to strike mail or a tough wooden shield with a metal boss and rim.

In today's time, three edges are often used for katanas. The "battle" edge, the "social" edge, and the "competition edge." The latter one is used for cutting competitions on tatami mats, bamboo, etc. The thinner edge allows the swords to cut better. However, it is not as strong as the other two.

Middle Eastern swords, such as the shamshir, the yataghan, the talwar and kilij, have edges very similar to European blades. This is because mail was worn a great deal, and although the mail was lighter than the normal European mail, it was still iron or steel.

PHYSICS OF CUTTING

Simple laws of physics will tell you that the greater the speed, the more force generated. The greater the mass, ditto. Combine the two and you can get impressive results. But there are limits to each of these, and these limits are set by the human body. There is only so much speed that can be generated, and only so much mass that the muscles can handle. The effective sword is a combination of these factors plus edge, blade geometry, the individual swinging it, and—one that everyone seems to forget—the item being cut.

It is generally agreed that the best blade angle for a knife edge is approximately 17 degrees, and this would also be true for most swords. This allows you to cut flesh and bone without doing damage to the sword when the cut is properly made. Should you be required to cut something that is reinforced, say with leather, heavy clothing, or mail, you need a thicker edge. The most effective of this type of edge, as discussed in the chapter on katanas, is referred to variously as an "appleseed," a "channel," a "rounded," or today, a "Moran edge," in honor of Bill Moran, the noted knife maker. This edge has the cutting bevel rounded, and gives a lot of strength to the edge of the sword. A chisel edge is also effective, but the minute shoulders, small as they may be, still offer some drag to the penetration of the blade.

For demonstration purposes, many swords will have thinner edges, which allow them to cut more smoothly. Remember that the cut is a wedge in action, and the material cut must slide over the blade unless there is tension pulling the cut material apart. This means that any raised surface on the blade will offer some resistance.

An appleseed edge (top) and a chisel edge (bottom).

From a purely practical standpoint, those swords with raised central ribs are just as effective a weapon as a flat-bladed sword. The rib will make it stiffer in a thrust, and while it will offer resistance to cutting deeper, you can still cut several inches into the body, and that's enough to discourage most people.

For modern competition purposes, some swords are made with very sharp, and also thin, edges. This makes them devastating in cutting through bamboo and tatami mats. Frankly, they would also be quite devastating against an unarmored opponent as well. Just do not plan on trying to cut mail or armor with one.

TYPES OF CUT

In my own mind I have always differentiated various types of cut. A blow that is straight down, whether used with one or two hands, I have always considered a crushing cut, and can easily be called a "chop." A slashing cut is one that is designed to go through an object (whether it does or not) so that you are in a position to counter or continue the cut in a different direction. A "pushcut" is a cut where the sword is pushed forward on the blow, acting as a slice, whereas a "drawcut" is when the sword is pulled back from the object in a "drawing" motion. There is also the "snapping cut" where the blade is thrust forward and then the edge is snapped to the target.

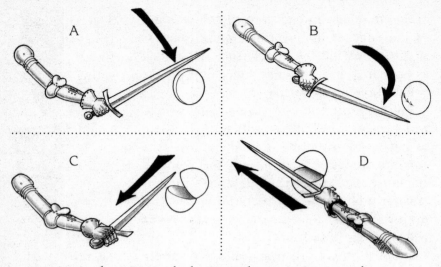

A) A *chop*. B) A *slash*. C) A *drawcut*. D) A *pushcut*.

While the terms "drawcut" and "pushcut" are terms in common usage, chopping and slashing are somewhat arbitrary terms that I use for my own understanding. These are not to be taken as hard and fast settled terminology.

A drawcut is quite interesting. In real swordplay with the katana it was quite popular. As the blow is made and connects, the arms do not follow the straight downward path with which the blow was launched. Instead they are drawn back across the body, thus adding a slicing motion to the blow. This is very effective against flesh and bone, less so against armor. But it is not only effective for increasing the power and the depth of the cut, it is also effective in returning the sword to an attacking or defensive position.

This drawing motion was also popular in the Near East. The

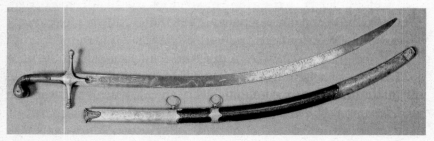

Antique shamshir, circa 1800, 36 inches overall length. HRC39.

Persian shamsir, which is a rather late sword, was designed with the drawcut in mind. It has been correctly stated that the shape of this sword gives you the longest possible cut when the arm and wrist is used in the most natural motion.* This seems to imply a strange and different form of swordplay. Regretfully this is one area that I have been unable to follow up or to figure out how it might have been used. I do feel that it was different than Western saber fighting.

It has been said that the drawcut was unknown to the West. I find this hard to believe. The West has also struck me as being preeminent in the various ways to kill one's fellow man, so I doubt that it was not known. It may not have been *used* much, but not unknown.

The pushcut was used, but it is not as effective as the drawcut. In the pushcut, the edge is pushed forward when contact is made. Due to the mechanics of striking, the force available is not the same as the drawcut. Better control and somewhat more power can be delivered in the drawcut than in the pushcut.

The slashing cut is just as it is called, a slash. The direction of the blow can be diagonal, and either up or down. This is a simple cut where there is no action of the blade in a slicing motion. This is probably the most common blow used in swordplay.

The chopping type of cut is one that is primarily used in a downward stroke. Although it is possible to strike this way in a horizontal motion, downward is preferred, as it allows a great deal more force. This is the type of blow one might aim at a helmeted head, where force is very necessary to do damage.

SECRETS OF CUTTING

You will hear of the "secrets" of learning to cut. As far as I've been able to ascertain, there is only one "secret" to the art of cutting well. *The edge of the blade must be perfectly aligned with the direction of the blow.* If the edge is misaligned even one to two degrees, the cut will not be effective. Interestingly enough, in many of the Icelandic sagas you will hear of swords that fail to

---

* Stone, George Cameron, *A Glossary of the Construction, Decoration and Use of Arms and Armor.* Jack Brussel, Publisher, New York, 1961.

"bite." This is attributed to sorcery usually, but sometimes the reason is that it is a poor blade. I suspect that often it was grip that had turned, or an edge that was misaligned. Edge misalignment is all too easy to achieve. Merely sharpening the sword on one side only can cause this.

Another problem is the failure of the grip to be aligned with the edge. This is also a problem that can occur easily. The wood of the grip can gather a lot of moisture from sweating and the atmosphere, and then when it dries it can shift position very slightly. This will throw off the alignment.

I cannot stress the importance of this enough. Failure can result in two things, both bad. One, you can ruin a really fine sword by cutting and having the edge not hit properly. If it fails to cut into the object, then all of the energy generated is transferred to the front of the blade, and the sudden force can cause it to bend. Second is more embarrassing: the sword slips, and the cut you make is lousy. This is really bad when giving a demonstration. I've had it happen and it upset me

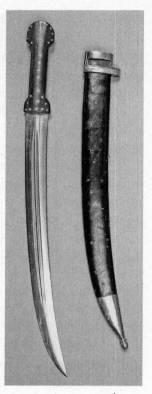

Antique sword with oval grip, Caucasian kindjal, 25 inches overall length. HRC551.

and the audience. In retrospect, I think the audience was more upset when I fell on the floor screaming, kicking my feet, and then holding my breath. Rather than repeat this embarrassing episode, I now always try to make sure the sword I cut with is properly aligned.

As you can see, the grip of the sword must indicate the location of the edge. Most European grips are oval, with the long axis in the plane of the edge. There are many Middle Eastern swords with boxlike grips, with the long axis at right angles to the plane of the blade. This

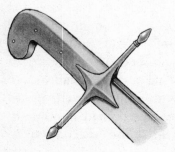

A kilij with box grip.

Modern mace. HRC50.

is very true with many kilij, shamshirs and kindjals. This is not hard to get used to, and there is no chance of mistaking the edge, for then you can easily see you are holding it wrong. The worst is a round grip. This will not tell you where the edge is, and it can easily turn in the hand. Al-Kindi, in the Arabic work on the sword, warns against this, and rightly so. So always beware of a round grip. It's okay on a mace, but not on a sword.

HOW TO PRACTICE CUTTING

To begin practice I would suggest tapping a piece of balsa wood to make sure you are holding the sword correctly and hitting the edge squarely. Balsa, being quite soft, will register the cut, and you can see if one side is indented more than the other.

Before going into the physical mechanics of cutting, let's look at what is available for cutting. The Japanese use a reed mat for cutting practice. These mats come in various sizes and can be purchased from several companies. These mats are soaked in water for a specified time, allowed to drain for a period, then cut. Sometimes a wooden dowel is inserted to represent bone.

Since starting Museum Replicas, Ltd., I have used cardboard tubes in my cutting. The ones I use at present are the cores for large paper rolls. They have a wall thickness of about a quarter inch. They are tough, but not too difficult to cut. Still, I would caution everyone in cutting cardboard. Do not use a highly polished sword, or a blade whose finish you value. Small bits of silica are common in cardboard, and they will scratch the blade. I use blades with a satin finish, which I prefer, and they rarely show any scratches. But a highly polished blade is likely to be marred by the cut.

One item that is quite tricky to cut is a kid's toy plastic tube. These are long tubes of plastic foam, and are popular toys around swimming pools. They have almost no rigidity, and the sword has to be quite sharp to cut cleanly. It also has to be moving fast. A slow cut or a dull blade will cause the tube to bend or the cut to change direction as the tube bends under the impact.

I have often heard complaints about swords being damaged when cutting into trees. Swords were made to hack the limbs of men, not the limbs of trees. For that you can use an axe or a tough machete, but not the usual European or Japanese sword. Small saplings can be used. I don't recommend it, but they can be used. Nothing over two inches in diameter should be attempted. Soft pine is preferred, and try to avoid all hardwoods. Live saplings are much like bone: when alive they are relatively easy to cut, but when they dry out, become quite tough.

Rolled newspaper is an excellent cutting material. It is cheap, plentiful, and its level of difficulty can easily be adjusted by the size of the roll attempted. Each individual will have to adjust the roll to his ability and the difficulty desired. A very loose roll, and the paper will likely bend as it's being cut, and will usually tear. The tighter the roll, the harder it is to cut, so that you can make a very tight and very large roll, and no one can cut it. Since it is so cheap, I would suggest experimenting until you find the right combination. I always used masking or cellophane tape to keep the roll together. Depending on the thickness of the roll, you can use small cans or tubes to put the paper in, and this usually works just fine.

Newspaper has one advantage over other materials. It is easy to tell just how sharp the sword is. Once you have cut through the roll, examine the two sections. If the sword is full sharp, you will not see any tears on the edges. Even a good sharp sword will usually tear the last couple of sheets of paper, so it takes a *really* sharp sword not to leave any tear (and also a very good cut).

SAFETY

Let's quickly get into some safe practices here. No, I am not a politically correct namby pamby type. But—I have a very good friend, an expert with knife, axe and sword. While he was cutting one day the axe flew out of his hand, straight at my head. I moved aside, but had I not seen it, or been a little less quick, it could have been right unpleasant. (No, he didn't do it on purpose. I know because I owed him money at the time.)

So, first, when attempting to cut through something, make sure you know what is on the other side. It's very similar to shooting a pistol. You need to know where the sword is going to end up. Having someone watch who is standing just a bit too close can be quite messy, and really hard to explain to the police.

Second, always have a loop around the sword and your wrist. Losing your sword while in the midst of a cut makes you look really silly and incompetent. It can also be dangerous. But even if no one is there but you, you will still feel silly and incompetent. After all, Conan never lost his sword.

Third, when cutting in front of an audience, always cut with the audience in front of you, with your sword ending up pointing in the opposite direction. Gasps of awe at your performance are much better than gasps of fear while ducking flying swords.

STANCE

In any martial art what you need first is a firm foundation. Therefore it follows that the stance is of great importance. (I am given to bad puns. No, I'm not sorry.) When delivering a strong solid blow, it is necessary for you to have your feet firmly planted, and to be able to put your whole body into the blow. The exact spread and position of the feet will vary from person to person,

Cutting with a katana.

but above all, you must be comfortable. Later you will learn to cut with the arms alone, but that is in the future.

For example, when cutting with a katana, the whole body will move. The arms and shoulders start the action. While the body bends forward at the midsection, the knees bend slightly as well as the hips. The whole force of the body is put into the blow, and as your blade encounters the object to be cut, the arms, shoulders, and even the hips will rotate slightly back and down so that the blade is pulled through. The force generated by this action can be quite awesome.

Very similar movements will also be done with European blades, both one- and two-handed weapons. Unless the sword is slightly curved, the drawing movement is not used. Although it will work, it will not work quite as well.

Would you get an opportunity to actually use this movement in a real fight with swords? Suppose you were transported back into time, could you use this technique then, and would it work? Sure it would work, but you probably wouldn't get a chance to use it in a real fight. Real fights were quick, and that is why you also need to learn how to lash out with just arm power and still inflict a deadly cut.

I have to confess, there is another secret. That secret is practice. Like most human endeavors, the more you do something, the better you will be at it.

HOW TO PRACTICE

My suggestion is to first use rolled newspapers. (I use the *Wall Street Journal*, as it is heavy reading, and not frothy like many newspapers.) Start with a roll about 1¾ inches in diameter, and of medium tightness. Roll it so that the folded sides are on the outside. Once the roll is completed, use some tape and tape the edges about every 5 inches. If you roll the paper along the long dimension, you should be able to get about 4 cuts per roll. Stand the roll upright, and proceed to cut. The tube can be secured several ways; I often use a small soup can and add some padding to make the tube fit tightly.

If you like a katana, then practice this cut to start with. The drawcut utilizes the whole body, and while it is slightly more difficult to learn, once you have mastered it, other cuts are easier.

Remember the drawing motion. The whole body properly moves when the cut is made. Whatever the results of your first cut, it will improve with practice.

The snapping cut is also a move that works very well with a katana. It is not particularly impressive in any sort of demonstration, but it worked pretty well in combat, and you can score points with it in a tournament with padded weapons.

The sword is held overhead and the blow is made. As the leading arm comes down (usually the right), the other hand snaps the grip up. This forces the blade of the sword down quickly, adding both speed and force to the cut. A slight variation to this move is having the sword held before you in a guard position. Rather than raising or lifting the arms, the arms are extended quickly. The right wrist snaps down at the same time the left arm lifts the grip. This snaps the blade down. While the force is not near the same as a full cut, it is sufficient to cause a great deal of damage in an actual fight.

Hank cutting mats.
Photo by Peter Fuller.

This type of cut is also quite useful in learning exactly where your edge is. By learning this cut, and learning to stop the right arm at a specific point in space, you can then learn to cut precisely.

Both the drawcut and the snap cut can be used with one-handed swords. The drawcut works better with a curved blade, but even a straight European-style knightly sword can be used.

The trick of the drawcut is much the same as with the katana. The cut is made, and while the blade is in motion, the wrist is firm, and the blade is drawn back toward the body. The snap cut is quite useful with the single-handed sword. Using it, a blow with considerable power can be generated. As with any full power cut, the cut draws on the power of the body as well as that of the arm. As the arm descends, just before the blade makes contact, the wrist is snapped forward. This extra speed generates a surprising amount of force, and its use can enable you to make a strong cut using only the force of the arm and shoulder.

There is another aspect that has to be mentioned. Anytime you are making a strong cut at a specific object, your concentration should be on cutting past the object. It is easy to concentrate on the object, and what usually happens is that your arm stops close to the surface. But if you look past the object, you will cut through it. This is just like throwing a punch—it is thrown through the opponent.

This section is not designed to be an end-all treatise on cutting. Hopefully, it will give you something of the basics. You can practice on your own, and then if you so desire, seek some professional instruction.

Suggestions for further reading from Hank:

Hoyland, Robert G. and Brian Gilmour, *Medieval Islamic Swords and Swordmaking: Kindi's Treatise "On Swords and their kinds"* (edition, translation and commentary). The E.J.W. Gibb Memorial Trust, Oxford, 2006.

Suggestions for further reading from the editors:

Anglo, Sydney, *The Martial Arts of Renaissance Europe*. Yale University Press, New Haven, 2000.

Waldman, John, *Hafted Weapons of Medieval and Renaissance Europe*. Brill Academic Publishers, 2005.

Williams, Alan, *The Knight and the Blast Furnace: A History of the Metallurgy of Armour in the Middle Ages & and the Early Modern Period*. Brill Academic Publishers, 2003.

Fighting with the Sword

Although I cannot imagine being interested in swords without also being interested in the combat potential of each weapon, some people feel differently. In a conversation with Ewart Oakeshott, he mentioned a well known sword authority (who shall remain nameless) who commented that he wasn't interested in the blades of swords at all, but only in their hilts! This was someone who had held many old and splendid blades in his hands, and who never once thought of them as weapons? Now, I do believe that he said it, I just don't think that he meant it. Possibly he was embarrassed that a man of his standing still held a sword and thought of "Raw, Red War!" After all, war isn't considered a pleasant subject and these days it is thought crass to say you find the subject interesting or exciting.

But like it or not, good, bad, but never indifferent, swords were weapons, made for young men to use when killing other young men. No matter what is thought, no matter what euphemisms are used, this is the basic fact. They are weapons, and how they could be used as weapons depends on many things.

It is undoubtedly presumptuous and may even be insolent for me to write on fighting with the sword. I have never led a charge of cavalry, or a Viking raid on England, nor stood in the front ranks of a Roman legion. I never stood in a shield wall screaming my defiance at the enemy or, I might blushingly admit, never fought a duel with either katana or rapier. But I did grow up in the 1940s and '50s, when schoolyard fights and barroom brawls were considered part of growing up, and I've had my share of those types of encounters.

And I have over the years played at fighting with a large number of people. In the late 1960s I was lucky enough to locate some other sword nuts who lived close by, and we spent a lot of time sparring and getting bruised. There was time spent in the Society for Creative Anachronism, as well as studying various fight manuals from Europe, Japan and China. Over the intervening years this research has taken many forms. I have cut into pork shoulder bones, armor of all types, other swords, tatami mats, newspapers, and many more items. In addition, I've studied a lot of literary material, medieval and Viking sagas, archeological reports, and spoken with curators, police officers and wound experts.

So I do have some firm opinions regarding swords and sword use. The strongest is very simple. There are no experts in this field. It is simply too varied, with too many different types of swords, too many geographical areas, and entirely too much of a time frame in which these weapons were used. I am not an expert by any means, and what follows are my own opinions.

How well this minor amount of knowledge relates to fighting with swords it is difficult to say. Many of the things you will find in this section will apply to real sword fights with real weapons and with real serious intent to harm. But it also applies to many other types of contests, not only physical, but mental as well.

But one thing it has taught me is that in actual combat, things do not go as predicted in manuals and instructional books. Even today, what happens in a barroom brawl is not quite the same as what occurs in the dojo. It has often been said that all battle plans go astray the moment the first shot is fired, and I believe that is true in all forms of combat.

There is something else that must be emphasized. A full scale battle was completely different than a planned duel, or a chance encounter, or even being attacked by footpads. And each encounter would always be different from any other encounter. Whether you were an English longbow man, a Swiss pikeman, a samurai or a French knight, whether you had fought in battle once or twice before, or if this was your fifth or sixth encounter, each battle was different.

This is also true for individual duels; each was an encounter within itself, and while experience is always helpful, what worked in the past might not work now.

In today's society there is an unconscious assumption that all people are the same. There is also the belief that all men feel and think as we do, with the same basic values. This is simply not true. For an example, how many men, having accidentally committed a severe breach of etiquette, would commit suicide as a way of expiation? None in our current society, but it was quite common in medieval Japan.

We live in a society that places a high value on human life, but sadly places very little value on the concept of honor. In the past a man would die to uphold his honor, and now honor is considered a rather outmoded concept. To say that you would rather die on your feet than live on your knees is a comment that brings out snickers in many sections of our society.

But this book isn't about social ills or changes, it's about swords. I do feel that it is very important to understand that what is considered proper today does not apply to other times and places.

I have often been asked about how you fight with swords. Usually I try to answer this question by asking what sword they are talking about and in what context. By the time they puzzle out what they want to know, I'm no longer around. It isn't that I am reluctant to talk about the use of swords, or to share what little knowledge I may have, but rather many persons do not actually know what they are asking.

It should also be noted that most of this section will deal with combat between individuals. Actual battles are another thing entirely. As strategy may win a war, tactics may win a battle. This section is not about either. In my opinion each battle was a thing unto itself. Even those that appear similar, such as the battles of Cannae and Adrianople, are different. In each the Romans were surrounded and crushed together so tightly they were unable to use their weapons, and many actually smothered to death. If a time traveler could actually take part in each battle he would find that each had its own flavor, if you will, each its own feel and ambience. Of course this is also true of individual encounters. No two will ever be exactly alike; if they were, they would be easy to prepare for.

Another facet that has to be mentioned is the difference between real combat and simple contests. Although in the past "swordplay" and "sword fighting" meant the same thing; in this chapter I will be using them differently. "Swordplay" means just what it says, play with swords. There is a vast difference between the play and fighting. Since it is highly unlikely that any of us will ever have to actually fight with swords we can only guess at the effectiveness of the training.

Miyamoto Musashi's excellent *Book of Five Rings* deals with many things, but the essence of the book can be distilled down to a simple phrase, "The object is to cut your enemy." Of course Musashi is not the only one to set this out. All of the European masters have said the same thing. Your object is to win. While this is true in war, in contests there are rules. These rules are there for many reasons, but when you enter into these contests, you have agreed to play by the rules. If you dislike them, then you have two options: you can lobby to have them changed, or you cannot play. To play and try to "game" the system or to circumvent the rules or to actually cheat is, in my opinion, dishonorable. In a contest I would rather lose with honor than win by cheating. However, in actual combat I can assure you that I would do whatever I can to make sure that I walk away while my enemy doesn't.

Now kind reader, if you will put up with my long winded comments, I will try to tell you some things that I know, some things that I suspect, and then you can figure out what you may have garnered from this and your own experiences.

PHYSICAL CONDITIONING FOR SWORDPLAY

Obviously physical condition is important, but in certain circumstances that pales beside the need to just have a physical body there. An example is the Battle of Visby, a battle that has already shown up in this book. Many of the skeletons unearthed were of older people, and many had been crippled in the past, either by

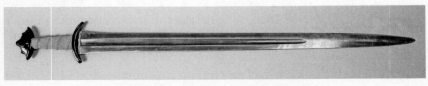

Reproduction Viking sword. HRC19.

disease, accident or combat. But when the Danes invaded, the city needed all the help it could get, and so they called on everyone who could bear a weapon. A lot of the skeletons were of young men, and this was probably their first, and last, combat.

We consider physical conditioning very important and there are countless gyms and dojos in this country promoting it. And well they should, for this is very important to your physical well being. But consider why they have to. We have cars, TV, radio, movies, enormous quantities of food, and huge amounts of leisure time to enjoy all of these "benefits" of this society. After all, we only work about 40 hours per week, and in some countries, it is only 35–37 hours per week.

But before the onset of the industrial revolution these benefits were not available. You walked or rode a horse. A few of the very wealthy rode in carriages, but they too had to walk. In short, these people may have suffered from more diseases and injuries than we do, but for overall condition, the ability to keep going, to suffer hardships and continue and yet still survive, they were much stronger and tougher than we are. I can remember when I was young, and a product of the city. Even though I was something of an athlete, wrestling, running, lifting weights, boxing, and so on, there were young farm boys who had not done any exercises but were at least as tough and strong, and quite formidable.

Consider this. Archery is a sport that I dearly love. (Regrettably, I am also lousy at it.) In my youth I shot a heavy bow, an 86-pound Kodiac Magnum from Bear. I was the only one I knew who could pull it. Today many shoot "heavy" bows, compound bows with draw weights of 90 and 100 pounds, yet with *holding* weights of only 45–50 pounds.

Consider the bows taken from the *Mary Rose* (a ship of Henry VIII that was sunk in 1545, and recovered several years ago). Experts went over the bows, and while there were a few that drew only about 80 pounds, many had draw weights of about 125 pounds, and one or two whose estimated draw weights were about 160 pounds. The Mongol bows are believed to have draw weights quite similar to these. Certainly the recurve will outshoot a longbow pound for pound in draw weights. Some scientific tests done about twenty years ago showed that a recurved composite bow of the type used by the horse archers of Central Asia can discharge an arrow roughly 20 percent faster than a longbow of

Antique German stiletto circa 1600, 15 inches overall length. HRC35.

the same draw weight. The recurve also has a slight mechanical advantage due to the angle of the string to the nock. This makes it somewhat easier to draw.

Now, I am aware that these archers learned their craft from an early age. But it also reflects the fact that in their society they were merely archers, and not noted strong men.

But now back to combat with swords and other hand weapons.

As has been stated elsewhere in this book, the Icelandic sagas are an excellent source of information for fighting with sword and shield and combat in general. One thing that I found interesting is the number of encounters between groups of men. More often than not they talk of several people fighting, with men from the opposing sides merely looking on. Then suddenly one will start to fight, while another, having severely wounded or even killed his opponent will take a break. Rarely do we hear of everyone fighting at one time. I found this curious until a TV documentary on gang fights in various parts of the country reminded me of my own youth, when I witnessed several fights between groups. They were the same as was shown on TV, and the same as many of the fights described in the sagas.

Several guys would be fighting, while others looked on. Then one would jump in, beat on someone, then jump back out of the fight, posture a bit, and sometimes go back in, and others just wait. It also looked a great deal like chimps involved in a raid, particularly the posturing.

In *Njal's Saga*—there were lots of fights recorded in *Njal's Saga*—Gunnar, Hjort and Kolskegg are involved in such a melee. They are attacked by a group of men led by Starkad. Gunnar defends himself with his bow and kills several from a distance when Starkad decides that if they stay within range of that bow they are in deep trouble, so they press the attack quickly. Then Gunnar drops his bow, and grabs a sword and halberd. Kolskegg was armed with sword and shield. Bork and Thorkel ran toward them. Bork swung at Gunnar, who parried so hard with his halberd that the sword flew from Bork's grasp. Then Gunnar pivoted and cut Thorkel on the neck with his sword so hard that he cut Thorkel's head off. Kol Egilsson said, "Let's attack Kolskegg," and lunged at him with a spear. Kolskegg had just killed somebody and was caught off guard. The spear hit the outside of Kolskegg's thigh and cut it deeply. Kolskegg whirled, swung his sword and cut off Kol's leg. "Did that one handed?" asked Kol. "That's what I get for not having my shield with me," he continued, as he stood on one leg, looking down at the stump. "It's just like you think, the leg's off," was the reply from Kolskegg.

When Egil, Kol's father, saw his son die, he then attacked Gunnar. Gunnar countered with his halberd, stuck it through Egil's stomach and threw him into the river. Thorir, an Easterner (i.e. Norwegian), had been standing somewhat idly by and Starkad called him a coward. This angered him. He jumped up and attacked Hjort (who had already killed two men), stabbing him in the chest, which killed him instantly. Gunnar saw this and attacked the Easterner. With one swipe of his halberd Gunnar cut him in two at the waist. Then Gunnar threw the halberd at Bork, sending it right through him and pinning him to the ground. Kolskegg cut off Egilsson's head and then Gunnar sliced off Ottar Egilsson's forearm. All in all, not a good fight to even be standing around near.

Although I have no way of proving this, I feel that in many battles much the same thing took place. You would fight in the line, then slip back and take a break before continuing the conflict. This is provided that your line is holding; once it broke, most ran like hell. Wasn't a question of cowardice, more like running from a dam that has broken.

Single combat is where skill is the most important. And we will deal with the physical requirement first. Specific conditioning is something that must be left up to the individuals and to their choice of weapons. What I have heard from the many people I have talked to over the years is that most want to be proficient with many types of

Reproduction spetum. HRC253.

swords, daggers, staff weapons and spears. Obviously sparring and practicing with these weapons is a necessity, and this will also help somewhat in the cardio conditioning, and a small amount in the muscle conditioning. But more is needed in both aerobic and anaerobic conditioning.

For the modern practitioner of swordplay, a strong heart and lungs is a must. Being able to move quickly on your feet is also a plus, and these can both be attained by various exercises. Doing the type of swordplay you enjoy is certainly one of the ways you can increase your endurance. However, this should be supplemented by running, stair climbing, duck walks or even the old football exercise of high stepping through squares. Cardiovascular conditioning has another advantage—it's also healthy.

Strong wrists and forearms are also needed. The ability to snap the sword forward quickly is valuable. While this does not require great physical strength, snapping the sword forward and then losing it because your hands are not strong enough to hold it is downright embarrassing. In the old days it could get you killed, today it will only get you snickers that are ineffectively hidden.

Obviously shoulder muscles are important, but you don't need to be Mr. Universe to have shoulders strong enough to wield a sword. Most of the power in a sword stroke is generated by triceps and forearms, with only the initial movement started by the deltoids. In some blows the hips and back play a role, but only in massive cuts where there is no necessity of being prepared to recover and guard.

Still, the basis of all individual power lies in the back and abdomen. This is the center of the

Arm wielding a sword, with musculature shown.

human body, and both arms and legs depend on this section for support. No matter how strong the legs and arms, without a strong back and stomach, they are essentially weak. Before Man developed the luxuries of modern civilization, normal everyday activities, such as walking, running, and lifting, kept these parts of the body strong. Now we have to make a conscious effort in order to attain this.

Basic reflexes cannot be changed. While it is not possible to change slow twitch fibers into fast twitch, the actual movement can be improved in speed and accuracy. This is achieved by practice. Practice of individual movements can be noticeably improved with repetitive practice of each movement. This helps not only in the individual movement, but in the body's overall reaction time. If, as an example, you learn to throw and pull back a straight punch, and you practice so that you become faster than when you started, you will find that the ability to throw the arm up to block a punch will also be improved.

Footwork is also quite important. It is surprising how many people can manage to fall over their own feet. Kendo has a definite style of footwork. This consists of lifting the feet only slightly from the floor and almost gliding. It is surprisingly fast and effective in closing with your opponent. Fencing, on the other hand, advances with strong forward steps, almost kicking the front leg forward. This is also quite effective in quick closing. Although it may seem strange at first glance to have two different methods of advancing, it is due to the weapons. With the rapier the body is turned sideways, and with the katana the body is full face.

Sparring is a necessity for learning to use the sword. Free-form sparring is probably best, specific practice moves being second, with katas* being third. While katas are an important training device, too heavy a reliance on them can be detrimental. The problem with doing only katas is that it is all too easy to train the body to move in a specific way. If the opponent realizes this, then he can take advantage of it.

Care must also be taken in the use of the practice weapon. As of this writing there are no satisfactory sparring weapons on the market other than fencing blades such as the double wide epee blade. Wooden wasters are dangerous, and so are blunted steel or aluminum swords. Each can be quite harmful and even deadly if improperly used. Although there are a couple of practice swords being worked on, so far they have not been released to the public.

I would very strongly suggest that anyone reading this (whether interested in actually sparring or not) who smokes, to quit. I

---

* Katas: Martial arts body positions and exercises, as in karate.

—Jerry Proctor

smoked, and had convinced myself that I was one of the lucky ones who was not affected by smoking. I was running two miles a night wearing a 28-pound mail shirt, and could be on the field all day with no problem. So we delude ourselves. I came down with emphysema in my early fifties. Had I quit before, I could still go out and spar most of the day. I move pretty well for an older guy, but I have one problem, I just can't breathe. So quit.

Alright, I'm done with preaching, on your own head be it. Now let us get back to the use of the sword.

MENTAL ASPECTS OF SWORDPLAY

The mental aspects of swordplay must not be overlooked. While it may be of supreme importance to the competitors to win a backyard match, a national title, or even an Olympic gold metal, it is not the same as using real weapons where people are going to die. I do not think it is possible to define the type of outlook one should have when involved in a real life or death struggle. The feelings are personal and they will be dictated by the circumstances of the encounter, and the culture in which the individual was raised. Certainly a life and death struggle was not that unusual to a Viking or a samurai. It is also certain that there were both cowards and heroes in all lands and times. It is also a fact that many went out deliberately seeking violent encounters for the sheer adrenaline thrill, for money or for reputation.

There are certain abilities that I feel were necessary for these individuals to succeed, and they are also abilities that will win bloodless contests as well.

Awareness. This covers not only the area and landscape of the contest, but the intentions of your opponent as well. With practice anyone can learn to observe his surroundings in a quick glance. If you can quickly place in your mind the location of obstacles you can avoid being forced into them, and you may be able to force your opponent into one. You must also be aware of your opponent's intentions. Obviously his primary goal is to win, but you must be aware of the methods he will try to use in order to achieve that goal. You see the blow aimed at your head, but is he going to suddenly drop his arm and hit for the leg? The thrust is coming straight at you, but when you parry will he let his blade drop and

Modern Hank-type sword.
From the collection of Whit Williams. Photo by Adam Lyon.

rise on the other side of your blade and complete the thrust? These are things that must be learned, but cannot really be taught. This is instinct and experience. It *is* possible to develop a feel for this sort of thing. It never works one hundred percent of the time; nothing does. But if it happens frequently, then you will be a winner.

Calmness and Serenity. I have never read a treatise on any of the martial arts that did not emphasize calmness of mind. If it didn't, it wasn't worth the paper it was printed on. The Japanese, in their delightful way, might refer to this as "The Still Waters of the Mind" or "The Serenity of Acceptance," while the West, in a more direct approach, will call it coolness under fire.

There have been a number of tests where adrenaline was injected into people who were then asked to perform certain neuro-muscular functions. When the adrenaline level was high, they did not do them well. It did adversely affect fine dexterity while giving greater speed and force to larger actions.

This may appear to contradict the idea of calmness, but in reality it doesn't. If you can keep your calm and relax mentally, then you may take full advantage of what the additional adrenaline can give you. You will also be able to make your actions more efficient by recognizing the threats you face and countering them.

Awareness and calmness are actually linked together. The calm allows you to be aware of what is happening. If your mind is filled with rage or fear, then it becomes cloudy and you cannot see things clearly.

You will read of warriors filled with rage striking about at every side. On the other hand, take Thorolf, Egil's brother in *Egil's Saga* and Skarp-Hedin in *Njal's Saga*: each is described as filled with a burning rage. But this does not mean that they lost contact with what was happening around them. Instead, it is my opinion that this was a cold rage that gave their actions more strength and speed, and that their minds were calm and each blow was done

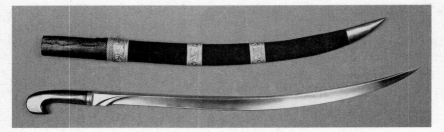

A favorite modern sword. HRC400.

deliberately. Indeed, anyone who gives way to rage often ends up striking wildly, and doing very little damage in the process.

You can win on emotion, but in order to be really good at something you have to learn to control those emotions. Often I have watched a football game and have seen the underdog in the contest come out blazing with fire and emotion. They dominate for a while, but then the fires burn low, the energy is used up, and if the other team continues to play a sound solid game, they eventually win. I have seen the same thing happen in both play and real fights (the real occasion was a brutal street fight). Emotion is fine, and it provides a lot of stimulus, but it must be controlled. Once it gains the upper hand it becomes a very dangerous friend, one that controls you, and that can be costly.

The combination of awareness and calmness allows you to see what your opponent is doing, but this is coupled with the art of seeing and not seeing. I hate to get into some of the Japanese mysticism, but in essence this is what you do. Some have called it the thousand yard stare. In short, your eyes are not focused on any one thing. They are not focused on the sword, the feet, or the eyes of your opponent. To focus on any one thing is to allow yourself to be deceived. If there is a sudden movement of the sword, and your eyes inadvertently follow it, you can be hit with a shield, or a dagger. Unfocused eyes allow you to pick up all movement and because your eyes are not focused on one thing, they can see other movement.

DECEPTION

One extremely important aspect of sword fighting, real or play, is deception. Actually deception is the key to most any contest or endeavor. You never want to advertise your moves or your intentions. It does not matter whether you are in a sparring match in your backyard, trying for a hostile takeover of a large company, playing a poker hand, or engaged in a major armed conflict. You never, ever advertise your moves, you always deceive.

At first this seems to be basically unfair. We Americans have all grown up with the concept of sportsmanship and fair play. And while this may not be true in actual combat, we still feel that it should apply in contest of skill and in sports. But consider this: a quarterback fades back, looks right and throws left. A running back jukes to the left, cuts right. A chess player offers a pawn in what appears to be a mistake, it is taken, and then the trap is sprung. You create a diversion on one flank to make the enemy think that is where the attack will fall, while your army masses on the other side to overwhelm the fewer number. You plant fake messages and even a corpse to convince the Germans that the invasion is going to be at Calais instead of Normandy. War is filled with deception, and so is personal combat and swordplay and sword fighting.

There are many tricks and moves that can be used, and fighting with sword and shield gives opportunity for all of them. A look at the leg, the sword flashes down, only to curl up at the right moment and strike the helmet. A downward slash that is designed to miss brings up your opponent's shield and this allows you to use your shield to lift up his even farther and stab upward, your sword, having traveled downward, being in a perfect position for an upward thrust.

There are so many deceptions inherent in the field of swords that it is impossible to list them all. This book is not intended to teach swordplay, but to give the basics. For in-depth study you need a good instructor. Let me recount a couple of things that the reader might find interesting.

Close to twenty years ago a good friend and superb martial artist brought a young fellow by my house. The boy was on his way to take part in a large tournament, and if my memory serves me, it was a ken-jitsu tournament. We talked and sparred a little bit. The guy was very athletic, very quick and aggressive and showed a lot of promise. But it was also obvious that there was a lot he didn't know. He asked if I had any advice.

I told him that in many matches, there is a quiet moment

when one of the combatants will step back, slightly lower his sword and take a deep breath. When this happens the other will invariably do the same, and then they will renew the action. I suggested that should he observe his opponent take a deep breath he should attack rather than mirror his movement. A few days later I got a call that he had won, and the match point had been achieved doing what I had suggested. (I never claimed to be a nice person.)

A few years ago there was a series of science fiction novels written by E.C. Tubb that I enjoyed a great deal. There were several duels with knives, and our hero moved exceedingly fast. There was one duel where the guy he was facing in the arena is handed his knife by his manager, who drops the knife. The duelist reaches down and grabs the knife before it hits the ground. This is staged, and was designed to impress the opponent with how fast he is. The books were good, but he had that sequence all wrong.

It was okay to drop the knife, but the duelist should have reached for the knife, missed it, and maybe even added a stumble or so. This to show the other how slow and clumsy he was. Nothing better than to have your opponent underestimate you.

It is with vast modesty that I recall a time many years ago when I was accused of having low animal cunning. One of my friends quickly spoke up in defense of me, and stated that "Hank's cunning is much lower than any animal, and we refer to it as low Hankish cunning." I blushed becomingly as I gracefully accepted the accolade.

In any swordplay contest I would suggest that you deceive, deceive and deceive. But never cheat. That is merely contemptible. This is one of the major differences between swordplay and sword fighting.

CONFIDENCE & TOUGHNESS OF SPIRIT

One of the most important components of a tough mind is confidence. True confidence comes from achievement. I don't mean merely winning. I have known people who won various things, but had no confidence at all. They would convince themselves that it was merely luck. I have known some guys who lost a lot, but had a lot of confidence in themselves. They were confident that they had given it their best shot, and that they would again and again. They would continue to learn, and they would never quit. Practice with a good teacher, good self-discipline and a willingness to try; these are the things that can instill confidence.

When a man begins a task, whether it is swordplay or sword fighting, or even a business deal, he must approach it with the knowledge that he is very capable, strong, tough and determined enough to overcome the obstacles that will be placed in his path.

I do feel that it is better to have your opponent think you are frightened, as this builds his confidence, and sets him up for a shocking realization. But no matter what demeanor you display on the outside, inside you must have two feelings that appear to be opposites. You must feel that you are the toughest and the best (at whatever the contest is) that the world has ever seen. But you also realize that your opponent is the most dangerous you have ever faced, and is quite capable of winning unless you give full attention to the work at hand. Now it really doesn't matter who you are facing, it can be a 10-year-old-child, or a 90-year-old-woman. If you don't pay very close attention, you can be looking up at an elderly grandmotherly type who is shaking her head at you and saying, "Sonny boy, you just don't get it."

In 991 AD, the year the battle of Maldon took place between some raiding Vikings and Byrhtnoth, leader of the Saxons, a poem was written regarding the battle. It seems to imply that Byrhtnoth was a heroic fool for letting the Vikings cross a stream and then square off. Although chivalrous, it also subjected his subjects to the murderous frenzy of the Vikings who were victorious. Ewart Oakeshott, in his wonderful book *The Archeology of Weapons*, quotes the ending couplet of the poem. I would like to do the same here.

> *"Thought the harder, Heart the Bolder,*
> *Mood the more, as our might lessens."*

If there was ever a poem or line that exemplifies the warrior spirit, it is that couplet. The Saxons chose to continue fighting until they died rather than surrender. But the couplet is not just about fighting. Rather, it can be used to govern one's whole approach to life, not just fighting, whether play or real. The stronger the opponent, the stronger you must be, the tougher the task at hand, the tougher you must be. These are not just physical attributes, they are mental! Toughness of mind is what allows a man to do and to endure.

Now, this is not to say that all of our ancestors had this ability, this strength of mind. No, there were cowards then, there were weaklings, and this will always be true. But in a less coddled society, this mental toughness existed in people in greater numbers.

But it can be developed. It takes more effort today than it did in the past. In the past physical hardships were part of life and that made it easier to be tough simply because if you were not tough, it is likely you wouldn't survive.

RHYTHM

Rhythm is very important but not in the way you might think. To use football again: how many times do you hear about a quarterback, "He can't get into rhythm"? Or that the other team won't let him establish a rhythm? The same is true with boxers and fencers; they engage their opponent at their rhythm and this allows them to gain a slight advantage, and be able to judge the proper time to land a hit or blow.

But what is true is that in physical contests involving direct confrontation, when you fall into a rhythm you are simply asking to get beat. Rhythm is easy to pick up, and just as easy to disrupt and then attack into the opening. You are essentially telling your opponent what you are about to do.

Incongruent rhythm coupled with deception in your movements can be devastating in the attack. In short, your opponent simply cannot tell what you are about to do, or when you are going to do it. In my humble opinion, establishing a rhythm is a sure road to disaster. A lot of this is from my own experience. I have no rhythm at all. I can't keep a beat going more than two or three beats before I lose it. My wife has despaired of ever making me a ballroom dancer, and at a showing of the musical *Stomp* during the part where the audience participates, she made me sit on my hands!

But what I have been able to do is foul up someone else's rhythm. It was always easy for me to see someone getting into a rhythm, as it allowed an opening, and using some speed, let me be able to take advantage of it. Frankly, I never realized that I was so devoid of rhythm, I only knew that I was able to take advantage of others, and was rather proud of my discovery. Then I read a couple of Chinese and Japanese texts where this was discussed, and the student was advised not to develop a rhythm. Or at least to develop one, then quickly change it. So much for discovering something new under the sun.

I think this applies more to specific forms of both swordplay and sword fights. Single sword contests, with katana, saber, rapier, and the like, lend themselves more to developing a rhythm than do fights with sword and shield. But the basic concept, that of keeping your opponent off balance, will always apply.

INTIMIDATION

Intimidation is another aspect of the mental game that needs to be addressed. It should be absolutely impossible for anyone to intimidate you. Size, strength, muscles, appearance, reputation—these are merely characteristics, and have nothing to do with the business to be done. The only thing that matters is performance, and that hasn't happened yet. But it is very easy for you to intimidate yourself. No one is perfect, and no one is invincible, but that not only applies to you, it applies to your opponent as well.

I dislike giving personal examples, and I will not go into details on this one, but there was a time I was in a "contest" with a guy much bigger, and stronger. (He was 6 feet 5 inches at 250 pounds, while I was 6 feet and 200 pounds.) He was also younger, and no one expected me to win; in fact, I was advised to run away. He lost, and badly. He was overconfident, and was used to intimidating others. I frankly just didn't care about his age, size or weight. In short, I was not intimidated. Had I been, I would have lost.

Another example is the boxing match between Mike Tyson and Buster Douglas. Tyson could hit like a big mule kicking, and most boxers were scared when they went into the ring with him. I had commented on that several times, and shortly after the fight started I pointed out to my friends also watching, that

Douglas simply didn't give a damn and was not scared at all. Douglas knocked him out.

Intimidation and confidence are two sides of the same coin. If you can't handle them properly, it does not mean you will lose, but it does increase the chances of a defeat by half.

Intimidation on your part is something else. If you can intimidate your opponent, do so. Curiously enough, the intimidation can take many forms. I've mentioned earlier a duel reported that took place in the mid-16th century. The challenged party was not particularly anxious to fight this duel, but he agreed. On the day of the duel he showed up with his hair and beard dyed a bright red. It was also stiffened into projecting points all along his head. It must have been a fearsome sight, as his opponent called off the duel and actually refused to fight him. This is a good example of someone intimidating himself. The challenger was still meeting the same person that he had challenged. The hair configuration in no way improved his ability to fight.

You should realize that with a trained fighter, intimidation probably won't work. If it doesn't work on you, why should it work on him? It is my opinion that a calm impassive look is usually the most arresting. Certainly it is better than the glaring, snarling and growling that some use.

TIMING AND DISTANCE

In all of the martial arts there are two physical actions that must be honed to a fine degree. No matter the mental state, your individual strength or your conditioning, without a good sense of timing and distance you are not prepared.

Timing is closely related to rhythm in the sense that you can perceive the rhythm and time your strike. Obviously there is a need for physical speed, but even someone with very fast reactions will fail unless the timing is there. Timing is something that must be practiced. Even a natural sense of timing can be improved with steady practice.

Distance is equally important. No matter how fierce the blow, how sudden, or how tricky, if it doesn't land it is worthless. A blow that doesn't land requires more effort to stop and control than a blow that is blocked.

It is also important to make your opponent miss. It is much better to have him miss by a small margin than by a large one. If he misses by a small margin then you are in a good position for a counterattack. However, if you have leapt back and he misses by a large margin, then you have a greater distance to cover to get to him. That requires more time, and it also gives him more time to recover and makes your attack far less likely to succeed.

There is an interesting tale of the old Japanese samurai who was visited by an old friend. The friend inquired as to how his host's young sons were doing in their training. The old samurai stated he would show him. Whereupon he placed a small paper lantern over the door so that it would fall when the door was opened. He closed the door and called for his youngest son. The young man entered, the lantern fell, and quick as lightning he drew his sword and struck. Then in the embarrassed silence he picked up the pieces and bowed to his father. The visitor nodded his approval. The old samurai once again placed another lantern in the same position, closed the door, and called his next son. The older son entered, the lantern fell, the son drew his blade swiftly, then saw the lantern and sheathed the sword, picked up the lantern and handed it to his father. Again the visitor smiled, but this time the smile was broader.

Once again the lantern was set. The eldest son was called for. He entered, the lantern fell, the son reached for his sword, saw the lantern, reached out and caught it, and then presented it to his father. The visiting samurai this time grinned, and commented, "The training goes very well!"

This tale has been told so often that it has become somewhat corny to many who hear it more than once. But if you examine the whole parable, you then see why this is important. Each son has reacted in his own level of maturity and wisdom. Although it is necessary that you be able to react swiftly, there is an even greater need that you know when to react. React inappropriately and you leave yourself open for a counter, react too swiftly, and your speed can be used against you. To bring up football once again: How often do you see a defense that is very fast come roaring off the line, smashing through, only to see the runner taking off in a different direction entirely? Their speed was used against them.

I had this happen on a personal level. I had a friend who really was not interested in any of sort of combat. He cheerfully admitted that he was too slow, and much preferred to be a cook and a lover rather than a warrior. But one day he decided that he wanted to spar with me using dummy knives. I was preparing to teach a class, so I agreed. He was really slow. He made a cut at my stomach. I snapped my arm out to block and counter, only to realize that he was *so* slow that my arm had missed his completely. His arm and hand, with the dummy knife, were still completing the cut. I panicked and was able to suck in my stomach enough so that the cut missed. But I had violated all of the principles that I knew very well. I had underestimated my opponent. He was so slow that my attitude was casual, and I had merely moved fast, without any awareness of where I was going to end up.

DIFFERENCES BETWEEN EAST AND WEST

A thorough study of the various written works on fighting with the sword will show an interesting dichotomy between the East and the West. Now, I have not read *all* of the available manuals dealing with swords that have recently been translated and printed. There are a surprisingly large number of them, written in many European languages. By and large these manuals deal with various attacks, counterattacks, footwork, parrying and all of the usual things that you might expect to find in a book on swordplay. One thing none of those that I have read have addressed is the mentality of combat, either real or play. They deal strictly with the physical aspects of swordplay, and often the advice given is stated in such a way as to be somewhat confusing or ambiguous. There may be a motive behind this, which we will deal with later.

In the past several years these many European "*fechtbuchs*" have been translated and have been made available to those interested. I have read only a few of them and plan on reading more. However, I have a healthy skepticism regarding most of these books. Any manual that has you holding and using a sword so that the sharp point is directed at you causes me to twinge. This is true with knives as well. (As a side note: Most European manuals dealing with knives show the daggers with an ice-pick grip. This makes sense when your opponent is wearing fairly heavy clothes, or possibly mail underneath his outer garments, but not otherwise.)

Let me explain my hesitancy in embracing these manuals with wholehearted enthusiasm. First, these books were written several hundred years ago. Language and convention have changed considerably since that time. It is quite possible that comments were not made in the books simply because everyone at that time knew what the author was talking about. It could also be that some things were left out deliberately so as to gain students where these things were explained by personal instruction. Above all, these manuals are not clear in their depiction of movements from one position to another and thus many of the movements are not fully explained.

However, many people today will look at one of these manuals and proceed to state that this is *the* way swords were used at the time of the writing. This is equivalent to reading a modern martial arts manual and drawing the conclusion that this is the way street fights are conducted, from someone who has never been in a street fight. Watching many of these drills and exhibitions taken from the manuals, I will admit that they look pretty good, but a close examination will show that these are well choreographed, and bear as much resemblance to actual combat as do fights in the movies.

What all of these seem to be missing (at least in the ones I have read), is training in the improvisation of attacks. Following a set scenario of moves is a definite invitation to get killed. These things may be used in a fencing match or contest where one is there to demonstrate form and skill, but it has no place in a life or death contest.

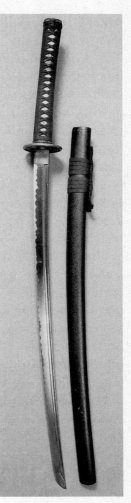

Reproduction Japanese sword. HRC106.

There is one thing that is absolutely true, and that is that you cannot learn to fight by merely reading a book. Not boxing, wrestling, any of the Oriental martial arts or swordplay. There has to be some hands-on sparring.

The Japanese manuals that I have read (always in translation) rarely, if ever, deal with any of the physical aspects of swordplay.

Instead they deal with the mental side. They stress the development of the mind and the spirit, and to the Westerner, this is rather confusing, as it is stated in terms of Zen and many of the other spiritual concepts. It is sometimes stated that these concepts cannot be properly explained in writing, but require a teacher.

Now, a cynical person might say that this was done in order to encourage individuals to enlist in the school that the writer favored or even taught. I have no doubt that this was true in some cases, but I also feel that many merely wished to share knowledge. It is also true that some things have to be demonstrated and even explained in person. Therefore, it is up to the individual to draw his own conclusions on the works that he might encounter whether they be Western or Eastern.

There is no question that the most difficult manuals to understand are those written in the Far East. There is the real poetic terminology which, when coupled with Zen Buddhism, can present quite a challenge for the Westerner. Terms such as: Moon in the Water, Beating the Grass to Scare the Snake, The Empty Mind or The Stillness of the Placid Pond. These are lovely phrases, and once you understand what is meant, why, they all make sense. But it can require a great deal of effort to learn what is meant, while in the West information is imparted in a much plainer fashion. Here I will attempt to give you my thoughts on this.

GETTING TO THE ZONE

I have encountered many variations on what you should watch in any physical contest. Many boxers will tell you to watch their feet, some swordsmen, old and new, will say watch the sword, his hands, his eyes, and when using the katana it is often said to watch his elbows.

Frankly, I don't believe in any of those. As mentioned above, I feel that if you focus on any one subject you can become fixated and you will lose sight of other attacks that may be launched. I much prefer not to focus on anything. This requires practice, but you undergo this in any eye exam where the examiner will tell you to stare directly ahead and then signal when you see a flashing light. This is done to determine your peripheral vision. Now if your attention is focused on the center you will not notice the blinking dot. However, if you merely look at the center, you will see the blinking light.

The fact that I needed glasses was an advantage to me. I didn't see well enough to focus anyway without my glasses. As a result I was able to pick up movement slightly quicker. This is definitely an advantage. This also led to a small but successful tactic. When I noticed someone watching a particular part—shield, sword, eyes, etc.—I could feint with that part, and launch an attack from another angle. Although vision is not a mental attitude, it does require a specific mental effort to keep from concentrating or focusing on what you perceive as the major threat, and is an important aspect of swordplay.

In the West we have the description of someone being "in the zone." Many people have experienced this, and it is a time when everything is going perfectly. Your body moves with ease, everything works, and you don't have to think about it. You are fully concentrated, and yet you do not feel it. You are merely "doing." In Zen this is known as the state of mindlessness.

I have in the past made some mocking comments about some of the Eastern terminology. Yet as I have grown older sometimes the Eastern terms are the only ones that fit. Consider "Empty Mind." I have to confess that in my 72 years I have encountered many people that were essentially mindless. But this is not what I mean. Rather this is a state where the knowledge imparted to the body and absorbed by the mind flows freely, and without any conscious control. You simply are; and are simply doing.

One way to put this is that frequently the body knows what to do, particularly if it has had training. But all too often the mind will interfere with the body by simply "thinking" of what the body should do. This is wrong. Let the body respond as it has been taught. Properly taught, it is amazing how quickly and simply the body can react as needed. Let me add a quick warning here. The physical limitations that we all suffer from can be alleviated but cannot be denied. On this down note we will now go to something else.

Before going any further into comments on mental conditioning, it has to be emphasized that physical training and practice are required to achieve any level of proficiency, particularly in the field of swordplay. There may be natural killers, there may be natural fighters, natural lovers and natural con artists. But there are no natural swordsmen. Each weapon has its own style of usage which is optimal for that sword. The greatest weapon that Man possesses is his brain, his mind. It has allowed him to develop weapons that have insured his survival in a harsh world. Using mind and knowledge also allows for excellent swordplay.

I prefer the phrase "the calm before the storm" instead of "Empty Mind," for I think it communicates the feeling I wish to describe. The body should be still and calm, but more important, the mind should be still and calm as well. But maybe the term "Empty Mind" should also be used as well, for the mind must be devoid of conscious thought, conscious plan or intent. It should just "be." This is a difficult concept to get across, but on reflection I think that everyone has experienced awareness without thought. This is not meditation which tries to divorce the mind from its physical surroundings. Rather this is a state where you are intensely aware of your physical surroundings, have accepted them, and are prepared to take whatever action is required, but without having to think about it.

This cannot be emphasized enough. There are many ways to becoming good, there are many ways to becoming excellent; however, to become great you must be able to react without conscious thought, and react correctly.

The body must be relaxed and calm as well as the mind. I know this sounds silly when one may be talking about fencing, with lightning quick movements and constantly shifting positions for any small advantage it can give. But the truth is that you move better when you are relaxed. When tense, muscles are poised for action in one direction; in order to change direction they must first relax and shift position, and this requires time.

If you are relaxed prior to the movement, you can strike quicker and harder and more accurately. If you tighten up, harden your muscles preparatory to striking, you will do two things: one, you will give warning that you are about to strike (and often where), and two, you will not strike as quickly. Muscles are easier to control if they do not have to be relaxed before the blow. This problem is most common in the upper body, where shoulders, triceps, forearms and wrist are the primary muscles being used (hip and body movements add tremendous force to a blow but the muscles holding and guiding the sword are the primary movers). When these muscles are tightened up, other muscles, such as the biceps, are also involved, and these muscles must be relaxed before the other muscles can move properly. So be relaxed, you can do much better.

Consider this. When a weight lifter approaches the bar for a clean and jerk, he positions himself, concentrates his force on one explosive movement to bring the weight to his shoulders, then a quick concentration to force the weight overhead. During the setup, his muscles are tense, preparing for that explosive action. But should he suddenly be told that he has to do a snatch instead, he has to then readjust, for his muscles and mind were set for another action. This is always true of swordplay, as you never know where or how you will have to move.

It is a simple fact that you can move quicker in spontaneous action with muscles relaxed than with muscles tense and tight. So in order to be prepared for whatever happens, both mind and body must be relaxed and calm.

You can be born with confidence, you can learn it, you can lose it, you can regain it, it can be false, misplaced, or true, but it is something that you need. It is also something that your opponent must sense and realize when you first meet. Some attempt to impart this by scowling, snarling, growling or glaring. This might impress some people, but for those who are truly competent all it says is that he is trying to scare me because he is not confident that he can win on skill alone. It is much better to be simply calm and impassive. There is no need for any of these silly histrionics.

Let me go back to Mike Tyson once again. I admired him as a fighter, and one thing that I liked was that I never saw him glare or scowl at any opponent. Instead he was always calm and impassive, and also implacable. He gave the impression that he was there to do a job, and he would do it as if it was no big deal. His opposition found this very intimidating. I do not know if this was planned or that it was simply the way he was, but it worked very well, at least until he met Buster Douglas.

CAUTION

But required along with confidence is caution. I do not mean the caution that breeds fear, but rather the caution that fosters awareness. You are the best at what you do. No question, you

Hank-type fantasy cutting sword. HRC106.

are the best. The person you are facing is the second best, and is very tricky. If I am not totally aware, he could win, so I must not let my guard down.

The problem is not so much overconfidence as in underestimating your opponent. Fights, battles and wars have been lost because someone underestimated their opponent. No better example can be used than WWII. Japan was supremely confident in their fighting ability, and completely underestimated the will to fight of the American people. On top of that they underestimated the industrial capacity of the US. Never, ever, underestimate your opponent.

I have had people say that this is contradictory, but it isn't. If you do not have complete confidence in what you are doing, you shouldn't be doing it. But having complete confidence in yourself does not mean you have to belittle or ignore your opponent. It means that you will be able to see what is happening, and will be able to counter the attacks.

This leads to a real striking difference in contest and actual swordplay. (Pun again intended with no shame or remorse.)

In real combat the action is not finished with just one blow. Instead it continues until the winner is assured that his enemy can no longer function. Dead, in short. We read of fights where many blows are struck. In *Egil's Saga,* Egil starts a duel dealing so many blows so quickly and ferociously that the guy he is fighting doesn't have time to return blow for blow. There is a break, and then Egil again attacks the same way and kills the other.

But while this happens in real fights, it is something that cannot be allowed to happen in sparring matches and contests in the various medieval and role playing groups we have today. There is simply too much of a chance for injury. Some may argue that this does not represent real combat, and they'd be right about it. No form of sword "play" can compare with actual combat.

†   †   †

Many many more pages could be written about the required mental attitudes and physical training needed for sword fights, whether real or in play. It is not the purpose of this book to detail all of the concepts, but I hope the above will give the reader who is interested a good idea of what is involved.

Suggestions for further reading from the editors:

Liddell Hart, B.H., *Strategy*. Penguin, London. First published 1954, revised 1967.

Musashi, Miyamoto, *Book of the Five Rings*. First published 1643.

Potter, Stephen, *Gamesmanship*, first published 1950, *Lifesmanship*, first published 1951, *Oneupsmanship*, first published 1952. These books are humor, but also give practical examples of how to get inside your opponent's head and were favorites of Hank's.

Tzu, Sun, *The Art of War*. First published possibly 403–221 BC.

▶ Note on Illustrations ◀

The illustrations were selected by the editor after the author's death; if there are any errors the blame falls to the editor.

All interior photography is by Suzanne Hughes unless otherwise indicated. "HRC" in the caption indicates that an item is from the collection of Hank Reinhardt, and the number given is the collection number. All interior drawings are by Peter Fuller.

Measurements of antiques are listed but not that of reproduction weapons. Note that Hank usually refers to blade length in the text; measurements given in the captions are for overall length, following the standard convention for use in identifying individual items.